Your Towns and Citie

Aldershot
in the Great War

Your Towns and Cities in the Great War

Aldershot
in the Great War

The Home of the British Army

Murray Rowlands

Pen & Sword
MILITARY

First published in Great Britain in 2015 by
PEN & SWORD MILITARY
an imprint of
Pen and Sword Books Ltd
47 Church Street
Barnsley
South Yorkshire S70 2AS

ISBN 978 1 78303 202 6

Printed and bound in England
by CPI Group (UK) Ltd, Croydon, CR0 4YY

Typeset in Times New Roman by Chic Graphics

Pen & Sword Books Ltd incorporates the imprints of
Pen & Sword Archaeology, Atlas, Aviation, Battleground, Discovery,
Family History, History, Maritime, Military, Naval, Politics, Railways,
Select, Social History, Transport, True Crime, and Claymore Press,
Frontline Books, Leo Cooper, Praetorian Press, Remember When,
Seaforth Publishing and Wharncliffe.

For a complete list of Pen and Sword titles please contact
Pen and Sword Books Limited
47 Church Street, Barnsley, South Yorkshire, S70 2AS, England
E-mail: enquiries@pen-and-sword.co.uk
Website: www.pen-and-sword.co.uk

Contents

Acknowledgements

Above all to Wendy without whom this book would not have appeared.
Hampshire Library and Archive Service. Particularly in this connection the staff of Aldershot and Farnborough Libraries
Mr David Strong for his help and support
Paul Vickers and the staff of the Prince Consort Library
The Imperial War Museum
FAST Museum and Ian Fagg in Farnborough
The News Group – *Aldershot News*
Surrey Archive Centre, Woking
St Michael's Church, Aldershot
St Joseph's Church, Aldershot
Holy Trinity Church, Aldershot
The Aldershot Command
The Heritage Centre, Bramshott
The Royal Military College Library

Finally, thanks and acknowledgment to Gillian Barnes-Riding and Surrey Heath Museum for permission to publish the paintings and drawing from the German POW Camp at Frith Hill, Frimley.

M C Rowlands
March 2014

MAP OF ALDERSHOT COMMAND.

SUPPLEMENT TO THE MONTHLY OFFICIAL DIRECTORY.

EWSHOTT.

BLACKDOWN, DEEPCUT and BISLEY

BORDON and LONGMOOR.

REGISTERED COPYRIGHT.

MAY & Co.,

Army Printers and Publishers,

ALDERSHOT.

WHERE THE UNITS ARE QUARTERED.

5. R.F.A., Marlboro' Lines.
8. 2nd R. Dublin Fusiliers.
9. 1st Irish Guards.
10. 1st Norfolk Regt.
11. 1st Cameron Highrs.
12. 1st Scots Guards.
24. Royal Engineers.
31. Army Service Corps.
34. K.O. Yorks L.I. & A.O.D.
46. R.A.M.C.
48. 1st Gordon Highlanders.
49. 4th Royal Fusiliers.
50. 2nd Lincoln Regt.
54. 4th Middlesex Regt.
57. R.F.A.
58. R.H.A.
59. 1st Leicestershire Regt.
60. 1st Royal Irish Fusiliers
61. 1st The Buffs.
65. 19th Hussars.
66. 7th Hussars.
67. 3rd Dragoon Guards.

BLACKDOWN.
2nd York & Lanc. Regt.
2nd Royal Irish Regt.

BORDON.
1st E. Yorks Regt.
1st R.W. Kent Regt.
1st Worcestershire Regt.
3rd Rifle Brigade.
R.F.A.

DEEPCUT. R.F.A.

EWSHOTT. R.F.A.

LONGMOOR.
Mounted Infantry.
R.E. (Railway Cos.)

WOKING. East Lanc Regt.

---

1. Government House (G.O.C.-in-Chief).
2. Queen's Hotel.
3. Officers' Quarters and Messes.
4. Wesleyan Soldiers Home.
5. Lille Barracks. R.F.A.
6. Married Soldiers Quarters.
7. Tournay Barracks.
8. Blenheim Barracks.
9. Malplaquet Barracks.
10. Oudenarde Barracks.
11. Ramilies Barracks.
13. Garrison Church.
14. Connaught Hospital.
15. Brigade Offices.
16. Blandford House.
17. W.D. Nursery.
18. Vine Cottage.
19. Army Athletic Ground.
20. Gymnasium.
21. Swimming Baths.
22. Royal Engineer Establishment.
23. Royal Engineer Theatre.
24. Gibraltar Barracks, R.E.
25. R.E. Workshops and Stores.
26. St. George's Church.
27. D.A.A.G.'s Quarters.
28. Headquarter Offices and Camp P.O.
29. Military Police Barracks.
30. Army Service Corps Establishment.
31. Buller Barracks, A.S.C.
32. A.S.C. Training School and Offices.
33. Army Service Corps Theatre.
34. Mandora Barracks.
35. Central Electric Light Station.
36. Supply Depot.
37. Mechanical Transport Training Depot.
38. Camp Farm.
39. Isolation Hospital.
40. Mechanical Transport Service Corps.
41. Hay Pressing Establishment.
42. Military Cemetery and Chapel.
43. Ordnance Stores.
44. Louise Margaret Hospital.
45. Cambridge Hospital.
46. McGrigor Barracks, R.A.M.C.
47. Fire Stations.
48. Maida Barracks.
49. Corunna Barracks.
50. Barrosa Barracks.
51. Albuhera Barracks.
52. Officers' Club.
53. Prince Consort's Library.
54. Moore Barracks.
55. Army Accounts Offices.
56. School of Sanitation.
57. Waterloo Barracks, R.F.A.
58. Waterloo Barracks, R.H.A.
59. Talavera Barracks.
60. Salamanca Barracks.
61. Badajos Barracks.
62. Wellington Monument.
63. All Saints' Church.
64. Wellesley House.
65. South Cavalry Barracks.
66. West Cavalry Barracks.
67. East Cavalry Barracks.
68. May & Co., Army Printer.
69. Police Station and Court.
70. Banks.
71. General Post Office (Town).
72. Aldershot Theatre.

Preface

When Pen and Sword suggested I write about Aldershot in World War One I assumed that because the town and camp was the home of the British Army, much would have been written about what happened during the war.

I quickly discovered that no history had been written. Colonel Cole, who published the only history of the town, devoted hardly any space to the period of the town's history when it occupied a pivotal position in the Allied powers' conduct of the war.

There are likely reasons for the dearth of information about the years 1914 to 1918. The first is that under the Defence of the Realm Act there was an absolute freeze on any communication of information about what was happening in Aldershot. This was to such an extent that one director of the military publishers Gale and Polden, based in the town, went to prison for two months for publishing information they had gleaned from the War Office. It appears that Aldershot resembled a closed town in the Soviet Union during the Cold War.

The second reason relates to the fate of Gale and Polden itself. It was taken over by Robert Maxwell, the publishing mogul, and closed. At the time of its closure there were reports of its bank of archival material being taken to the local tip. Only a record of the *Aldershot News* published by the firm remained, and I am deeply indebted to this source for providing me with a starting point.

I made a remarkable discovery writing this book. No reliable list existed of the names of the fallen from Aldershot. This was reflected by the town's war memorial having no names on it. My wife and I therefore made a strenuous effort to produce a reasonably reliable list.

Winchester School Army Cadets in Camp, Aldershot 1912.

General William Knollys, reforming Commandant.

Queen's Lancers on parade for King's birthday 1912.

*King George V with
Staff Officers
watching manoeuvres
above the Long Valley
1914.*

*Postcard 'Greetings
from Aldershot'.*

Cavalry training at Long Valley.

Aldershot Garrison Church.

Lady Dorothy Haig, General Haig's wife, known for her philanthropic work in Aldershot.

Aldershot Railway Station.

Miss Daniell's centre for soldiers in Aldershot.

Lt.-Gen. Sir Horace Smith-Dorrien, reforming Camp Commandant.

King Edward VII's visit to Aldershot 1909.

Aldershot Command Headquarters 1908.

An Aldershot group pre war.

The Church of England Institute building which played a crucial role in the town's political and social life.

Riflemen from the London Rifle Brigade in training in Aldershot 1863.

Layout of camp with cadets training.

Aldershot children in pre-war classroom.

Talavera Barracks pre-war.

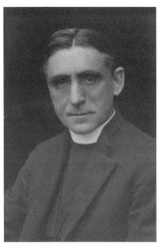

Rev'd F.O.T. Hawkes, Vicar of Aldershot.

The Fire Station in Aldershot.

Balloon being prepared by Army Balloon Corps in Aldershot (FAST).

Francis Cohen, Aldershot's first Jewish Chaplin.

General Haig with his staff at Aldershot in 1912. From L to R: Captain Baird, General Robb, General Haig, General Davies, Captain Charteris.

Introduction

In the beginning – the creation of Aldershot

In the beginning the British Army created the barracks on the earth and in the heavens an aircraft factory. As a town, Aldershot was an artificial creation built to support a small standing army. The Duke of Wellington at the end of his life opposed the creation of a garrison town built on unattractive, largely scrub land on the borders of Hampshire, Surrey and West Sussex. It had the advantage of the Basingstoke Canal running close to it and the strategic value of being in a position to offer protection for London to any invading army. Queen Victoria had reviewed troops at nearby Chobham Common and, from the outset, not only Victoria and Albert but other members of the Royal Family were aware of the proximity of Windsor to a proposed camp.

Lord Hardinge, the commander in chief of the army, shared the concern in government circles about the acquisition of power by another Napoleon in France in the early 1850s. An approach was made to the Bishop of Winchester, the owner of some of the land, for the purchase of 100,000 acres at an agreed price of £12 per acre. Building of the camp started at a fortuitous time, for the Crimean War against Russia broke out in 1854. The construction of a camp of 1,200 huts was supported by Prince Albert, the prince consort, who played an active part in the design of quarters for the soldiers. Each hut was designed for twenty soldiers relating to the number in a battalion. We shall see in the crisis of accommodation associated with the recruitment of Kitchener's new army that fifty men were squeezed in when the new volunteers arrived in late 1914 and early 1915.

By 1914 Aldershot was the centre for training army school mistresses. They had to be between 20 and 22 years of age and possess necessary physical and educational standards. Training in the town was for a year. The army forbade them to marry a soldier below the rank of sergeant and they were expected to retire when they were married. Their role was administered by the Corps of Army Schoolmasters, but they had an independent existence as far as pay and conditions were concerned. Because they were neither civilians nor military they suffered the disadvantages of both. The War Office dictated where they served, at home or abroad. As they were not an army unit they had no uniform and their pay was never raised in line with army pay. By 1919 they were receiving the same pay as a lance corporal.

Much of the building of the infrastructure of Aldershot was initially down to George Kemp and, subsequently, to the firm Kemp-Stroud Ltd. Some of the firm's buildings include the YMCA Building, All Hallows School, the entrance to the town's market, the General Post Office, St Michael's Church of England School, council housing following the war, the Alexandra Cinema, the County Secondary School, to name just a few. The company constructed a new sewerage works for the growing town and camp. George Kemp was followed by his son into the business. The company became Kemp-Stroud when Stroud, a new manager, joined the firm. Stroud was born in India and arrived in Aldershot in 1908.

This book will concentrate on the men and women whose lives were associated with these barracks, be they Wellington Lines, Maida, Mandora, McGrigor, Corunna, Barossa, Buller, Malplaquet, Lille, Ramillies, Warburg, Oudenarde, Beaumont, Waterloo, Salamanca and Albuhera. The Aldershot command spread for miles around the surrounding area from Woking to Reading. It took in Bordon and Longmoor, where land was purchased in 1880. It included land at Ewshot originally part of the Ewshot Estate, which became the base for the New Zealand Artillery in 1916, and Bramshott, where the Canadians were based. The commanders who presided over the growth of Aldershot exercised great power over the lives of everyone in Aldershot, soldier and civilian alike. Very often as the Great War progressed it was the wives of Aldershot's commanding officers who played a leading part in the necessary humanitarian and social provisions for the town. This was the case with both Smith-Dorrien and Haig's wives. Through the period of the war it was not only Queen Mary and the spouses of commanding officers who supported the soldiers' wives, the wounded and the orphans of the war, but many local women who devoted their lives to the often unrecognised task of helping victims.

The tradition of evangelical Christianity was still very evident in wartime Aldershot with a plethora of churches of all shades of opinion. This is reflected in the period in command of General Sir James Hope Grant GCB from 1870 to 1875, who took steps to stamp out immoral behaviour among the troops. In 1860 an iron church was built, beginning military church history in Aldershot. Two churches designated Chapel Schools were built to cater for the spiritual needs of the camp. In 1856 another church, which may have been originally intended to be a hospital advocated by Florence Nightingale, was constructed. By 1913 there was a substantial Catholic Church, St Joseph's, reflecting the large number of Irish soldiers serving at Aldershot. Methodist and Wesleyan churches, along with the others, were constructed that offered social support to mitigate the often brutal conditions experienced by the soldiers and their wives in the camp.

In Aldershot there was a growing Jewish population marked by the building of a synagogue. Not until 1889 had Judaism received formal recognition by the British Army as a *bona fide* religion for serving soldiers. Jewish soldiers were simply entered as C of E. When in 1889 Judaism was recognised by the army, only nineteen soldiers chose to register. There were at least five times that number of Jews in the ranks. In 1892, Rev'd Francis Lyon Cohen was appointed as the first officiating Jewish chaplain to the forces. He had been in Aldershot in 1862 and growing up there was aware of the prejudice against his religion forcing many to conceal their belief. From 1892 he was conducting church services simultaneously with those offered in other faiths.

Both the *Aldershot News* and *Sheldrake Military Gazette* reflect the evangelical concerns of these churches within the Aldershot community. As we will see the Vicar of Aldershot, F.O.T. Hawkes, was the leader of a philosophical debate about the nature and character of the war. Much of the commentary on the role of religion in Aldershot has been content to show the buildings where worship took place, but not to discuss the role these churches played, especially during the war in offering spiritual, physical and social support. Such is the case of St Augustine's in the then isolated remote working-class hamlet of North Town, separated from the rest of the town by the steep slopes of Redan

Hill. Its remoteness convinced the town's planners that here was the ideal place for a cemetery built in 1860, to be followed by an isolation hospital in 1900, a gas works in 1865 and the sewerage farm. In 1913 North Town's local church St Augustine's welcomed a new vicar, Rev'd Edward Stephen Gladstone Wickham, the grandson of William Gladstone. Like his grandfather he was a high church Anglican and because of this wanted to be known as Father Wickham.

While his predecessors had chosen to live in the more affluent parts of Aldershot, Father Wickham lived in the White Swan public house in North Town. By the standards of the time Wickham did everything wrong, such as taking members of his Sunday school hop-picking at a time when the temperance movement was at its height in order to raise funds for the church's building funds. In June 1914 he welcomed Princess Beatrice, Queen Victoria's youngest daughter, whose son would be killed at Mons a few months later, to open the hall attached to his church. Certainly, in the early part of the war, the churches of all denominations played a significant role in the ethical and social life of the town.

Lieutenant General Sir William T. Knollys, commander during the period from 1855 to 1860, discovered that many of the troops in his charge lacked even the elemental ability to pitch a tent. Instruction in this and the beginnings of medical services resulted from his time. Lesser officers, such as Lieutenant Colonel Frederick Hamersley, commenced the camp's pre-occupation with physical fitness by constructing its first gymnasium at the South Camp in 1861. Field Marshal Earl Douglas Haig, general commanding officer in the period leading up to the war, saw physical fitness coming through games and sporting activity as a crucial part of military training. Thus, even in the blackest period of the war, 1917 to 1918, sports such as cross country running and rugby were focused for the Aldershot command in the town.

The physical shape of Aldershot was dramatically affected by Field Marshal Sir Evelyn Wood, VC GCB GCMG, in the period from 1889 to 1893 through the rebuilding of the existing wooden huts of the South Camp in brick and the replacement of the huts in North Camp with much improved accommodation. But it was in the area of discipline that change reflected on the whole character of the camp. Before the abolition of flogging for soldiers serving at home the public could witness the disgusting sight of men being flogged with up to fifty strokes. This was used to reinforce the discipline maintained by pickets, NCOs who roamed around the camps picking up drunken soldiers frequenting the fifty inns that had sprung up in the camp. However, the well-regarded Lieutenant General Sir Horace Smith-Dorrien abolished the practice and took steps to recognise the right of soldiers to be trusted to behave in a civilised manner in the town. It should be mentioned that stringent field punishments such as tying to a wheel were still open to authorities. A military prison called The Glasshouse was built in Aldershot in 1856 in the South Camp, capable of housing 200 prisoners. It was rebuilt in 1970 in a manner resembling a Victorian prison.

What Smith-Dorrien did in office from 1907 to 1912 did not find favour with his predecessor Field Marshal Sir John French, GCVO KCB KCMG, who saw his reforms as a poor reflection of what had happened during his own leadership of the camp. Only Smith-Dorrien seemed aware of the horrors the war was about to bring. Speaking to gung-ho cadets from public schools at a camp in Aldershot in 1914 he described in vivid detail the reality of the war to come. Smith-Dorrien's wife continued to play an active role in the humanitarian and social affairs of the town after he moved to his post in Gibraltar. Of greater significance was what Field Marshal Earl Douglas Haig, KGB KCIE KCVO, was saying in the Royal Pavilion to King George about Field Marshal French, the man chosen to lead the British Expeditionary Force from Aldershot Military Camp. Haig's time at Aldershot from 1912 to 1914 was mainly occupied with the logistics of putting together a force able to move after the declaration of war on 4 August 1914. Haig's wife did much to make up for her dour husband's inarticulate failings in communication with people in Aldershot.

The late Victorian period, Edwardian era and the years immediately prior to the war can be seen as ones of superficial prosperity. The town attracted workers from the surrounding area previously dependent on the wages paid for farm labour. The crudest aspects of the town were revealed in the prostitution and diseases caught from liaisons in music hall back rooms. At the same time a growing middle-class providing services for a more sophisticated clientele chose to move away from Aldershot, with its poor sewerage system and high level of disease, to nearby Farnborough. The more enlightened commanders recognised that a way to combat illegitimacy and venereal diseases was to allow soldiers leave to marry. Where it was permitted for men in barracks the women lived on the strength of the regiment, and drew rations from the soldiers' entitlement at no extra cost. In return they cleaned and did laundry duty.

In response to public concern about the bad habits of idle soldiers, the Prince Consort paid for a library for the camp. The Royal Family had their own residence at The Pavilion, from where Queen Victoria, Edward VII and George V could review the frequent parades, displays and manoeuvres. Apart from the honours investitures that took place during the war it was not until 1919 that the famous Aldershot tattoos took place. The colours associated with the parades and displays of the turn of the century were replaced by a universal khaki just before the war. In Lynchford Road, marching Highlanders in their kilts could be seen. All about the town would be spotlessly clean and colourful uniformed men with their white puttees and waist belts. Because of the Royal Family's abiding interest in Aldershot they brought to the camp a succession of royal visitors. In August 1894 the German kaiser, Wilhelm II, attended a royal review and extensive field day. There seems to be no comment about the irony of this when the *Aldershot News* recorded the first trains full of wounded soldiers arriving in the town in late August 1914. Two decades previously the station where they arrived had been decked out for Wilhelm II's arrival with flags and Prussian colours, the platform laid with crimson cloth right out to the station yard. His arrival was via a special train from Portsmouth and he went through streets bedecked with bunting and flags to Laffan's Plain, where an assembly of 12,000 troops was waiting to greet him.

The same *Aldershot News* that would be calling for a boycott of all traders with even remote German or Austrian connections in 1914 was ecstatic about the sight. 'The scene was an extremely brilliant one, the prancing horses, the bright hues of the uniforms, the glitter of gold lace and decorations, the glint of silver and the flashing of steel formed a grand spectacle.' In 1914, the kaiser was to refer to the British Expeditionary force created by Haig as a 'contemptible little army'. The *Aldershot News* advanced this prospectus of Aldershot in 1909:

Few places in the South of England can compare with Aldershot in the advantages it possesses as a residential district. Situated at a high altitude in the midst of pine and heather, and adjacent to the most beautiful part of Surrey, it is almost unrivalled for health-giving and social facilities. The proximity of a world-famed camp supplies interest and amusement for almost all classes of residents, and both in the town and the district around there are many well-built conventionally arranged residences, which are let at rents which compare very favourably with other places of less importance and possessing fewer attractions. The rates are low, while the sanitary conditions in the town and the water supply are excellent. It was these circumstances which decided the authorities to make the permanent garrison here, and the health statistics show that their decision was a right and a wise one.

Besides the numerous social advantages which appeal especially to those who have interests or associations connected with the army, the cost of living is a question which may decide many people in favour of residence in Aldershot.

The fact that the army needs are so great enables traders to buy in the best markets, and not only can household provisions be bought cheaply, but luxuries of all kinds are available at a moderate price. Furniture and drapery establishments, jewellers, and similar traders cater for all classes of customers. Coals and all necessities of life are comparatively cheap owing to the considerable trade done, and this circumstance may well decide those seeking for a place of residence to choose Aldershot. In addition there are undeniable benefits of Aldershot. Sport of all kinds is continually going on in 'The Camp' and the district. The educational resources of Aldershot and the district are being rapidly developed. There are several high class private schools, and the provision of a large secondary school and teachers' centre will shortly provide the necessary facilities for middle-class education.

New measures have recently been taken by the traders in town to develop further the commercial possibilities of Aldershot. It is not generally recognised as it should be that the town offers unique facilities for shopping. A new movement which has been set on foot promises speedy developments commercially, and the remarkable growth of Aldershot will no doubt be even more marked in the future than in the past.

In 1911, around the time this advocacy for Aldershot was published, its population was 35,175, including 15,711 South Camp personnel. The published life expectancy of soldiers in the camp was half that of the civilian population, so perhaps claims for a healthy environment might be questioned. Within a short time of war being declared a real crisis developed as far as housing was concerned as many workers supporting the army are drawn into the area. By 1917 the *Aldershot News* and *Sheldrake Military Gazette* were demanding urgent action to build more houses. There is a class bias in the piece reflected in the *Aldershot News* until about 1916, when it discovers working people deserve a place in the sun. In 1915 it publishes figures from the trustees of the Farnham Workhouse revealing that it has 265 in residence. There is a clear market argument in relation to economies of scale to attract newcomers. However there is little recognition of what might happen when the numbers of troops in barracks is reduced – something that happened post-1918.

Gale and Polden, the publishers of the *Aldershot News*, played a highly significant role in the life of Aldershot from the time they moved into the Wellington Works in 1893. In 1894 they published the first edition of *Aldershot News* selling more than 12,000 copies. Their market was set at selling specialist books to the army and to the navy, with its Nelson Works set up to trade at Chatham and Portsmouth. The firm established a link with the Royal Family in being selected by Queen Mary to print her Christmas cards. Much interpretation of what happened in Aldershot is dependent on its publication of the *Aldershot News*. However, even they are frustrated by the level of censorship imposed on both the town and the military command. The paper comments how much it wishes to print but is unable to because of censorship. The reality of the controls the government possessed is well-illustrated by the prosecution brought against a clerk in the War Office on 24 March 1916, who had been sending information to the *Military Mail* published by Gale and Polden. Lupton Maude was arrested and charged with sending personal information to Charles Mattocks, who lived at Kenmore in Cargate Avenue. Both were taken before Sir John Dickerson at Bow Street Court and placed on bail and charged under the Official Secrets Act. Lupton Maude had been a regular contributor to the *Military Mail* and Charles Mattocks was deputy chairman of Gale and Polden. The latter was a highly respected

Aldershot figure and president of Aldershot Chamber Of Commerce.

Despite this, he and Maude appeared before Mr Justice Darling on 26 April 1916, pleading guilty to communicating and receiving information covered by the Official Secrets Act. This appeared in a column marked 'Heard in Whitehall by Mars'. In some cases the actual words in the official documents appeared in the column. Both men were sentenced to two months in prison. This indicates the genuine difficulty the press in Aldershot were experiencing reporting what was going on around them. The *Aldershot News* promised to write these stories after the war, but it never did. The catastrophic fire that destroyed its works will be described in the section of the book devoted to 1918.

One event that was a harbinger for the future, not only World War One but also World War Two, was the arrival of the Canadian Army in 1910, as part of their nation's efforts to build its armed forces. To follow them would be New Zealanders, Australians, Indians and South Africans. The fulsome words of welcome given to the Canadians reflects the view of people in the town of soldiers coming from the empire. 'We are not unmindful of the ready help given to the Mother Country by the forces of Canada in time of need, and you may rest assured that services so nobly rendered in the past were deeply appreciated by Englishmen and the spirit of unity which was then exemplified gives us the confident hope that if ever our Empire is attacked by foes or the liberty of our Anglo Saxon race is threatened, England with its colonies will stand shoulder to shoulder in defending the Empire which we one and all love so well.' This was in a speech of welcome by a mayor prior to the war.

Perhaps it's the Anglo Saxon bit that reveals that until very recently the memorial to soldiers from the Indian sub-continent killed in World War One was neglected. The War Office's original plan had been to create a burial ground for Muslim soldiers at Netley. However, a section of Brookwood Cemetery at Woking was found for them but suffered from neglect and lack of interest from the time a memorial had been built.

The growth of Aldershot coincided with the outcry about the failures of the British Army to provide adequate treatment and care for its soldiers. As far as the hospitals were concerned, prior to 1854 virtually nothing existed. There was the Hospital Hill or Union Workhouse since 1692, but this was hardly a response to the needs of a large army town. The traditional approach to nursing and social care had previously been seen to rest with regiments of the army such as the cavalry, artillery and the infantry. Despite at first there being hutted hospitals at North and South Camps, Florence Nightingale's campaigns about the shocking conditions for the wounded during the Crimean war had shown how inadequate these were. There was a reluctant acceptance that these should be replaced. Plans for a general hospital proposed by Florence Nightingale in 1857 never came to fruition.

However, her ideas about the elements required for a hospital capable of responding to the needs of the wounded such as airy wards with efficient ventilation, access to sunlight, properly plastered walls, did form the basis for how hospitals at Aldershot were to be built. In 1875 the foundation stone for the Cambridge Hospital was probably laid by the Duke of Cambridge. Its initial cost was £45,758. New innovations were introduced, such as a lift to take food from the ground floor to the first floor, a fine principal corridor of 528 feet long, and seven large wards each with twenty-four beds. There was an officers' ward of 92 feet by 24 feet. Provision for heating was achieved through ducting and two gas stoves. Louvres were created for fresh air, and hot and cold water was available throughout the hospital. New chambers were added, reflecting the growing size of the camp and the town. A female hospital was also added, supported by the Sisters of Charity and, in 1898, a mother and child unit.

For the people of Aldershot the Cambridge Hospital played an iconic part in their lives. The bells that would ring out from its clock tower were silenced following complaints from the sick and wounded in the hospital. Stories include the existence of a ghost, possibly one of the thousands of soldiers who passed through during the course of the war. From the first trainload of wounded brought back from France at the end of August 1914 until well into 1919, Aldershot's hospitals played a significant part in thousands of soldiers' lives.

As well as the Cambridge, some eleven central hospitals were under the jurisdiction of the Aldershot command. In addition, there were twenty-nine auxiliary hospitals set up during the war. From this the scale of numbers of wounded and ill soldiers returning to the Aldershot area can be appreciated. In 1918 the Spanish flu epidemic imposed an almost impossible strain on the provision, particularly the Cambridge's sister hospital in town, the Connaught. As with Brockenhurst Hospital in the

New Forest, where a private hotel was taken over for officers, a similar officers' hospital, the Wellesley, was created. With young men pushed together in overcrowded accommodation, a breeding ground for a whole range of contagious diseases, such as measles and mumps, was created. It was necessary to open an isolation hospital. Conditions also saw many cases of TB and consumption that had to be treated. As the war progressed the Aldershot community was forced to come to terms with the omnipresence of venereal disease and clinics were set up in the face of some hostility. But because of the size of the demand for medical services after the Battle of the Somme in 1916, hospitals associated with barracks such as the ones at Bramshott and Mandora had to be created. Bramshott and Bear Wood Hospitals treated wounded Canadian soldiers. In the 30-mile radius twenty-nine hospitals and centres for convalescence were brought into being, most of which are barely remembered today. In the absence of modern drugs, even a superficial wound might take months to heal, if it ever healed at all. Many convalescing soldiers were dressed in a blue uniform that does not appear to have changed since Dickens witnessed them in Aldershot in 1859.

> The old red brick poor-house has been taken possession of by the parochial authorities as a hospital for invalid soldiers. Walking in a small dusty garden or sitting on benches under the shadow of side walls, are a number of convalescents, dressed in light blue serge trousers, jackets, and the night caps, which make them look like comic performers of the Pierrot class in a circus of French horse riders.

As Aldershot town grew in prosperity around supplying an enlarged camp, so too did its middle-class. The original Cartgate of the pre-camp days became Cargate and the location for wealthier home owners. There you might find Mr Taplin the solicitor, George Kemp the builder, the families of George Digby and Henry Wyatt who were furnishing suppliers. Most of the homes had servants' quarters. In roads such as Crimean Road and Sebastopol Road were the houses of craftsmen, such as gunsmiths, blacksmiths, shirt collar makers, and of coachmen and grooms. But the industrial company that went well beyond the other occupations of the town was Gale and Polden. They arrived in Aldershot in 1888 and set up a shop in Wellington Street. The firm were publishers and booksellers to the army and navy. They were able to produce specialist publications, something that had hardly existed at all. There was an absence of officially printed forms for parade states, ration returns, crime and sick reports, which were usually produced by hand. Gale announced that: 'A selection of several hundreds of most modern and popular books will always be found in stock and, having made arrangements for receiving parcels from the principal London Houses daily, the book that should happen not to be in stock could be obtained immediately.'

In 1893 the firm moved their works at Chatham to Aldershot. They chose a site close to Aldershot Station on a small market garden. The proximity to the rail head was invaluable because the company's large machines could easily be moved to the new site. Not only a major employer, they began to challenge the *Sheldrake Military Gazette*, the existing local paper, by publishing the *Aldershot News*. By 1892, from their Wellington Works, the company was supplying 400 canteens, 100 officers' messes, 200 sergeants' messes, 250 libraries, recreation rooms and regimental institutes throughout the service as well as other strong commercial connections. The company's series dealing with army educational issues was in use by military educational departments and school boards both around the country and the empire. As the war progressed so did the names of the men employed by the firm appear as either dead or wounded in the paper. The disastrous fire that gutted the company's premises in 1918 occurred at the darkest time of the war and seemed to heap more misery on the town.

The growth of the camp and town was also reflected in a demand for transport. The chosen place for the camp had the virtue of wide open spaces. Unfortunately this meant town and camp were off the beaten track and effective means of communication had to be established. At the time of the establishment of the camp the nearest station was at Farnborough on the South Western Railway Company line. There was a station at Farnham on the South Eastern line taking in Guildford, Wanborough, Ash Green and Tongham. There was an absence of any form of public transport from these stations to the camp. In 1856 a horse drawn omnibus was taking passengers from Farnham to the camp. In order to effectively build the barracks a single track railway line was laid down between the nearest station, Tongham, and the South Camp. By the time Charles Dickens visited the town and wrote his description for *All the Year Round* magazine, he described the scene with the railway in the following way:

> Along the High Street of this military village runs a single line of railway devoted to the carriage of coal and building material for the large barrack streets that are still being erected for the accommodation of future cavalry regiments. Every hour a train of luggage trucks is panting along the tramway and the only wonder is, that the driver who conducts the engines is not attired in some variety of military undress costume.

However, the growth of the town and camp following the Boer War created a demand for a distinctive company known as Traco – The Aldershot and District Traction Company. Formed in 1906 as the Aldershot and Farnborough Motor Omnibus Company, it won the franchise to run a bus service through the camps. Two buses were purchased from the Hastings and St Leonards Bus Company and starting on 1 June 1906, a service began between Aldershot and the Queen's Hotel in Farnborough. A previous attempt to run a tram service covering the same route had not succeeded. Routes vital for the Aldershot command into the surrounding area, such as one to Ash and Farnham, were established. However, the level of demand in the area found the company lacking the resources to undertake new routes. As a result the company was purchased by the British Automobile Traction Company and the New Central Omnibus Company Ltd, who expanded the original bus depot in Halimote Road with vehicles to cover Fleet, Farnham and Haslemere.

By the outbreak of war, bus services had been established from Aldershot to Guildford, Pirbright and Ash. When the spread of the Aldershot command's tentacles throughout the area is considered, this service was vital to the process of linking army and civilian services. Coverage of the area was further increased in late 1914 by a takeover of the Guildford and District Motor Services Company operating out of their base in Guildford. Contracts with the War Department resulted in the purchase of motor lorries and steam wagons to service a growing parcel service. From a goods vehicle base at Haslemere, further expansion took place down to Midhurst and Sussex. In 1915 services were purchased from other operators, enabling the taking-in of Basingstoke and Reading.

Despite a great shift to motorised transport by both army and commercial services, there remained a considerable dependence on the horse. In the pre-war period it was a matter of controversy that General French had purchased a car. This conservatism was reflected in the opposition to Aldershot District Council purchasing a motor fire engine for £850. A committee was formed at South Farnborough to organise a protest against the proposal in 1913. They claimed that 96 per cent of those approached with their petition against the motorised vehicle were willing to sign, and they had won the support of people from North Farnborough as well. A public meeting was held in early September against the 'infernal machine'.

As far as the Basingstoke Canal is concerned, which runs through the centre of Aldershot, after a brief renaissance through its use to convey materials to build the barracks in the 1850s, no one appeared to bail it out and turn it into a profitable concern. Attempts to use it for pleasure boat hire, for water and for some commercial carriage were tried. During the war the Royal Engineers employed it to carry supplies, not only to Aldershot but also to Crookham and Deepcut. However, it was the railway that was most deeply embedded in the culture of transportation for Aldershot. If there was a case of sexual molestation reported to the Aldershot magistrates it happened on the line between Farnham and the town's station. Above all troops came and went in a never ending stream from the station at the end of the aptly named Station Road.

Perhaps as well as its military aspect we should look to its pubs and its music halls to discover its essence. Here again is the ever-present Dickens commenting on the town's musical scene as early as 1859:

> The British soldier is not entirely of a musical turn, and though he is to be seen through many tavern room windows standing up against the fireplace, with his eyes fixed upon the ceiling, in a rapt and enthusiastic manner, singing sentimental songs for the amusement of his comrades, or leading a wild chorus in which they all endeavour to join, he likewise haunts the roadside in little knots, which looks at a distance like a bed of geraniums, and he marches in along the dusty main road in groups of ten, or twelve, as if he had been on an evening walk to Farnborough or some adjacent town.

Dickens goes on to point to The Red, White and Blue Music Hall in the High Street opposite the police station yard, which was the principal watering hole of NCOs at the time. He describes how, like many other pubs that were to become a feature of the town's life, it was fitted with a stage and that with the simulation of gunfire the popular show came to an end sharply at nine-thirty pm. The popular comic singer then received the congratulations of the military audience before being marshalled back to barracks by pickets patrolling the streets, a practice discontinued by the general in charge, Smith-Dorrien, before the war. A whole range of buildings of this kind gave Aldershot its character.

There was The Alexandra at the corner of Alexander Road and Barrack Road. It was next to the public house of the same name and where Charlie Chaplin gave his first performance at the age of 5. Invariably, performers faced an audience of hostile soldiers only there to jeer. His mother, who he was travelling with, was incapacitated through periods of melancholy and depression. In her absence one night in 1894, Charlie went on stage and announced he would only sing in response to money. His coarse audience was so taken aback by this that they took him to their hearts and money was forthcoming. Much to their amusement he stopped the song he had begun singing and concentrated on picking up the money that had been thrown on stage. A more upmarket institution reflecting the town's growing prosperity was the Hippodrome. Built in 1913, even during the war the Carla Rosa Opera Company was appearing there performing grand opera. Visiting reviews also performed at the theatre. A number of theatres like the Palace changed from offering music and theatre to cinema. The Theatre Royal, which grew out of an officers' club, became famous for an exciting event in 1912. In one of the boxes of the theatre, S.F. Cody was observed by the audience and invited to come onto the stage and speak about the role the aeroplanes he was seeking to develop could play a crucial role in time of war. He advertised his flying school on Laffan's Plain. In a grim paradox, his son Sam Cody was killed in action during the war fighting four German aircraft, and Cody himself was to die in an accident the following year. His two other sons, Leon and Vivian, worked in the production of aircraft at the aircraft factory.

The character of the town and camp was represented by its scores of pubs and hotels. Among these were the Alliance (1859), Army and

Navy (1859), The Beehive (1852), Crimea (1859), Elephant and Castle (1859), Florence Nightingale (1872), the Fox and Hounds (dating back from Tudor times), Golden Lion (1787), Prince of Wales (1859), Red Lion (1852), to name just a few. At the time of the creation of the camp only a handful of inns were located in the area. Publicans followed the soldiers amply illustrated by the dates they were set up. Their number produced debate between reformers and traditionalists as to whether regular soldiers could be trusted to behave in a civilised manner and whether harsh penalties were required against drunkenness and debauchery.

As events between 1914 and 1918 unfolded, we witnessed profound changes in the community of camp and town that make up Aldershot. The Liberal politician promised a land fit for heroes, but after the war the town that achieved Borough status subsisted on bread and circuses – when the depression took hold in the late twenties and early thirties, there was precious little bread. The circuses took the form of vast expensive military tattoos, which seemed to be an attempt to justify the bloodletting of the war. By 1916, due to organisation for war requiring collectivist activity, the political and military establishment had to acknowledge the existence of organisations representing the interests of working people. As able-bodied men were sucked up for the mincing machine of the Western Front, Italy and the Middle East, replacement workers had to be found for the Home Front to remain viable. Woman stepped forward to take over the jobs once seen as the exclusive province of men.

In the beginning, the presence of women in the camp was barely tolerated, wives living in shared accommodation in the rudimentary wooden huts. The Wood and Smith-Dorrien reforms improved their lot, but there were still commanding officers who believed there should be no women in their men's accommodation right up to the outbreak of the war. The position of women in Edwardian society meant that career opportunities for the majority from working-class backgrounds were to either go into service or work in factories as manual operatives. Following the education reforms of 1872 and 1902, there might be opportunities to become school mistresses in state schools for those from middle-class families. In Aldershot their situation was worsened by paternalism, with the army deciding that a woman born into a family where the father was in the lower ranks was seen as little more than a camp follower. Middle-class women such, as Miss Daniells, who in 1872 established a centre at the Aldershot Institute to ameliorate the bleak conditions found in the camp, might involve themselves in social care linked to churches, such as the Wesleyans. By 1913, a small Suffragette group had been formed who were first denied access to Queens Road by the police during one of the king's many visits and then shouted at and abused by the parading troops.

All this had changed absolutely by 1918. The crisis with food supplies had led to the creation of the Women's Land Army. At first local farmers refused to accept women workers, but as the war progressed they played a vital role in farm production. Hundreds of women in the Aldershot command area were working in war-related industries. This was particularly true of the Royal Aircraft Factory at Farnborough. Many joined Voluntary Aid Detachment groups (VAD). From a position where any presence within the army had been an anathema a Women's Auxiliary Army Corps had been formed to join the Royal Air Force and a fellow service organisation the Women's Royal Naval Service. It became obvious in Aldershot that women could carry out clerical work for government departments and local government. With the advent of rationing and provision for childcare, the clerical aspect of this work was invariably done by women. In 1917 the formation of the WAAC indicated that the government had belatedly recognised that manpower-planning should be person-power-planning. Haig had resisted the employment of women as clerks and in domestic service, claiming that the kit was likely to cause 'sex difficulties' at army depots. By the end of the war, however, women in uniform were an acceptable facet of society

Convention has it that a grateful nation rewarded its womenfolk with the franchise and greater employment prospects in 1918. At best this is only a half truth. Lloyd George's Khaki Election of 1918 gave the vote to women over 30 in Aldershot and, as with men, provided additional limitations about their having to be identified with a particular place of residence. For women over 30 in the camp, who followed their partner from posting to posting around the country, this resulted in that they were unable to vote for the first time because they lacked an acceptable place of residence. The jobs many women now occupied disappeared as returning soldiers were given preference. For hundreds of married women their role was now unpaid carers for wounded and traumatised men returning from the trenches. Because military hospitals had been overwhelmed with the number of wounded, the homes of many wealthy women were turned over to care and convalescence for the duration of the war. The perpetual work carried on during the war to provide materials for the troops and to raise money for support of the troops dominated many local women's experiences of the war. The psychological response to these changes is best summed up by the local paper running a competition for who would be the first to have their ticket punched on an Aldershot and District Traction Company bus.

Aldershot has one thing in common with Paris. Much is made of its cemetery. It occupies 15 acres within the camp and was created in the 1870s with a chapel of remembrance added in 1879. Buried here are the men who played significant roles in the creation of the town, such as Evelyn Wood, who rebuilt the camp's wooden huts as substantial and habitable brick barracks. At his insistence the barracks were renamed after significant battles fought by the British Army. His burial in 1911 would be the occasion for massed ranks of soldiers marching up the hill to the cemetery accompanied by the swirl of the bagpipes playing Flower of the Forest. Buried here is General Gordon of Khartoum fame, and Edward Busk, the RAF test pilot who proved the danger of planes carrying a reserve tank of fuel when fuel in one tank was transferred to the other. Throughout the war an analysis of deaths reveals how many were related to bolting horses and similar mishaps. Lieutenant Beresford was faced with a bolting horse dragging its rider along one of the roads in the camp. He deliberately placed his own horse in its path and suffered fatal injuries. Disease was to take a grim toll of soldiers in the camps of World War One. Commemorated in the cemetery are the Cameron Highlanders who died in an outbreak of typhoid in 1910. W.D. Bissett, who was awarded the VC during the war, was given a non-descript grave compared to that of Cody, who has a large statue over his grave. Stretching over a large section of the cemetery are the graves of Commonwealth soldiers who died in the Cambridge Military Hospital or smaller hospitals close to Aldershot. In recognition of her work at the Aldershot Institute, Miss Daniells' grave may also be found here.

How far did events following the Boer War represent a move towards a militarised society and a militarised town? The National

Service League set up in 1901 was campaigning for universal national service and compulsory military drill in schools. Lord Roberts, former military commander in the Boer War who had close links with Aldershot and is buried in its cemetery, was one of the leading advocates of the move. As early as 1911 a vote in the House of Commons on conscription was supported by 177 members. The view of the Church of England, reflected by statements from Aldershot clergy like Rev'd F.O.T. Hawkes and Rev'd T. Senior, stated 'War is not murder but sacrifice, which is the soul of Christianity.' Despite this, military participation in 1914 depended on volunteers and great efforts were made to identify and recruit volunteers from all sections of society. From the officer training courses there was easy movement to the Royal Military Academy at nearby Sandhurst. Baden-Powell, in setting up the Boy Scouts, deliberately excluded military drill from activities in order to broaden its appeal. However, he took pride in 70 per cent of scouts going into the army and being bricks to shore up the wall of empire. In Aldershot few scruples existed about the dangers of inculcating militarism at an early age, witnessed by the ease with which young men recruited into cadet groups moved on to active service.

Even in a community so dominated by militaristic attitudes there is some indication that boys and young men were not as affected by jingoism as was previously assumed. However, the rush to the colours in August 1914 must be proof that patriotic groups had managed to instil a sense of what was regarded as duty among working-class men. Years of exposure to imperial propaganda, invasion literature, militaristic organisations and popular songs had overridden natural caution. An indication of how attitudes towards war service became embedded can be seen in the way cadet groups were created in nearby Camberley and Frimley. These grew from the boys in bible class groups. With the patronage of Lord Roberts and his National Service League from 1908, 100 boys from churches of all denominations, from Frimley, Camberley, Yorktown and St Paul's were drilled on Barossa Common and taught to shoot at Bisley. In 1912 the groups were affiliated with the Territorial Army and attached to the Queen's Royal West Surrey Regiment. Each cadet corps received 5 shillings per cadet recruited. The day war broke out, on 4 August, the cadet group in Camberley were preparing to go off to a camp in Eastbourne. With the outbreak of war, 100 joined up and those declared medically unfit found war-work in munitions at Crayford. Only when appeals against enlistment were heard from 1916 at tribunals in Aldershot and Farnborough did arguments against stripping the community of most of its skilled adult male workers come forward.

The story of the war in Aldershot is a story of people who went from hard times before the war into even harder times when it happened. Take George Clarkson whose father was a serving soldier and because of an accident was forced to leave the army two years before he could draw his pension. His mother died when he was 7 and his father was left to bring up a large family. There was a severe trade depression in the period leading up to the war, which produced much unemployment in Aldershot. He remembered having nothing to eat all day and things did not improve when his father married again. His stepmother had no time for him or his brothers and sisters. Although his father was quick-tempered, he was not vindictively cruel like his stepmother.

George remembered one summer going to swim in the Basingstoke Canal and someone stealing the towels off him and his brother. They were given only bread and water for the next two days. He was given the opportunity to apologise, which he readily accepted, but his brother, who resented being punished for something he had no responsibility for, was forced to suffer the bread and water diet for more than a week.

When he was 12 he was top boy at Newport Road School and his teacher wanted him to go on a scholarship to Farnham Grammar School. This was out of the question because of his family's poverty, so he started work as an errand boy at International Stores. Then there was a job with a building firm in Ash requiring a 3-mile walk to get there to start work at 5.30 am. However, his stepmother insisted on him wearing hobnailed boots, which caused him so much pain he had to drop out of the job. Other jobs, such as working with a Canadian blacksmith who went bankrupt, followed until he joined up. Even in later life he was still bitter at not being able to take up his scholarship. In Bill Cotton again, someone who overcame a life of poverty to make the most of the opportunity the army presented to develop his full potential. Jobs were hard to find but he opted for one in a garden shop because it was in the open air. Bill was closely attached to his church and became a Sunday school teacher as well as playing an active role in the scouts' and cadets' groups based around the church. When he joined-up in 1913 and was attached to the McGrigor Barracks he chose the Royal Medical Corps because of an interest in physiology and the workings of the human body. Bill was fortunate, and getting there before the huge enlistment associated with the creation of the new army meant there was a uniform and equipment available for him. His early weeks were devoted to drill and route marches of 6 to 8 miles in and around the camp, together with rifle practice on the Lee Enfield. He enjoyed the tuition on the structure of the body in order to deal with the wounded, together with applying a tourniquet with gauze bandaging to stop bleeding. Finally there was a severe test to prove they could carry this out under the pressure of the battlefield.

The food troops received in the barracks was barely adequate and had to be supplemented with what they could purchase from the canteen on the 1 shilling a day they received as pay. He believed the discipline was hard but fair. When he got a two-day leave pass before Christmas he chose to go to the Union Jack Club in London where he could get a good nutritious meal rather than go back home because his parents' house was so small there was no room for him. In April 1914, he was selected for the military police, the Red Caps, which involved guardroom duty on Saturday nights and dealing with the drunks. War came as a bolt from the blue and he was attached to the 7th Brigade of the Royal Horse Artillery. On 15 August, he left Aldershot with his approved supply of scissors, morphine, dressings, aspirins, iodine all packed on his pony and trap after being inoculated for typhoid.

Why is so little known about what happened in Aldershot during the Great War? A short comment from a frustrated journalist on the *Aldershot News* provides a crucial clue. Following the outbreak of hostilities he laments his inability to report in full detail what is happening in Aldershot and the camp. The Defence of the Realm Act (DORA) had come into effect on 8 August. It stated that no one was allowed to talk about naval or military matters in public places or to spread rumours about military matters. There was a ban on buying binoculars in the town. Guards were put on railways or bridges with the immediate consequence of the death of an innocent civilian in the early months of the war. The melting down of gold or silver was forbidden, restricting the work of jewellers in the town. Guy Fawkes Day was a non-event on 5 November, because the lighting of bonfires or setting off of fireworks was forbidden. If there was any surplus bread for feeding horses or chickens, this was outlawed, as was buying brandy or whisky in a railway refreshment room. The church bells in Aldershot were forced to go silent until November 1918.

The government had given itself the power to take over the factories and workshops of the town, take anyone breaching the terms of the Act to court and to censor newspapers like the *Aldershot News* or the *Sheldrake Military Gazette*. Not satisfied with this there was a promise of more Acts that would increase British Summer Time to improve worker output, and demand of brewers that they increased the water content of their beer during the war. During the hours of opening of the town's pubs it was forbidden to buy anyone any alcohol.

The closest parallel to Aldershot at this time is the closed cities in the Soviet Union. As war progressed, in the magistrates courts the police would bring charges against 'aliens' they considered having no right to be in residence in Aldershot. Among them were people of Belgian nationality on whose behalf the war was being fought. As well as those there were Americans, who the British were seeking desperately to enter the war on their side. That the consequence of the wholesale loss of civil liberties was not contested owed a great deal to the paranoia that had steadily built up about German spies and can be seen in John Buchan's book *The Thirty Nine Steps*. When the conditions in some of the officers' messes in the camps are described, absent are the Spartan conditions the government expected ordinary soldiers and citizens to live under.

Despite this, Laurie Lee's description of the excitement the atmosphere in Aldershot was able to engender among the public sums up the pre-war town.

I got to Aldershot too early so I walked about. We'd had rain and the streets were shining. When suddenly without warning marched a full dressed regiment of soldiers as I stood transfixed; all those men and just me. I didn't know where to look. The officer in front – he had beautiful whiskers – raised his sword and cried out 'eyes right' and would you believe the drums started rolling and the bagpipes started to play, and all those wonderful lads snapped to attention and looked straight into my eyes.

Who spoke for God in Aldershot in the Great War?
After months of searching for the parish journals for the churches of
Aldershot during World War 1, it was discovered that the home of the
British Army had two declared vicars: Rev'd F.O.T. Hawkes and Rev'd
Senior.

There were reports in the *Aldershot News* of the work Rev'd
Frederick Ocheloney Hawkes was doing in the institute attached to his
church to raise a whole range of social issues. Born in 1878, he was
educated at Magdalene College, Oxford, and was ordained in 1903. He
was designated as the Vicar of Aldershot. Rev'd Hawkes was a well-
recognised figure walking through the town and camp with his dog.
He remained a bachelor throughout his life, finishing his ecclesiastical
career as Bishop of Kingston. However, at a number of civic occasions
especially involving intercession about the consequences of the war,
Rev'd Senior's name appears as being Aldershot's vicar. His parish
church in Aldershot was Holy Trinity. In 1918 he nominated Lord
Wolmer from the Conservative and Unionist Party to be the town's
member of parliament.

It is not an issue of who exactly the town's vicar was but who was
the senior figure in the centre of the huge Aldershot command
operating out of an area spreading from the outskirts of London to
Southampton. This is illustrated by a parish magazine for late 1918
discovered at the Surrey History and Archives Centre in Woking. Rev'd
Hawkes had clearly moved from working among his parishioners in
Aldershot to a role as chaplain to the British Army overseas. He had
followed the army into Germany after the Armistice on 11 November
1918, and writes in a frank and objective style of what he found in
Cologne where he was based. Hawkes described seeing underfed
children, the direct result of over four years' blockade by the British
Navy of German Ports. Although fraternisation with the German
population was not permitted, he clearly discussed the war with
ordinary Germans. They were angry and disillusioned with where the
kaiser had led them and with the Prussian dominance of German
military policy. His enquiries revealed that they saw themselves as a
separate state with different values. They were in genuine fear of bandit
groups, or Friecorps, armed ex-soldiers at large in their region.

Hawkes had an opportunity to analyse elementary education in
Germany. He praised the provision of elementary schools he found

there. This was an interest arising from his close involvement with community education in Aldershot. It was Hawkes who asked how soon the billeted troops would be out of Aldershot schools in 1914/15 so education of the town's children could continue. The facilities enjoyed by German elementary schoolchildren were superior to those in Aldershot, but he doubts whether the town's ratepayers would pay to bring local schools up to the standard of the ones he'd inspected. Clearly this followed the work he did in Aldershot advocating greater state involvement in the care of children through nursery education both within the town and in the military camp. Here is someone offering a platform for George Lansbury, a socialist and future leader of the Labour Party, at his institute to speak on social and political affairs. The invitation was extended to Lansbury because of his Christian Socialist beliefs and also because Hawkes realised that after the immense suffering of the war, returning soldiers did not want to return to a town where the workhouse still existed.

What of his fellow vicar, Rev'd Senior? He wrote a commentary for the parish magazines for Holy Trinity and was clearly in competition with Rev'd Hawkes for the chaplaincy of the army. He expressed disappointment at not having secured the post. The difference in approach to the war between Senior and Hawkes might be described as that between the church temporal and the church spiritual. Whereas in all his sermons and public utterances about war and its consequences Hawkes is trying to establish a philosophical rationale for the war, no such doubts appear in Senior's writing. He extols the 'splendid patriotism' to be found at the recruiting stations throughout the Aldershot command. There is just a hint of puzzling as to why the Almighty is allowing the terrible conflict to take place, but 'it must be for some wise purpose'. In 1914 he was convinced throughout the war a true religious belief would return to national life.

Both men saw the availability of alcohol as being a great threat to national life. There were so many pubs in Aldershot quenching the thirst of the camp that one wonders if figures such as Mrs Elizabeth Hacher presiding over her Tavern in Grosvenor Road throughout the war, Earnest Hobbs at the Beehive in the High Street, Matilda Vinson at the Cambridge in Queen's Road or Emily Howe at the Crimean Inn in Crimea Road were in outright competition in shaping the lives of the men in the Aldershot.

Both men were at pains to argue against pressures from a wartime economy allowing trading on Sundays and the advent of Sunday newspapers. The real debate was between total prohibition and restricting the sale of alcohol. As the war continued into 1915, Senior expresses concern at the shortage of curates and Sunday school teachers. That he offered services to soldiers in the camp is evidenced by a letter written from the trenches to Miss Poole, one of his assistants. 'I cannot tell you how grateful I am to you for thinking of me in your prayers.' However, Senior's failure to cope with the demands and stress of providing spiritual succour to the thousands of men who poured into Aldershot is shown by the comment in his letter to his flock justifying a short holiday. 'I need this or else I will break down.' Senior wrote in 1915 that in the two-and-a-half years in post, he had preached 412 times at Holy Trinity and, if other sermons were included, 450 times.

In the church journal he claimed that the advent of war meant that more Christian men were now fighting at any one time since the world began. Presumably he means only in the British Army. The vicar goes on to condemn a strike by Welsh miners as creating a 'sorry picture' to the soldiers at the Front. He welcomes a Mr Goodchild, the new curate, but records that like many in the desperately overcrowded town the curate has been unable to find anywhere to live. In this holy war to maintain Christian values he claims the British Army of volunteers is the largest 'since the world began'. He demanded that a good soldier does not simply attend the services of intercession his ministry offers but approaches a programme of prayer in a similar way to his military training.

The true Christian ideal is not represented by occasional attendance at an intercessional service for the successful outcome of the war. 'Satisfactory drilling and preparation of a soldier is a lot more than his changing out of civilian clothes into a uniform and appearing on parade. Our religious life is suffering from a lack of a systematic approach to prayer,' Senior states, reflecting some impatience as the war drags on into the last months of 1915.

So much of church and civic life in Aldershot was devoted to the collection of money for a whole range of causes. The church magazine records how half the collection at services during the month of September 1915 would be sent to a field hospital in 'gallant Serbia'. Some of it would go towards the provision of church tents in Malta, Flanders and Egypt. Money had to be found for the maintenance of fifty motor ambulances. A continual demand supported by F.O.T. Hawkes was for money and foodstuffs to supplement the almost starvation rations endured by British prisoners-of-war in Germany. Because collection boxes were rattled for a whole range of war causes, necessary donations were reduced for the Aldershot civilian hospital, which relied on public philanthropy for its existence. Finance seemed to be the basis for the church's existence because, in every issue of the magazine, many pages are devoted to listing gifts and donations. As the war progressed the state stepped in offering war bonds to support the prosecution of the war.

In the congregations of both men, armies of women were working to produce bandages, splints, bed jackets, pillowslips and towels for local hospitals. A similar demand was coming from the new hospitals being set up in Farnborough by the Red Cross. However when the war entered 1916, Senior lamented how little religion seemed to be affecting life in Aldershot's camps. He did note, however, a comment by a military expert that people are now kinder to each other than they were before the war. As universal conscription is introduced he addressed serving soldiers as 'children of God'. The constraints of war were closing in on his parish as the size of its parish magazine was reduced drastically. In autumn 1916, there was a crisis in agricultural production because not enough agricultural labour was available to bring in the crops. In the *Aldershot News*, Hawkes wrote about the consequences of a change in women's labour towards forming a Land Army replacing men called-up for the army. His institute pushed at the narrow boundaries of conventional attitudes towards labour following gender stereotypes. Hawkes was, however, on record expressing doubts about how wisely women earning good wages will spend them and whether it will lead to immoral behaviour.

By 1917, Senior's drastically reduced magazine discussed the bread ration weighing just 4lb per week, ½lb per day. His congregation was supporting the Cambridge Military Hospital with foodstuffs indicated by a letter of thanks from the hospital expressing gratitude for eggs and fruit at Easter. A sum of £40 was collected for the supply depot for Aldershot's military hospitals. After the black period at the commencement of 1918, Senior counselled how victory would come quickly if we said our prayers. When victory finally came, there was a huge open air service on 11 November and another of thanksgiving on 17 November. Senior instructed his readers to vote in the hastily convened Khaki Election of 14 December, which the *Aldershot News* described as a non-event because so many of the electorate were excluded.

Our two clergymen provide differing perspectives of the post war world in welcoming home the town's soldiers on 12 March 1919. Senior spoke with disgust about the tyrannous regime in Soviet Russia and criticises the striking railway workers. On the other hand, Hawkes recognised the demands of working people for a reconstructed more equal society but with cautions. Both were united in a practical concern about memorials in their churches for how the sacrifice of the war would be remembered.

What of the other dominations? At the time of enlistment it was said that 75 per cent defined themselves as Church of England. In 1858, someone from the Wesleyans surveying Aldershot and the army made the following comment:

> The British Army is itself a class separated almost entirely from civil society. The soldier occupies a position of his own. Ordinarily he is under extremely demoralising influences against which the utmost effort to discipline are ineffective to counteract. There is constant neighbourhood of vice.

For the 15,000 troops there was no established place of worship. In response to this the Wesleyans appointed a minister, Rev'd Bachelor, who set about trying to establish a congregation for the camp and town. He encountered considerable opposition from the military hierarchy, who believed there was no role for non-conformist religion within the camp. Only C of E padres and chaplains could be paid for working in the regiments of the camp. An approach by the Wesleyans in 1858 for access to the army for one of their chaplains to the War Office was greeted with the response: 'I am unable to accede to your application.' However, each of the reforms to the army, such as the Cardwell Reforms of 1872 to 1873, resulted in a growing number of non-conformist chaplains being accepted into the army. By 1908, Wesleyan chaplains were playing an active role in the exercises of the Territorials, although there was a considerable debate about rifle practice taking place on Sundays. In the build-up to the war the non-conformist churches and their amenities providing vital social support were in place. An example of this was the Percy Illingworth Institute costing £5,000 set up by the Baptists and opened by Lloyd George. By 1915 the Primitive Methodists had set up eight huts offering support for the troops, while the Presbyterians opened the halls attached to their churches for a range of amenities. The Wesleyans pioneered the development of homes for soldiers, established temporary institutes linked to local churches and thirty-four semi-permanent huts. Despite all this activity, the C of E slipped effortlessly into providing the overwhelming number of chaplains in the army.

They shared Rev'd Senior's consternation that the advent of war had not bought with it a return to Christianity. Their role increasingly was a social one leading the struggle for awareness among the troops of VD, which was at one stage invaliding twice as many soldiers as the medical consequences of life in the trenches. The difference of approach towards religion in wartime transcended protestant sectarian divide. Asked how a chaplain would approach the last minutes of life of a mortally wounded soldier, Catholics and High Church Anglicans would give him the last rites while the advice of other chaplains was to offer him a cigarette. However, the Wesleyans, Primitive Methodists, Methodists and Baptists all represented in Aldershot were not invited to the Thanksgiving Service marking the end of the war at Westminster Abbey in 1919.

Frederick Hawkes went on to be Bishop of Kingston until he retired in 1952.

And in the heavens …
The British War Office was convinced there was a role for flight in the form of balloons through recognising the use made of them by Confederate forces in the American Civil War (1861–1865). By 1880 balloons were being used in the army's manoeuvres at Aldershot. Whatever brief the army had for balloons was focused on their role in colonial wars for vital observation. There, just over the bridge across the Basingstoke Canal, a balloon factory was established.

However, in the manoeuvres of 1890 balloons proved so useful that a balloon equipment store was set up in Aldershot near the Stanhope Lines and adjacent to the Basingstoke Canal. The thirty-three men and three officers could be described as the country's first working aviation unit. The School for Ballooning was also moved to Aldershot. This was in the belief that ballooning for observation should play a crucial role in reconnaissance. The balloon factory was born in 1892. Later, the factory also began the development of aircraft.

By 1899, balloons proved they could play a vital role in the Boer War. This resulted in a great demand on the factory to produce new equipment. It began to produce new balloons, and to employ engineers and scientific specialists in flight. In contrast to the National Physical Laboratory, who drew most of their personnel from Imperial College, the factory attracted scientists and skilled workers from Cambridge. Among these was D.H. Pinsent, a brilliant mathematician and personal friend of the philosopher Wittgenstein. He was killed in an accident in 1918. During the war, Hermann Glauert, an outstanding physicist, pioneered work solving the problem of spinning aircraft, one of the main causes for crashes. In just one month in 1918, of 106 flying accidents, forty-one were attributed to spinning.

With the appointment of Lieutenant Walter Templer, the serious role of a factory dependent on direct state funding commenced. A review following the Boer War suggested moving the factory from its existing site, which was now found to be too enclosed, to a new 22 acre site a few miles away at Farnborough. During the Great War there were distinct social and political implications of this that went beyond this physical move of locale.

The move coincided with experiments in man-lifting kites. Enter Samuel Cody, a man who was able to link the excitement of extra-terrestrial flight from the drawing board to Aldershot's imagination. He was born in Birdville, Texas, in 1861, as William Cowdery. He changed his name to Cody when he set up a wild west show that he brought to England. In many ways Cody resembled a modern day celebrity and it was this element in his character that endeared him to Aldershot. His competitions and stunts kept him in the public eye.

By 1901, Cody was offering his man-lifting kites to the War Office, aware of the role balloons had played in the Boer War. In June 1904, he was in Aldershot testing with the army one of his kites on a salary of £1,000 a year. He was given permission to base his workshop on Laffan's Plain and large crowds started to assemble when he tested his kites. Meanwhile, at the factory itself, experimentation was going on with aircraft as well as balloons and aerial photography. Their approach to aircraft development was in striking contrast to Cody's reliance on trial and error. By 1907, Cody achieved the first powered flight at

Farnborough on Cove Common, and the factory had produced Nulli Secundus, an airship that circumnavigated Farnborough Common at a height of 800 feet.

Although army minister R.B. Haldane originally denied any future for aircraft, the progress of Germany in aviation development reluctantly convinced him of the need. Behind the spectacle of Cody's new planes taking to the skies was the reality of an infrastructure to support powered flight being developed at Farnborough. In December 1909 the two elements of ballooning and the factory, were separated. Significantly for Aldershot, a visionary superintendent, Mervyn Joseph Pius O'Gorman, was given a seven-year contract on a part-time basis of three days a week on a salary of £950. At that time he had a staff of 100. He was 38 and a graduate in mechanical engineering from Trinity College Dublin. He was described as being brash, flamboyant and witty and filling the rooms he worked in with the smell of Turkish cigarettes. The aircraft factory was to concentrate on balloon experiments, research and testing, co-operating with the National Physical Laboratory. There should be no volume production at the factory, although O'Gorman campaigned to build his own aeroplane. He is reported as becoming increasingly irritated at the way sappers associated with balloons invaded his workshops. Under his auspice the factory spread and the land required for testing new planes grew. Part of his genius was that he discovered men who made outstanding contributions to the development of the British aircraft industry. However, there was continual opposition from private sector aircraft developers who saw the government subsidies he enjoyed as giving him an unfair advantage. The period of the war was to highlight how dangerous flying these experimental aircraft was. Even before the war an outstanding young designer, Ridge, was killed flying the SE1, one of the planes designed by another of O'Gorman's protégés, Geoffrey de Havilland. In the period before the war, William Cody's Cathedral design had won a competition for military design. Fortunately, wiser counsels prevailed at the War Office and the BE series associated with the factory was preferred. Despite continual hostility from other plane makers O'Gorman was given permission to go into production with his own plane on 14 November 1913. He was suspicious of people like Cody, who he referred to as 'enthusiasts', but in 1910 he became aware that his factory needed aircraft inventors so he appointed de Havilland in this role and as a test pilot. De Havilland met Fred Green, the factory's chief engineer, at the Motor Show at Olympia who, as well as offering him a job, persuaded O'Gorman to buy the plane de Havilland had just built. By the following year the factory was being carried along by de Havilland's work. In that year they developed a seaplane using the nearby Fleet Pond.

O'Gorman's staff grew to 4,000 including skilled draughtsmen who, unlike other manufacturers, produced drawings for all the component parts of his planes. These were supplied on request to commercial aircraft manufacturers. However, he was restricted by a War Office ruling forbidding spending on aircraft research resulting in any work having to be done, although repairs were made on existing aircraft. It would become clear that he represented a new age of war-related industrial production. This would bring him into conflict with some of the traditional policies and attitudes that dominated military thinking.

When he took over, the factory consisted of one large shed (originally erected on the Aldershot site in 1900 for balloon making), one airship shed and a small machine shop. His total staff was fifty men and fifty women employed in a drawing office, workshop and for administrative functions. O'Gorman restructured the workshop to reflect the technical requirements of a new industry. He created scientific specialisms in chemistry, physics, engine technology, metallurgy and wireless. Apprenticeships were offered in the new range of skills demanded by flying. In this way he introduced a genuinely scientific approach to the design, construction and flight testing needed for the air industry. The factory was now focused on the construction and repair of aeroplanes.

By 1910, de Havilland's more practical and reliable plane had been purchased. This was reflected in the name of the factory being altered to the aircraft factory the following year. But O'Gorman was coming up against the army's determination to restrict experiment and development of new aircraft at the factory. They conceived his role as providing technical support for the range of aircraft in which the army was now investing.

Parallel to this Cody was capturing the public's attention by entering the many competitions offered for aircraft development. In 1909 he entered his flying Cathedral based on a French design in the Michelin Cup. It crashed on Laffan's Plain in 1911. In 1912, de Havilland's BE2 plane achieved a record height of 10,000 feet. The failure of many of the aeroplanes of the period was attributed to unsatisfactory engines. O'Gorman successfully bid for his factory to produce a better engine, which it produced in 1913.

Cody had won trials with a biplane beating thirty other French and English competitors in 1912 on Salisbury Plain. He was working on pioneering ideas for an air ambulance carrying a table, doctor, assistant and an anaesthetist. He lost his life when flying his latest aircraft, designed as a private entry in the *Daily Mail* race on 7 August 1910 around Britain. The aeroplane broke up and he was catapulted 300 feet to the ground. The sense of loss in the Aldershot community was reflected by the 100,000 people who attended his funeral. Clearly he was regarded not only as a local but a national treasure. A national paper described his death as 'one of the greatest blows which aviation has sustained in recent years'. He was given a full military funeral and is buried in Aldershot Military Cemetery.

Despite some grudging belated recognition that aircraft would play a significant role in modern warfare, the factory and what was to become the Royal aircraft factory was inadequately equipped for the demands that were soon to be made upon them. The state of the aerodrome they operated out of was dangerous because of the obstacles to flight posed by un-cleared trees and shrubs. Despite this the Royal aircraft factory produced the BE2c, which entered service in 1914 and was the first aircraft to intercept and destroy a Zeppelin. Throughout the war the conflict of interest between O'Gorman's rational, scientific establishment and an army administration fighting a war of attrition in France became very apparent through demands that young skilled scientists, engineers and tradesmen who worked at the factory be conscripted into the army. There was also a desperate need for an adequate engine to power British planes, which desperate attempts to prohibit discussion about new design through the Defence of the Realm Act did not help. As war approached the War Office realised that there were dangers relying on the private sector to produce the aeroplanes they required. The development of the aircraft factory at Farnborough brought with it an industrial/military relationship.

Aldershot Command Units, August 1914

Division	Brigade	Unit	Barracks	Officers	WOs	Sergeants	Trumpeters, Drummers, Buglers	Rank and file	Total all ranks	Comments
Aldershot Garrison										
	1st Cavalry Bde	2nd Dragoon Guards	Willems Bks	24	2	44	6	524	600	
	1st Cavalry Bde	5th Dragoon Guards	Warburg Bks	19	2	43	5	536	605	
	1st Cavalry Bde	11th Hussars	Beaumont Bks	27	2	44	6	577	656	
		15th Hussars (detachment)	Beaumont Bks	13	0	17	1	235	266	
	1st Cavalry Bde - attached	Royal Horse Artillery, IV Brigade, J Battery	Waterloo Bks West	5	0	9	2	159	175	6 guns
	1st Cavalry Bde - attached	Royal Horse Artillery, VII Brigade, I and L Batteries	Waterloo Bks West	14	1	19	5	311	340	12 guns (6 per battery)
	1st Cavalry Bde - attached	Royal Engineers, 1 Field Squadron, 1 Signal Troop	Gibraltar Bks							*See total for all RE*
1st Division	1st Infantry Bde	1st Bn, Coldstream Gds	Blenheim Bks	30	1	41	13	595	680	
1st Division	1st Infantry Bde	1st Bn, Scots Gds	Ramillies Bks	29	1	41	20	594	685	

Division	Brigade	Unit	Barracks	Officers	WOs	Sergeants	Trumpeters, Drummers, Buglers	Rank and file	Total all ranks	Comments
		Total manning all RE units		72	7	139	10	1,312	1,540	
		Royal Garrison Artillery, 1st Heavy Brigade, HQ plus 26, 35 and 108 Batteries	Possibly Redan plus other locations	17	1	21	7	386	432	12 guns (4 per battery)
		Mounted Military Police	Military Police Bks	2	1	6	0	48	57	
		Military Foot Police	Military Police Bks	0	1	5	0	38	44	
		Army Service Corps, Horse Transport Companies: 1 (Transport Depot), 7, 9, 10, 16, 20, 26, 27, 28, 31, 35, 36	Buller Bks							*See total for all ASC*
		Army Service Corps, Mechanical Transport Companies: 52 (MT Depot), 53, 54, 57, 58, 59, 60, 61	Buller Bks							*See total for all ASC*
		Army Service Corps, Supply Companies: A (Supply Depot), C	Buller Bks							*See total for all ASC*
		Total manning all ASC units		99	33	225	13	1,517	1,887	

Division	Brigade	Unit	Barracks	Officers	WOs	Sergeants	Trumpeters, Drummers, Buglers	Rank and file	Total all ranks	Comments
2nd Division	6th Infantry Bde	1st Bn, King's (Liverpool) Regt	Talavera Bks	24	2	39	15	734	814	
2nd Division	6th Infantry Bde	2nd Bn, South Staffordshire Regt	Badajos Bks	23	2	37	16	457	535	
2nd Division	6th Infantry Bde	1st Bn, Royal Berkshire Regt	Mandora Bks	24	2	38	16	707	787	
2nd Division	6th Infantry Bde	1st Bn, King's Royal Rifle Corps	Salamanca Bks	25	2	39	15	597	678	
2nd Division	Divisional Troops	Royal Field Artillery, XXXIV Brigade, HQ plus 22, 50 and 70 Batteries	Waterloo Bks East	17	1	30	7	396	451	12 guns (4 per battery)
		Royal Artillery Mounted Band	Waterloo Bks	0	1	3	0	57	61	
2nd Division	Divisional Troops	Royal Engineers, 5 and 11 (Field) Co, 2 Signal Co	Gibraltar Bks							See total for all RE
	Army Troops	Royal Engineers, A Signal Co, 1 Bridging Train	Gibraltar Bks							See total for all RE
		Royal Engineers, Training Depot for Field Units	Gibraltar Bks							See total for all RE
		Army Signal School	Stanhope Lines							See total for all RE

Division	Brigade	Unit	Barracks	Officers	WOs	Sergeants	Trumpeters, Drummers, Buglers	Rank and file	Total all ranks	Comments
1st Division	1st Infantry Bde	1st Bn, Royal Highlanders (Black Watch)	Oudenarde Bks	24	2	37	21	551	635	
1st Division	1st Infantry Bde	2nd Bn, Royal Munster Fusiliers	Malplaquet Bks	23	2	39	16	662	742	
1st Division	2nd Infantry Bde	1st Bn, Loyal North Lancashire Regt	Tournay Bks	29	2	38	16	646	731	
1st Division	Divisional Troops	Royal Field Artillery, XXVI Brigade, HQ plus 116, 117 and 118 Batteries	Lille Bks	17	1	29	7	429	483	12 guns (4 per battery)
1st Division	Divisional Troops	Royal Engineers, 23 (Field) Co, 1 Signal Co	Gibraltar Bks							See total for all RE
2nd Division	5th Infantry Bde	2nd Bn, Worcestershire Regt	Corunna Bks	24	2	38	16	538	618	
2nd Division	5th Infantry Bde	2nd Bn, Ox and Bucks Light Infantry	Albuhera Bks	22	2	39	13	535	611	
2nd Division	5th Infantry Bde	2nd Bn, Highland Light Infantry	Maida Bks	25	2	38	21	519	605	
2nd Division	5th Infantry Bde	2nd Bn, Connaught Rangers	Barossa Bks	25	2	38	16	574	655	

Division	Brigade	Unit	Barracks	Officers	WOs	Sergeants	Trumpeters, Drummers, Buglers	Rank and file	Total all ranks	Comments
		Royal Army Medical Corps, 1, 2 and 3 Companies	McGrigor Bks	40	6	31	2	272	351	
		Royal Army Medical Corps, A, B and C Depot Companies	McGrigor Bks	50	1	28	14	514	607	
		Army Ordnance Department, Companies 1 and 4	Stanhope Lines	0	4	65	1	149	219	
		Army Veterinary Corps, 1 and 2 Sections		21	1	9	0	30	61	
		Army Pay Corps		0	2	20	0	0	22	
Total Aldershot Garrison		3 x cavalry regiments; 13 x infantry battalions; 12 x artillery batteries; 5 x RE Co.s plus minor RE units; 22 x ASC Co.s; 6 x RAMC Co.s; 2 x Ordnance Co.s; 2 x veterinary sections; military police; plus other support and minor units and detachments		764	91	1,289	300	15,199	**17,643**	

Division	Brigade	Unit	Barracks	Officers	WOs	Sergeants	Trumpeters, Drummers, Buglers	Rank and file	Total all ranks	Comments
		Army Ordnance Corps (detachment)		0	0	1	0	0	1	
Total Sandhurst				0	0	4	0	2	**6**	
Various stations										
		Royal Artillery Clerks' Section		0	2	12	0	1	15	
		Royal Engineers Clerks		0	0	10	0	5	15	
Total Various				0	2	22	0	6	**30**	
Total Aldershot Command		4 x cavalry regiments 21 x infantry battalions 30 x artillery batteries 9 x RE Co.s plus other units 23 x ASC Co.s plus detachments 6 x RAMC Co.s plus detachments 2 x Ordnance Co.s plus detachments 4 x RFC Squadrons plus other units 2 x Veterinary sections Military Police (mounted and foot) Pay Corps detachments		1,169	124	1,945	459	23,548	**27,245**	

Information compiled by Paul H. Vickers, January 2014. Sources:

Army List, August 1914
Distribution of Regimental Strength of the Army, August 1914
Barracks Finder, Aldershot Military Museum website
Order of Battle of Divisions, Part 1 - the Regular British Divisions. Official History of the Great War, HMSO 1935

Division	Brigade	Unit	Barracks	Officers	WOs	Sergeants	Trumpeters, Drummers, Buglers	Rank and file	Total all ranks	Comments
Farnborough										
		Royal Flying Corps, HQ, Airship Detachment, Kite Section, 1, 5, 6 and 7 Squadrons, Aircraft Park		43	4	47	0	470	**564**	
Blackdown										
1st Division	2nd Infantry Bde	1st Bn, Northamptonshire Regt	Dettingen Bks	25	2	39	9	588	663	
1st Division	2nd Infantry Bde	2nd Bn, King's Royal Rifle Corps	Alma Bks	23	2	38	15	624	702	
Total Blackdown		2 x infantry battalions		48	4	77	24	1,212	**1,365**	
Deepcut										
1st Division	Divisional Troops	Royal Field Artillery, XXV Brigade, HQ plus 113, 114 and 115 Batteries		21	1	32	7	405	466	12 guns (4 per battery)
1st Division	Divisional Troops	Royal Field Artillery, XLIII (Howitzer) Brigade, HQ plus 30, 40 and 57 Batteries		18	1	31	7	407	464	12 guns (4 per battery)
Total Deepcut		6 x artillery batteries		39	2	63	14	812	**930**	

Division	Brigade	Unit	Barracks	Officers	WOs	Sergeants	Trumpeters, Drummers, Buglers	Rank and file	Total all ranks	Comments
Bordon										
1st Division	3rd Infantry Bde	1st Bn, Royal West Surrey Regt	Guadaloupe Bks	26	2	39	11	629	707	
1st Division	3rd Infantry Bde	1st Bn, South Wales Borderers	St Lucia Bks	23	2	36	14	535	610	
1st Division	3rd Infantry Bde	1st Bn, Gloucestershire Regt	Quebec Bks	22	2	37	16	549	626	
1st Division	3rd Infantry Bde	2nd Bn, Welsh Regt	Martinique Bks	25	2	38	15	504	584	
1st Division	Divisional Troops	Royal Field Artillery, XXIX Brigade, HQ plus 46, 51 and 54 Batteries		19	1	28	7	412	467	18 guns (6 per battery)
1st Division	Divisional Troops	Royal Engineers, 26 (Field) Co		3	1	12	2	100	118	
2nd Division	Divisional Troops	Royal Field Artillery, XLI Brigade, HQ plus 4, 16 and 17 Batteries		17	1	29	7	385	439	12 guns (4 per battery)
		Army Service Corps, 13 Co (Horse Transport)		4	1	13	1	82	101	

Division	Brigade	Unit	Barracks	Officers	WOs	Sergeants	Trumpeters, Drummers, Buglers	Rank and file	Total all ranks	Comments
		Royal Army Medical Corps (detachment)		3	0	2	0	4	9	
		Army Ordnance Corps (detachment)		0	0	6	0	0	6	
Total Bordon		4 x infantry battalions; 6 x artillery batteries; 1 x RE Co; 1 x ASC Co; plus support units		142	12	240	73	3,200	**3,667**	
Woking										
1st Division	2nd Infantry Bde	2nd Bn, Royal Sussex Regt	Inkerman Bks	29	2	39	13	639	722	
		Army Service Corps (detachment)	Inkerman Bks	1	0	1	0	4	6	
		Royal Army Medical Corps (detachment)	Inkerman Bks	1	0	1	0	4	6	
		Army Ordnance Corps (detachment)	Inkerman Bks	0	0	1	0	0	1	
Total Woking		1 x infantry battalion; plus support units		31	2	42	13	647	**735**	
Ewshott										
2nd Division	Divisional Troops	Royal Field Artillery, XXXVI Brigade, HQ plus 15, 48 and 71 Batteries		17	1	30	6	395	449	12 guns (4 per battery)

Division	Brigade	Unit	Barracks	Officers	WOs	Sergeants	Trumpeters, Drummers, Buglers	Rank and file	Total all ranks	Comments
Camberley										
		Royal Engineers (detachment)		6	1	3	0	12	22	
		Army Service Corps (detachment)		0	0	0	0	1	1	
		Royal Army Medical Corps (detachment)		0	0	1	0	2	3	
Total Camberley				6	1	4	0	15	**26**	
Pirbright										
2nd Division	4th Brigade	2nd Bn, Grenadier Guards		28	1	41	16	649	735	
		Army Service Corps (detachment)		0	0	2	0	4	6	
		Royal Army Medical Corps (detachment)		3	0	1	0	5	9	
		Army Ordnance Corps (detachment)		0	0	4	0	0	4	
Total Pirbright		1 x infantry battalion; plus support units		31	1	48	16	658	**754**	
Sandhurst										
		Royal Engineers, Staff		0	0	2	0	0	2	
		Royal Army Medical Corps (detachment)		0	0	1	0	2	3	

Division	Brigade	Unit	Barracks	Officers	WOs	Sergeants	Trumpeters, Drummers, Buglers	Rank and file	Total all ranks	Comments
		Royal Field Artillery, XLIV Brigade, HQ plus 47, 56 and 60 Batteries		18	1	29	7	429	484	12 guns (4 per battery)
		Royal Army Medical Corps (detachment)		1	0	1	0	2	4	
		Army Ordnance Corps (detachment)		0	0	1	0	0	1	
Total Ewshott		6 x artillery batteries; plus support units		36	2	61	13	826	**938**	
Longmoor										
		15th Hussars		13	2	25	5	246	291	
		Royal Engineers, 8 (Ry) Co, 10 (Ry) Co, Railway Depot, 1 Signal Sqn		14	1	19	1	250	285	
		Army Service Corps (detachment)		0	0	1	0	1	2	
		Royal Army Medical Corps (detachment)		2	0	1	0	4	7	
		Army Ordnance Corps (detachment)		0	0	2	0	0	2	
Total Longmoor		3 x RE Co.s plus minor RE units; 1 x cavalry detachment; plus support units		29	3	48	6	501	**587**	

CHAPTER 1

1914
It all Begins

For all we have and are,
For all our children's fate,
Stand up and take the War,
The Hun is at the gate
– Jack Cole

Who was there?

On 4 August the commander in chief of Aldershot, Lieutenant General Sir Douglas Haig, was in Government House, Aldershot, waiting for the news that the ultimatum sent by the British requiring German troops to leave Belgium had run out. He had known for some time that the country was on the brink of war. The telephone rang just before midnight. Headquarters duty officer Captain John Harding-Newman told Haig that war had broken out with Germany. He was to command one of the two corps of the Expeditionary Force and should come up to London for a meeting of the War Council in Downing Street the following afternoon.

The War Office had anticipated the worst and had ordered a general mobilisation sending out a one-word telegram, 'mobilise' under the signature Troopers, the secretary of state's code name. In his diary Haig claims that everything had been well-thought out and foreseen.

Maurice Dease, a young reservist with a private income, describes the process of procuring the element vital for any mobilisation to take place. On 4 August for the Fusiliers he was charged with procuring at the greatest possible speed sufficient horses for his regiment. At 6 pm he was in Blackwater negotiating to buy horses only to discover that his purchasing officer, 'an old dodderer', had mislaid the regimental chequebook. He had to borrow cheques in order to buy the whole range of horses from hunters to draught horses that he required. He did a round of local stables paying on average £45 and selling his own prize hunter Palm for £60. In the countryside he met opposition because the draught horses were required for the harvest, which was just being brought in.

A young reservist comments on the days before mobilisation:

> Having a house in Fleet that summer, I cycled over to beyond Camberley one day, just at the stage when coming events were beginning to cast their shadows before and after the Sarajevo assassinations, to watch the Aldershot command at work. And to talk to many members of the command and with some of the Staff College personnel who had turned out to see the show. Some of them, for example Lieut.-Colonel Thwaites and J.T. Burnett-Stuart and Major (or was it Captain) W.E. Ironside, were all to go far within the next five years. But there were others that day who I met for the last time – Brigadier Neil Findlay commanding the Artillery, who had been in the same room as me at the 'shop' and Lieut.-Colonel Adrian Grant-Duff of the Black Watch, excusing his presence in the firing line on the plea that he 'really must see how his lads worked through the woodlands'; both had made the supreme sacrifice before the leaves were off the trees. How many are alive and unmaimed today of those fighting men of all ranks who buzzed about so cheerily amid the heather and the pine trees that afternoon and who melted away so silently out of Aldershot in a very few days?

Travis Hempson received a telegram to report to Aldershot immediately. He travelled to Aldershot with a Major Norrington from the Army Service Corps who had been in South Africa, and was depressed at the prospect of war. Unlike the contemporary opinion he stated that the war would be a long one and he was pessimistic of both he and Hempson surviving. On arrival at North Camp the two men shared a taxi to the Royal Army Medical Corps mess. Hempson went on to Redan Hill, where he found his regiment based in bell tents. That night, after a couple of blankets had been found for him, he slept on the ground in one of the tents. Swords that had at first been seen as an essential part of kit were soon discarded as unnecessary. Identity discs, field dressings and iron rations were issued. The iron rations consisted of a three-quarter lb of bully beef, four biscuits, two cubes of Oxo and a ration of tea and sugar. These were supposed to last for twenty-four hours. They were joined by their padre, who had been through the Boer War and was given responsibility for the mess. Hempson's pleasure at the good weather was rebuffed by an NCO who reminded him that winter was just around the corner. Many of the men were given anti-typhoid inoculations at the Cambridge Hospital, which made them unwell for several days. Throughout the night there was the noise of troops in training.

Hempson was informed that his group of the Royal Army Medical Corps would be leaving on 19 August. The 18th was occupied with the packing of wagons and the organising of a valise weighing 35lb.

Lieutenant Aldis comments:

The secrecy of everything was remarkable; I don't think our letters from Aldershot got home until after we had left. News of what was happening was mostly what we read in the papers when we got home, and there was little official information in these. The smooth mobilisation and departure of the original BEF has been so much written about. The fact remains that as far as the ordinary bloke could see of what was happening the whole thing was amazing apart from a little trouble with some of the horses. Many of them were huge beasts and could hardly hold their heads up in the cattle trucks. Entertaining instructions stated – 'if there is any trouble in getting the horse in, two drivers should lock arms above its hock and hustle him in.' Our Army Service Corps drivers were all very small, though tough, and it struck us as rather amusing to see two small men trying to hustle an enormous draught horse that had other ideas on the subject. The train left Aldershot at 2.30am. We didn't know where we were going but thought it would be Southampton. Though there was some talk of Bristol. I slept a bit on and off, in the train, but came to life about 10 miles from Southampton, a district new to me but recognised by others in the carriage. This proved to be our port of embarkation. The train ran along the quay, and was unloaded on the wharf'.

What really happened at Aldershot Station during the early days of August 1914? The unprepossessing Victorian pile had been the scene of wild events shortly after the turn of the century when the 'Soldiers of the Queen' were packed off to the South African War. Wives and partners of the soldiers had followed their men from the camps as they marched to the station screaming, and in some cases clinging to their men. Amongst the bunting, imperial colours and flags, regimental bands played and it seemed as though the whole town had assembled in Station Road.

The mystery is that commentators are unable to agree whether the same thing happened when the British Expeditionary Force, Kitchener's 'Contemptible Army', left for Belgium. At 6 pm on 3 August a soldier had appeared from the side entrance of Headquarters Building in the camp and hoisted three black balls up onto a flagstaff, officially beginning the mobilisation of British Forces. Reservists were called up as were Territorials from Hampshire. Guard duties were allocated such as ensuring the security of the aircraft factory, and vital communication routes, such as the railway lines. This resulted in a local tragedy almost immediately. Someone walking near a line in the evening did not hear the order to stop and was shot dead. A further tragedy occurred among the regular army, probably due to the prevailing spy mania. A sentry shot dead his brother-in-law claiming he felt certain he was a spy even though he could not see him properly.

Part of the feature of the well-oiled machine of mobilisation was that the Force would slip away in secrecy from the station on trains manned by railway staff sworn to secrecy about where they were going. Some reports suggest wild scenes as thousands of Territorials poured into the town and camps when the time came for their departure, in contrast to Haig's plans for a silent departure. Such was the enthusiasm that many Reservists reported without having received their call-up papers. Despite years of planning, the army struggled to cope and Aldershot became a vast tented city with canvas settlements stretching for miles around the town occupying every available green space in the camps. Fortunately, the period from mobilisation through October was featured by days of fine weather. Thousands of horses commandeered from around the country joined the troops on their journey first to Southampton and then across the Channel. The problem was that there was a shortage of harnesses and specialised equipment that went with an army whose whole power of movement depended on the horse. On the trains leaving Aldershot were 1,000 men from Aldershot, itself being part of the Hampshire Regiment. By 8 August, Kitchener almost alone in not believing that the war would not be over by Christmas had made one of his appeals for volunteers. It was the first of many. Such was the enthusiasm engendered by calls of this nature that in its vox-pop, the *Aldershot News* reports that the son of an important figure in Aldershot life was travelling back from Canada to join the British Army.

John Walters in *Aldershot Review* (1970) speaks of a type of hysteria that accompanied the declaration of war and of unbalanced emotionalism. Women and girls were seen kissing unknown soldiers. At the town's Hippodrome Theatre the performance was interrupted for the announcement of war, to be followed by repeated singing of *God save the King* and *Rule Britannia*. On 13 August, according to Walters, their departure was the scene of public lamentation from the soldiers' wives. On 14 August, Haig, after dining with the king, left for Belgium to take command of the First Army Corps. He was succeeded as commander of the camp by Major General Archibald Hunter.

Assuming that the Expeditionary Force slipped away quietly, a silent town and camp was transformed into the main training centre for the British Army. On 4 August 4 there were 174,800 troops in the camp. Within a few months Kitchener's new army had multiplied that number eight times over. The Salamanca Barracks designed to accommodate 800 men before the outbreak of war, by September housed 2,000. At Maida Barracks, the furniture for the Black Watch and Cameron Highlanders was removed so that the men could be packed in side by side. The experience of Aldershot and the wider command area was one indelibly linked to the culture of British life throughout the last century. The huge influx of volunteers swamped the military authority's ability to cope with them. New barracks were being erected around Aldershot at Chobham Ridges, Pirbright, Rushmoor, Twesledown, Frensham and Borden as hundreds of workmen were employed to build huts. No uniforms were available, apart from odd items conjured up from sources around the country. But recruits were given £10 to go and see if they could find appropriate clothing. Within a few weeks the civilian clothes the recruits were wearing were hanging off them in rags. Old Post Office uniforms were found and 50,000 greatcoats purchased. It was spring before khaki uniforms began to be issued. The footwear they were wearing was bringing their feet up in blisters because of the route marches that were part of their training. One report of a severely crippled volunteer records his refusal to complain about how severe his blisters were through fear of losing his place in his regiment. Huts designed to hold twenty now had fifty crammed in, and in the tents men slept top and bottom style in order to fit them all in. In some cases trilby hats had to suffice for regulation caps and a weird collection of water bottles and haversacks were handed out to some of the trainees.

Anthony Eden spoke of arriving as an officer for the new Kitchener army in late 1914. His view of the lines of huts, relics from the Boer War, left him much uninspired and complaining about their 'dreary rigidity' as midwinter approached. He was critical of the way in which the recruits were being trained for battle in open country, ignoring the reality of trench warfare in France. Eden told of the amateur approach of early training and of an incident with disastrous consequences. A 1lb bomb of TNT was placed on railway lines and exploded killing one of the men standing next to him. Edward Brittan, brother of Vera Brittan (*Testament of Youth*), wrote to his sister from Frensham Camp extolling the comfort of life under canvas with camp beds, sleeping bags and adequate blankets. He spoke of his personal servant and the excellence of food in the officers' mess. He was approached by the War Office to suggest names of friends from Oxford who might be suitable for a commission.

As far as weapons were concerned, at first drilling took place with poles instead of rifles. The country was searched for any form of weapon that would suffice until the standard Lee Enfield rifle became available. All the schools in the town were taken over for the use of the army, as were any halls or rooms. For training in artillery, field guns were constructed out of wood. In *A Tale of Two Captains*, John Baynes and Hugh Maclean describe suddenly being confronted without notice with 200 men from the Scots Rifles who they were expected to train and arrange accommodation for.

The order to take over all Aldershot schools had come to Aldershot District Council from the Local Government Board. However the town's education committee on 2 October protested that the committee had never been called together to discuss the move. A clash developed between the council's desire to help the army in any way to accommodate an estimated 100,000 troops and the education committee's belief that it should play a part in managing the occupation of the town's schools. It appeared that the council had usurped powers delegated to its education committee and had gone over that committee's head in turning schools over to the army. There is no indication that a serious effort had been made as of 2 October to find alternative accommodation for the town's children to continue their education.

The same difficulty arose in seeking accommodation for the wives of soldiers displaced by the need to accommodate new recruits. Wives were urged to depart from Aldershot. Grants were provided to assist them to do this, but there is little sign of counselling and effective advice on an individual basis. The Soldiers and Sailors' Families Association and kindred organisations were approached to help. Rail warrants were issued to these women together with a grant of £3 for the wife, £2 for the first child and £1 for each additional child. At the same time serious concern was expressed about how Aldershot's Refuge for Fallen and Friendless Women could continue its work now a grant from the Council's Extraordinary Fund was about to cease. Miss Avery, the superintendent of the charity, pointed out that the influx of young women into the camp meant a huge increase in demand for resources to help them.

The usually cautious *Aldershot News* carried this warning to those contemplating shopping in shops owned by Germans or Austrians:

> We have in this locality German and Austrian retailers such as butchers, bakers, hairdressers, etc. who trade to the detriment of our own businessmen. Beware of this peril. God save the King.

The case of A.R. Charles highlights the difficulties such strident attitudes would place a responsible newspaper in. He was the organist at All Saints' Garrison Church, the main focus for religious observation in the camp and the centre of many pre-war parades and ceremonies.

In addition he played an active part in raising money for the Aldershot Hospital. However, his name was really Leuthereusser, and he had failed to register his German origins under the Aliens Registration Order. Charles had lived in Aldershot for many years and was a well-regarded employee of a construction firm who did valuable work in the camp. He was taken to the police station and confronted with the fact that he had relatives living in London who were 'absolutely German'. In reply he said that he had come to England when he was 14, joined the Army Service Corps and later married an English woman. After leaving the services five years previously he had begun work with his current firm. He admitted that when war started he had lacked the courage to come forward and admit his German origins because of the consequences for his family and his son, who was studying through a scholarship in Winchester.

Providing him with a character reference, the manager of R. Dickeson and Co outlined Charles' exemplary behaviour and his lack of doubt that he was anything other than an Englishman. Taking all this into account the magistrates dismissed the case. A reader has to wonder whether it caused some reflection in the paper's newsroom about its previous editorial comments on all things German. Because of the fear of spies, anyone suspected of being an enemy alien was sought out by detectives in food shops, hairdressing salons, or anywhere in the camp and town. Stories circulated that Fritz, who cut hair in the camp, had smuggled a secret map of the area to the German high command. He was duly marched off into detention.

Local farmers undertook to keep the jobs of farm-workers open. The importance of agricultural labour became only too apparent from 1916 when German submarine warfare created severe food shortages. There was a call for children in state education to be conscripted into agricultural work to help bring in the harvest. It ushered in the Women's Land Army and a new role for women working in the agricultural sector. In expectation of having to deal with a large number of casualties based on the Boer War experience, in July the Princess Royal's Volunteer Corps had been practising nursing skills at a Reception Hospital at Pirbright Camp. They were also permitted to send a mounted squad of seven together with their field ambulances to a field day held by the First Division at Aldershot. Building on the success of this the surgeon general of the Aldershot command was able to secure recognition for the group known as F.A.N.Y. Unfortunately, the War Office was not able to use the group in any way but their leader, Mrs McDougall, crossed to Belgium and did invaluable work with the Belgium Red Cross. Witnessing the changing role they would play within a few weeks of the start of the war the *Aldershot News* reported that women were already replacing men carrying orders from local stores.

Men from universities were hastily enlisted and sent to The Royal Military Academy at nearby Camberley to train to be officers while new army cadets from the public schools were desperately pushed forward to be non-commissioned officers for the hundreds of battalions being hastily formed. Drafts were arriving in Aldershot from the depots established around the country for the new service battalions of the Second Expeditionary Force. The *Sheldrake Military Gazette* comments that the new troops in some cases present 'quite a respectable appearance on parade,' despite the absence of uniforms.

There were soon twenty-eight battalions of this kind being trained within the command, including twelve of Scottish infantry. In addition to these units there were three reserve regiments of cavalry, many thousands of Royal Engineers, Army Service Corps and other branches of the army who gravitated to Aldershot. A large group of Territorials had arrived at the command. For these men it was a routine of eight hours spent each day in drill and instruction together with lectures of one- or two-hours duration. An influx of this scale placed huge demands on the Army Ordnance Department for clothing and a whole range of equipment. It scratched around to produce old belts, braces and pouches. Despite all the shortcomings in kit and weaponry, the reporter commends the spirit with which recruits are approaching their training.

The town and command could look back in late September with some satisfaction at the way it had dispatched the Expeditionary Force to Belgium, rather in the same way it would play an important role in the dispatch of troops and equipment to the Falklands. In just sixty hours H.A. Walker, the general manager of the London and South West Railway, had provided 350 trains to transport the force. Trains were arriving in Southampton on the soldiers' first stage of their journey to the Front every twelve minutes at the peak of mobilisation.

Around the town there were meetings at which the valour of British troops was saluted following the battle at Mons and the subsequent retreat. Distinguished Conduct Medals were awarded to men like Sergeant Langford of the 5th Dragoon Guards for killing one officer, nine Uhlans and sixteen horses. Speaking in Aldershot on behalf of the War Office, Lord Desborough spoke in favour of the full mobilisation of the entire male population with military training for all men, even those working in exempted civilian occupations. On 25 October he indicated that the army was fully stretched dealing with the thousands of enlisted men who had rushed to the colours but that if there were 500,000 other men who were fit, and able to shoot, this would be very welcome by the War Office.

In Aldershot a scheme to provide military training to anyone who was unable to enlist was announced. Firms like Gale and Polden, Army and Navy Stores and the gas and water companies supported a company of around 400, who began training in the Drill Hall in the camp. The commander of the camp, Major General Anderson, had taken a personal interest in the volunteers but had stipulated that anyone between the age of 19 and 35 would be banned from participation unless they worked for the government or were engaged in government work. Further, no rifle drill was permitted. This brought the whole initiative to an abrupt halt and was a good example of the way the town and army were sometimes not singing from the same hymn sheet. Despite this the *Aldershot News* reports that a recruitment centre had been opened at the offices of the Aldershot Traction Company and delight is expressed with the general behaviour of the newly enlisted men who are arriving in the town and the way they are being licked into shape through their training. News that recruitment into the army is taking place among the footballers, cricketers, cyclists and golfers of the town is also saluted by the paper.

This was illustrated by the difficulty the town began to experience with the Water Company over providing water for washing facilities for the thousands of troops arriving. Councillor Harry Ainger, a local shopkeeper, raised the question of prosecution of a family involved in doing washing for the army and using an excess of water. Councillor Ainger stated that the army had no clear idea where it could get its washing done. The wives of serving men were being pressed into this work because of lack of money and were now being sued for arrears by the gas and water companies. Legal aid was not available for them.

The council indicated that it was powerless to assist any family taking in washing in this way from a surcharge for using excess water but that the military authorities should intervene in the situation. A similar problem arose with Aldershot Post Office as it sought to deal suddenly with 5,000 parcels. Hundreds of men availed themselves of the writing facilities provided by churches, such as the Presbyterians, to send heavily censored letters home to their nearest and dearest. Spare land had to be taken around the building to accommodate parcels of food being sent to prisoners-of-war in Germany who were barely existing on virtual starvation diets, not to mention the socks and gloves knitted under the jurisdiction of Queen Alexandra.

Life in the town was featured by stirring speeches, such as the one given to the military cyclists, who had their final dinner prior to their departure for the Front, and appeals of support for the hospitals and amenities for the troops being established. The *Aldershot News* reported 'Our territorials are eager for foreign service.' E Company, mainly made up of Aldershot volunteers, was responsible for guarding the aircraft factory. They were well-supported by the YMCA who, since war was declared, had opened 350 centres for recreation and refreshment. The paper claims that in proportion, Hampshire and Aldershot was contributing the largest proportion of men to the armed forces than any other county. At Farnborough a Red Cross hospital for wounded Belgian soldiers was set up at Farnborough Court. In October Belgian soldiers with wounds that had received no attention for days and were described as being in a piteous state, arrived from Ostend. Empress Eugenie was there to meet them in person. The more serious cases were dispatched to wards upstairs while those in the lounge chatted to their visitors. Most of the soldiers were married, some as young as 18, and they were cared for by three fully trained nurses. An appeal was made for donations so that the hospital could continue its work.

On 16 October, there is the first and only report of the arrival back in Aldershot of the ambulance train from the Front in the local paper. The train consisted of ten coaches with eight beds in each coach. It carried 130 wounded from Southampton. From the station they were transferred to the Cambridge and Connaught Hospitals. As it is reported, they were: 'Bright, happy, jovial fellows, brown faced, healthy looking heroes who but for their wounds one might believe they have just returned from autumn manoeuvres so brown and bonny were they.' The report admits there were some more seriously wounded than others and these required to be carried from the train on stretchers. The walking wounded were observed to have injuries to their arms and legs. The ambulance train from which they emerged is described as 'luxurious'. With the benefit of historical hindsight one could question how accurately this represented the real situation for men returning from France after the retreat from Mons and the privations of the early stage of the war. If many of their wounds were so inconsequential, why were they repatriated back to Aldershot?

Finally the fine weather that had seen in the commencement of the war broke in October when contractors still had to complete the huts for the new recruits. This meant sleeping on wet ground and training on parade grounds ankle deep in mud. The makeshift divisional brigade staffs were a mixture of retired and convalescent officers who had previously been in India together with reserve officers whose military experience was well behind the times. At the same time the requirement of aeronautics meant a whole new science of meteorology was opened up at the aircraft factory by men like Charles Cave. In April it began to be possible to track the path of thunderstorms and new development in aircraft photography meant cloud formations could be photographed.

A regular feature in both the *Aldershot News* and the *Sheldrake Military Gazette* is a Roll of Honour marking families distinguishing themselves through their contribution to the war. For instance, the Henley family were providing five members for the armed forces. Walter, the eldest son, was in the navy aboard HMS *Superb*; Herbert, who was just 19, was with the F2 Company of the Hampshire Regiment; Staff Sergeant Hewlett, the family's son-in-law, was with the Army Service Corps in France; another son-in-law, Will Kiernan, was with the Northumberland Fusiliers; while another son-in-law was fighting with the North Staffordshires. The Farrow family had five sons serving in the war. Edward, who was a sergeant in the Royal Garrison Artillery; William, a warrant officer in the navy serving on a torpedo destroyer; Ernest, with the Royal Garrison Artillery; Harold, E Company Hampshire Regiment; and Victor, a drummer in the Coldstream Guards.

On 9 October, the death of Sergeant Prince of the Royal Army Medical Corps was reported. He was killed when a German shell shattered the field ambulance to which he belonged. Prince was an England amateur footballer and played in forces football at the highest level. As an athlete he was army 440-yard champion as well as an excellent cricketer. In a town with deep connections with the army, such commitment to the war was commonplace. This made the consequence of death when it came so direct and all-embracing.

Other early deaths were reported. Corporal Fear, a well-known footballer in the town who was recently married to Miss Killingbeck. Sergeant A.F. Curry of the First Somersets, who was married in June 1913 to Miss H. Baker, was reported killed at Cambrai on 20 August after receiving a bullet in the heart. A further death reported is of Private H.C. Berry of the 2nd Highland Infantry, who was educated in the military school in the camp. News came that the family's other son was a prisoner-of-war in Germany. On 23 October, the death of Sergeant Jim Burrows, a member of the regular army, was reported. A death occurred closer to hand when Edward Black, who was just 20, from the aircraft factory, crashed his plane near Fleet Road in a burning mass of fabric. He was educated at Harrow and King's College, where he had been awarded a First in Mechanical Science.

Serving soldiers were quick to correct a claim in a letter to the *Aldershot News* that German soldiers were poor shots. 'Don't you believe it,' the letter says. 'I guess the fellow who wrote the letter has never been near the firing line. He's never smelt dead Germans in the trenches or being shown the white flag by the Germans and then being fired upon.' Private Duffield also wrote about the experience of being fired upon by your own artillery.

The town was preoccupied with the conflict between healthy upright behaviour, as exemplified by Major Chisholm's gym and a boxing contest at the Riding School in which Private Palmer of the 11th Hussars fought Private Donaldson of the Seaforth Highlanders, and the high level of drunkenness in the town. In striving for a healthy life they were supported by the campaign Rev'd Harry Carter was mounting against the town's pubs and grog shops. This was reflected in two prosecutions that were brought in the Aldershot Police Court on 16 October. The cases involved the sale of bottled beer in an off licence. Aylesford Hobbs had sold bottled beer to soldiers after 8 pm, when the sale of alcohol should have ended. Police reported a large group of soldiers and civilians in Victoria Road adjacent to the off licence drinking from quart bottles at the side of the road. A policeman reported seeing a member of the Highland Regiment leaving Mr Hobbs' premises with two quart bottles of beer tucked under his arm. Three other men wearing kilts were seen to exit the off licence carrying beer in a similar way. The policeman waited until 8.25 pm. He confronted Hobbs with what he had seen. However, in this case there was no absolute proof that the beer he had seen being consumed had actually been bought on Hobbs' premises. In a similar case, James Naylor, an off licensee, was fined £3.3s with 15s costs. Naylor claimed he was unaware of the rowdy drinking session taking place close to his premises as his wife and daughter did most of the serving, despite a claim by the police that a large group of men had been observed drinking for most of the afternoon. Mrs Naylor stated that she always warned her customers about drinking in the street. Any soldier indicating that he would drink beer in the street she would refuse to serve. However, magistrates did not believe her claims that she was not aware of what was happening in the vicinity of her husband's off licence. At the same time the Military Police initiated a campaign against soldiers using obscene language and were arresting ladies of possible ill fame for trespassing Defence Department land. Throughout the war there would be prosecutions of this kind against the ladies of the night.

The *Aldershot News* reports that drunkenness was bad during the first week in August for which the Scottish element was to blame. However, considering that when this was written 90,000 recruits were in place in the camp the subsequent levels of drunkenness might be acceptable. The number of public houses had been reduced but the town's clergymen called for the same controls on 'the dangerous trade' to be applied in the same way as they were in peacetime. Rev'd Hawkes pointed to the recreational outlets that had been opened at St Michael's, the Working Men's Club and a coffee bar at the West End Parish Church in North Camp offering an alternative to the pub as a social outlet.

Many local people gathered at Frimley Station to witness the arrival of one of the first groups of prisoners-of-war to arrive from the Front. Locals were impressed with the stature of the kaiser's imperial guards. In the group there were twenty who were wounded. The *Aldershot News* commented on their haggard condition and noted that some of the men were as old as 50 or 60. One of the prisoners confided that he had been a chef at the Savoy Hotel. All were pleased when they finally walked the 2 miles to Frith Hill, where their camp was located. Altogether 392 German prisoners were brought from Southampton that day.

As Christmas 1914 approached, the challenge to the Aldershot community was to ensure that its Old Folks' Christmas Fund was adequately supported, bearing in mind all the charities associated with the war. The officer in charge of the camp, Sir Archibald Hunter, is recorded as donating £10, and a sum of £3.15s was collected among the staff of Army HQ Aldershot. The fund sought to provide a bright half-sovereign for anyone over 60 in need in the town. On 4 December, an appeal was launched for these poor people who would be asked to a Christmas party when the money would be distributed. In the camp, special arrangements were made in order that Christmas dinner would be available for the troops. Residents were also urged to open their doors for soldiers to perhaps provide a meal over Christmas, as well as a bath.

Experiences of Aldershot

Returning to Bill Collins' story, his experience, like most working-class families, was that work fluctuated from one day to another. In the period of trade recession leading up to the war, his father's work as a scaffolder could never be relied on to bring in enough food to feed the family. When he left St Andrew's Church School, jobs were hard to find. At the time of joining the army in 1913, he was a Sunday school teacher and had the rudiments of drill from the scouts and church brigades. After joining the army he was attached to the McGrigor Barracks. He describes in detail the drill and route marches that formed part of his training. Private Collins easily passed first time the demands of accurate shooting. Contemporary reports picture Aldershot as a mass of soldiers marching, digging trenches and practising bayonet drills in their scarlet uniforms. By June the perceived threat of war meant that the simulation exercises such as stretcher-bearing and lectures on physiology given to the trainees took on a new reality. At the end of the process, Collins was put through a severe test, such as dealing with compound fractures and stopping bleeding, held at McGrigor Barracks. The food they were offered was barely adequate and they supplemented this by using 6 shillings of the 7 shillings they received as pay to buy food from the canteen.

Collins did not drink, was prepared to abide by the structures of behaviour he found in the army and welcomed the opportunity to participate in army football. When his first leave came round he did not go back home because, with four other children, there was no room for him. He made his way to the Union Jack Club in London, where a good bed and breakfast was available for just a shilling. He took what was said on his cap badge seriously, 'Faithful in Difficulty', and saw his distinctive role as looking after other people. In April 1914 he was selected to join the Red Caps of the Military Police. He was given responsibility for the Guard Room on Saturday nights, where he had to cope with the drunks. He describes war coming as 'a bolt from the blue', having to go down the hill to report to the 7th Brigade of The Royal Horse Guards and, by 15 August, was organising its medical supplies with stretchers, morphine, scissors, dressings, aspirins and iodine on to a cart to follow his regiment to the Front.

Even at this early stage, women like Kathleen Bottomley were swept up into active service. On 3 August, the day before war broke out, she had not yet left school. She was engulfed in crowds milling around Buckingham Palace shouting, 'We demand war with Germany.' For a brief period she worked at the general post office as a receptionist but left to join the WAACs, who were looking for cooks, waitresses, store women and receptionists. She neglected to tell her mother what she had done and found herself in Farnborough working as a waitress and cook for army officers. She was billeted close to an engine shed where engines were being tested all night, but was expected to be up early each morning for drills.

The King and General Haig inspect the "contemptible" original army early in 1914.

General Douglas Haig on horseback.

An earlier army departure from Aldershot Railway Station.

Aldershot volunteers for Hampshire Regiment.

Kitchener inspecting newly arrived volunteers, with the King 1914.

Soldiers from the 2nd Battalion Royal Munsters acclaim their General, 1914.

General Haig and King George V on parade in 1914.

Aldershot recruits joining the Hampshire Regiment in 1914.

Aldershot Institute.

CHAPTER 2

1915

When you see the names and numbers of men we lost, read them with pride for they died with pride and never flinched. So cheer up again and if I should fall you will have this satisfaction knowing I have done my duty and my best to keep the Huns from your home and let you live in decency

Private Oakley, Hampshire Regiment, 21 August 1914

With so many Scottish troops in the camp the New Year Hogmanay was marked by partying. The Seaforth Highlanders were entertained by Sergeant-Major MacKay with a smoking concert (a relaxed concert where men sat around smoking), followed by the officers for each platoon distributing gifts and partaking in a dinner of turkey and plum pudding. Similar celebrations took place involving the 8th Gordon Highlanders, 5th Cameron Highlanders, 8th Black Watch and 9th Seaforth Highlanders, concluding with a piper playing out the old year and ushering in the new.

Despite driving snow, sleet and rain, military activity for the year opened with a visit to Aldershot and the camp by Lord Kitchener, secretary of state for war, on 27 January. He was accompanied by M. Millerand, the French minister for war. The two men inspected parades of the new army, who were said to have endured the shocking conditions with 'good grace'. Whole divisions of the new army were drawn up on Laffan's Plain in sub-zero temperatures. In dead silence the Scottish troops assembled while behind them brigades of artillery and the Royal Engineers formed up, followed by the infantry brigades. The weather chose the arrival of the last group of men to change into a gale accompanied by cold, driving rain. The men were made to wait in these conditions until well after three o'clock, when an officer rode up warning of Kitchener's impending arrival. Kitchener passed among their ranks deep in conversation with one of his officers looking neither to left or right.

Following this, Kitchener's party made its way to the Royal Pavilion, where they were received by Sir Archibald Hunter, the officer in charge of the Aldershot command. Kitchener and the French war minister inspected a parade of Cameron Highlanders and, following a delay because their cars became bogged down in thick snow, they inspected another division at Blackdown Barracks.

The New Year was ushered in with the consequences of the restriction of the free movement of technical aeronautical information involving the aircraft factory. Lieutenant-Colonel O'Gorman, the inspirational and dynamic superintendent of the factory, had assembled a group of engineers, scientists and tradesman at the Farnborough factory. Within a matter a months the factory had played a crucial role in enabling the army to catch up on Germany in the manufacture of aircraft. As with all technological developments of this kind, those involved tended not to recognise the limits placed on the free flow of information demanded by controlling groups like the army. Those passionate about aircraft development had formed ad hoc groups that exchanged information about a whole range of issues around aerodynamics. Unfortunately, these did not square with the restrictions placed on those in the factory under the Defence of the Realm Act. Having operated night and day since the outbreak of war, the aircraft factory closed for a day giving a holiday to its 4,000 employees.

In March there was a royal visit to the town and camp. It commenced with arrival at the Royal Pavilion where the king, dressed in khaki, inspected a guard of honour. The king and queen then rode across to Ewshot to witness the Royal Military Corps undergoing training. Queen Mary made her way to the new YMCA hut to inspect the new building and the arrangements made for the comfort and recreation of the troops. She joined up with the king's party and went along Knolly's Road and Farnborough Road observing troops on parade grounds. They then went to the aircraft factory, where they were shown around by Mervyn O'Gorman, the superintendent in charge. This in turn was followed by an exhibition of flying by the Royal

Flying Corps. After lunch in the pavilion, the king and queen witnessed a cross country race on Queen's Parade.

The following day, a Sunday, the king and queen joined representatives from all units for a divine service at All Saints' Church. The service was conducted by Rev'd J. Benoy, senior chaplain of the forces in Aldershot. The Royal Artillery Band was conducted by the town's well known band master, Henry Sims, with arrangements from composers such as Bach and Mendelssohn. When they exited the church and walked along Farnborough Road, they were greeted by a large crowd who had come to see them.

William Roberts provides a graphic description of what it was like to join the Royal Flying Corps in 1915. When he arrived in Aldershot the only accommodation available was under canvas. He was to become a maintenance engineer at the factory. Planes being tested had to take passengers as ballast. On his first flight the plane turned over. 'Run away,' shouted the pilot, 'it's going to burst into flames.' An hour later he saw a Belgian pilot killed when his plane crashed. On 15 January, at Farnborough, Second-Lieutenant Gardner of the Royal Flying Corps suffered a similar fate. The extensive burns he received as the result of the crash made his body unrecognisable.

Another description about gravitating into work associated with the Royal Flying Corps is provided by Cecil King. After signing up for the army he was given a railway warrant for Aldershot. Initially he was allocated space in the barracks of the Black Watch. Conditions were primitive and the three meals a day were just sufficient to take the edge off their hunger. They were marched to the Farnborough base of the RFC, where they given largely menial tasks such as digging trenches and levelling off sites on the runways. They attended to planes that had taxied in and returned them to flying condition. Part of his training in the workings of aero engines involved being able to instantly name the parts of the engine after it had been dismantled and placed before them on the ground.

A female perspective comes from Constance Bottomley, who arrived in Farnborough after joining the WAAFs. They were kitted out in uniforms and allocated barracks at Star Hill. They were given lectures about something called VD which none of the women had ever heard of. At this stage she said, 'France seemed very far away.'

In the case of Victor Fagance, who joined the 10th Battalion Royal

West Surrey Regiment and arrived at Albuhera Barracks in December, his reason for joining up was because most of his friends had already done so. He found life at Aldershot hectic. Some of the NCOs were Boer War veterans who really knew what war was like. He described how it was discovered that men in his battalion had falsified their ages in order to join up and get to France. Due to a mistake, his name was missed off those being sent to France and he found himself with the 'lead swingers' in Northampton, which delayed his going to France. Fortune smiled on him because his regiment was decimated at the Battle of Loos.

Robert Parker was posted to North Camp and the tractor section of the Army Service Corps. Only six tractors existed and the test of efficiency involved reversing a tractor with a trailer attached. Further work involved working with tracked vehicles. He was given the task of moving the tractors from Aldershot to Avonmouth at 2½ miles an hour, which took him a week. Another marathon was performed by Charles Quenelle in a march from Folkestone to Aldershot, a distance of 115 miles. During the march small billeting parties would go ahead and secure billets for the men that included places like schools or mission halls. He recalled 250 men marching along the Hog's Back on the last phase of their journey and from there looking down on 'the holy city' of Aldershot. Quenelle said he hated the town, which offered no place to go except the barracks where they were located. They were located in huts that dated back to the Boer War. 'You were just a small cog in a very large wheel. No one ever explained what the purpose of the marches was you were required to do. Because of overcrowding you were never allowed to enjoy a full night's sleep.' One of the exercises they were required to do was attempting to fix barbed wire into the ground with a 4-inch-long screw.

The short back and sides administered by the army barbers made them all look like convicts prior to their departure for France.

Major General John Ford of the Royal Army Medical Corps came from an Aldershot command background. When he enlisted he was billeted in a tailor's shop. He talked about new recruits walking about sloppily dressed without uniforms and doing physical exercises on the parade ground. When he enlisted as a bugler he was in constant demand for regular church parades. Cecil Tubbs of the Somerset Light Infantry, arriving at the same time, said that new recruits judged their NCOs on the basis of their competence. Sydney Woodcock arrived in Aldershot with skills in machine construction engineering so that when he was asked to draw a hexagon as his test to join the Royal Engineers he had no difficulty in passing.

Eric de Norman was posted to the Buller Barracks in July. He was allowed a tailor's bill of £24 19s for his uniform. Much of his role was a supervisory one, going from tents to latrines and to barracks on a regular two-hour basis. He supervised meals as well as fielded complaints. Reflecting the growing need to ration his men, he was charged with weighing out meat and described the abattoir where the meat was stored as a horrible foul smelling place. The veteran sergeants made fun of a novice NCO if he got his cavalry drill wrong. Going into Aldershot was a nightmare because he found he had to salute all the time due to the number of officers based in the town. In comparison with the meagre rations available to the ordinary ranks, de Norman described the lavish fare, all served with silver service available in his mess with its fine oak panelling. Breakfast consisted of porridge, eggs, ham, sausages and bacon. For lunch a generous buffet was offered and on ceremonial occasions not only was there a mountain of food but also a wide selection of wines. Many of the officers he shared the mess with possessed their own cars. He was paid £11 12s a month.

Despite the perils of early test flying, the *esprit de corps* evident at the metalworkers' dinner indicates how well O'Gorman had succeeded in bringing together a group of skilled workers dedicated to the future of flying. He effectively dismantled the demarcation lines between the sheet metal worker and the coppersmith in the factory. However, life in the factory was not without crisis, as revealed by the fire on 12 March when the bells of the approaching Aldershot fire engine were confused with warning of an enemy air attack. Rather than taking cover, scores of people ran outside to discover what was happening. Aldershot was fortunate never to have had a Zeppelin attack, because its authorities struggled to establish an efficient regime to control the levels of lighting both in the camp and town.

The factory acted as a magnet to young men. On 10 December, Edward Norkett, a motor engineer, sued Colonel Charlton for the return of his apprentice who had falsified his age in order to join up. The court ordered that Ronald Jackson should be returned to his employer.

Patriotism v. Profit – how the War Office betrayed national trust
The local paper reported events in Parliament on 16 February 1916, surrounding the tale of what it believed to be jobbery and corruption, which had commenced this year.

The dispute between the War Office and Aldershot Council and business community centred on the activities of a Colonel Gascoigne. He had returned to the active list for the army, this coinciding with the securing of a valuable piece of real estate lying between the High Street and Wellington Avenue for the Army and Navy Co-operative for whom he had worked as a manager. The War Office had taken the land in 1875 and left it empty, despite requests that it might be used by the council or sold to town businessmen. But the War Office refused to give up the land.

Now the War Office sold the land for less than half its market value to the Army and Navy Co-operative for £4,300 under a secret contract. The local paper regarded this action as inexplicable, because the army itself was now desperate for space in which to drill the thousands of new recruits pouring into the camp due to existing drill areas being taken for barracks. Further, the War Office was paying large amounts of money to rent office space all over the town for the Army Pay Unit when this land could be used to centralise the process. In commercial terms, the action of the War Office represented favouritism towards one company, and the Army and Navy had been gifted a trading advantage over other retail firms in the town.

In a very weak response to complaints made in a speech by the town's member of parliament, Clavell-Salter, the minister stated that he simply had forgotten to inform the house of the transaction. However, he believed that members of all ranks serving in Aldershot would benefit from the presence of the store in the town. Both the business community and the council were unimpressed by this explanation, and the issue soured the relationship between the town and the War Office.

Settling where responsibility for paying for damage to the roads running through the camp as a result of intensive military activity resulted in differences of opinion between the army and Hampshire County Council, the local authority in charge of the camp's roads. On 19 February, Hampshire reluctantly agreed to pay £13,000 for road repairs for ten roads that were experiencing severe damage. The military authorities were not prepared to admit that damage to a major extent had occurred. Hampshire refused to accept that they should pay a contribution of £577 to repair the road running through Farnborough to the county boundary with Surrey. Representation to the army authorities was now to be made about meeting the additional cost of road maintenance consequent on the expansion of military activity in Aldershot and Farnborough.

From the start of the year, shortages of a whole range of things for civilised living began to be experienced in Aldershot. There was an acute lack of suitable housing for what the *Aldershot News* described as the working-classes. Because of the lack of skilled labour, either through recruitment into the services or deployment in building accommodation in the camp, a scheme to build affordable housing near to the Isolation Hospital was reported as making poor progress. A case brought by the council's environment officer highlighted this situation. A building contractor unable to find any suitable accommodation elsewhere had crammed his workers into an empty shop. In mitigation he pleaded that the shop was being used only for sleeping. As late in the year as July, the council was still debating how they could entice more money from the Local Government Board for a vital programme of house-building. The situation in Farnborough was no better because of an influx of skilled workers from around the country into O'Gorman's aircraft factory.

On 8 January, Aldershot is in the midst of a coal famine. With its price rising to 32 shillings a ton, it became unaffordable for poorer people at the coldest time of the year. This was partially the result of congestion on the railway. One of the vicars of Aldershot, Rev'd Senior, criticised the miners for militancy and taking industrial action. He conveniently forgets the mining disaster in the Welsh Valleys in 1913 that killed over 4,000 miners and that the mine owners insisted on opening the mine in question just a week after the disaster.

By October meat was in short supply and households were limited to ¾lb per week. However, the military censor intervened when a soldier writing home complained of the monotony of his diet in the camp consisting largely of bully beef and biscuits. Meanwhile, the price of bread and flour continued to rise.

For the children of the town there was a shortage of education. Their schools were systematically occupied by the army. For instance, on

2 February, Newport Road School had around 200 soldiers in residence and on 9 February, the East End schools were taken over to billet soldiers. As well as this, a shortage of teachers developed through some volunteering for the services. Reports of their deaths started arriving. C.W. Shanks, from West End Boys' School, serving with the Hampshire Regiment, was the first of these and Claude Elliot, born and brought up in Aldershot, was killed at Neuve Chappelle. All unmarried male teachers joined up during the year and the vacancies that were created were filled by women teachers. Although the schools were closed, nominally the numbers of children on roll increased by 414 because of the closure of schools in the camp. From 1915, maternity and childcare starts to become a major issue in Aldershot. The town was one of the first in the country to appoint a health visitor who had the responsibility for checking on children in their first year of life. By April a campaign had commenced placing pressure on the council to appoint another health visitor whose role was to provide assistance and advice to expectant mothers. Urgent work with children from 1 to 5 was identified. However, an approach to the army authorities for a centre to work from was met with refusal.

From a contemporary standpoint, the central role the churches played in the community of the camp and Aldershot is remarkable. In 1915, faced with the growing catastrophe the war represented for people's lives, the natural tendency was to seek comfort and guidance from religion. The *Aldershot News* reported on an increase in membership and activity in the churches. The challenge faced was not only to provide spiritual support to the thousands of men who flooded into the camp and town, but also to provide physical support in the form of pastoral care to these men. There was evidence of, in modern parlance, 'churches together', as sectarian divides were put aside in the face of the challenges the churches were presented with. At first there were very few resources available to respond to the social needs of men from the barracks. Novel ways were tried to raise money. Rev'd Senior tried a 'demanding toll' on everyone who visited him in his vestry at Holy Trinity Church. In this way by 17 March, he had raised £54. However, much of this money appears to have paid off debts already incurred for the church's activities, and less to support work for the troops.

From January, the combined churches began a temperance

campaign when the Bishops of London and Willesden were in Aldershot to speak on the issue. In response to the widespread drunkenness at the start of the war the churches were involved in tactical moves by the police and military authorities to improve the situation. At another meeting, a Colonel Boyrne spoke about the way in which even limited consumption of alcohol interfered with a soldier's training by reason of it making him incapable of making quick and rational decisions. In fact, it questioned whether he was capable of being a soldier altogether. He cited the outrages of German troops in Belgium after they had ransacked the stores and cellars of the country. He quoted a comment by a British general, Lord Roberts: 'Give me a teetotal army and I will lead it anywhere.'

However this view was challenged by a letter from the trenches claiming that the rum ration was the only way he could get through it all.

Rev'd Hawkes began a tradition of keeping philosophical discussion alive during the war with two meetings at his institute attached to St Michael's on 'The Church 1600 – 1660' and another relevant to understanding how and why war came on the great powers of Europe between 1815 and 1914. He chaired another meeting late in 1915 examining ways in which the desperate housing situation could be improved. From 1916, when the war started going very badly for the Allies, meetings and discussions organised by Hawkes would come to play a vital part in the town's life. On 12 February, at his Men's Conference in the parish hall, he came to grips with the question that although the war was wrong in the general sense, could it be justified in current circumstances? He claimed that Christ expressed neither approval nor disapproval of war. He examined the Quaker view of war, which held that it was against the will of Christ and involved the surrender of the individual conscience to those promoting war. He said he believed that for anyone joining the army in Aldershot this meant implicitly the orders of officers, which might be wrong and against a man's conscience.

Rev'd Hawkes stated that there were two good reasons against the Quaker view. Firstly, your whole existence in society was based on compromise with absolute conditions you were unable to effectively alter. For instance, there was the fact that many of the goods and services available were the result of exploitation of unfair labour. As an individual you could not simply withdraw participation in society because you objected to a small part of how it operated. Secondly, dealing with the Quaker view that war breached the fatherhood of God and brotherhood of man in a certain sense, some nations were justified in going to war. In the family of nations, the right existed to attack another nation and punish it for wrongdoing. War was wrong because of the misbehaviour of the nation that caused it. However, the use of force was wrong when the motive for employing that force was wrong. Rudyard Kipling was wrong when he said, 'The life of a warrior is the noblest one on earth.' Contrary to this it might produce a magnificent character but it undermined the family of nations. He rejected the Quaker argument against war but supported a Christian movement to stop war, perhaps prefiguring the ideas behind the League of Nations. In the next months, with the hearing of cases against conscription and conscientious objection, these arguments would appear in Aldershot and Farnborough again and again.

The year marked the forty-fifth anniversary meeting of one of the Freemasons Lodges within the camp. Its numbers had been boosted by the number of masons training there. It noted, however, that a shadow had been cast over the usual convivial new member-making ceremonies by the deaths that had already taken place among its members serving overseas. The meeting took place in the new Masonic Assembly Rooms over the Market Arcade in the High Street. The lodge had moved from its premises in Station Road because the masonic hall there had been placed in the hands of the receiver. Brother A.H. Smith extended a special welcome for all those in khaki attending the meeting.

A large part of Aldershot's economy depended on the operation of the Army Pay Department. However, a letter received by the local newspaper clearly indicates the Army Pay Corps was being so severely stretched by the extra demands made on its services by the surge in recruitment that the department appeared to be falling to pieces. The letter criticised the manner in which appointments into the corps had been made from the civil service, with no regard to the specialist skills involved in dealing with military pay. The correspondent complained about the lack of recognition accorded those who traditionally worked in the Pay Corps and were familiar with all the regulations related to its work. There was a complaint that the decision had been made to remove from each regiment its own depot with a record office. The justification for combining individual regimental based pay into a fixed centre appears to be to save money. In peacetime it worked after a fashion. The drawback is if information was required at the centre about a soldier, this was not immediately available but had to be sought from his barracks, which might be anywhere in the country. The letter complained that the civilian financial authorities were out of sympathy with the way a military pay section should operate. Faced with an outcry about its failure to manage military pay, the civilian financial authorities hurriedly drafted in untrained clerks. The new clerks had to be inducted into the Pay Corps systems, placing a great strain on the original pay clerks. Training of a pay clerk usually took five years, and yet the expectation was that the new appointees take up the reigns forthwith. The problem was further aggravated by a large number of specialist staff being sent to the Front to carry out pay duties there. This was one fifth of officers and a tenth of clerks. A further factor creating delays and mistakes for soldiers and their dependants in Aldershot was the number of changes in pay and allowances that were being produced as the war continued.

In August, Rudyard Kipling, on a visit to Aldershot, expressed concern about the gulf now beginning to develop between those who volunteered and those still not under arms. He had listened to the complaints of the men in the camp about the way those still not in uniform were prospering in their absence. Like many other commentators he was puzzled why underage recruits were not spotted by the professional soldiers responsible for their training. Also, in August, a recruit described how the 8th Light Division of the 9th Scots Division prepared to go to France. First there was the haircut, which resembled the American crew-cut of later years designed to avoid infestation by flies and lice. Troops were assembled on Aldershot Parade Ground with their Lee Enfield Rifle Mark IV, fitted with a single-blade bayonet. They carried 120 rounds of 303 ammunition and an entrenching tool. A water bottle in their haversack was an emergency day ration. In terms of clothing there was a greatcoat, a woollen shirt, three pairs of socks, a change of underclothing, a towel, soap and a comb. Around the pack was strapped a blanket roll and a ground sheet. Throughout the war questions around prisoners-of-war, both those in camps in and around Aldershot and those of Allied soldiers, would be a major concern. A letter from Private McDonald read to the group assembled in the Jubilee Hall Club seeking to encourage parcels for British POWs thanks the volunteers for the parcels that had been sent so far. He wrote of 'wearing away the weary days as we doing nothing here'. On 4 June, parcels of food organised by Dr Gibson were dispatched to Germany. This was in response to information that POWs there were receiving inadequate food. Food was being donated even from families in chastened circumstances themselves. The aircraft factory was commended for the extent of its giving. Parcels being sent consisted of a 4lb loaf, 1lb biscuits, 12oz cheese, two tins of condensed milk, cigarettes, a cake and a box of soap. Comments appeared in the *Aldershot News* about how well the enemy POWs are being treated in comparison with the Allied ones in Germany. Soldiers returning from a swap of prisoners arrived back wearing wooden shoes and much in need of decent clothing. Bugler William Berry reported that the lack of food given to wounded prisoners worsened their physical condition. But for the food sent from Aldershot, more of these men would have died. He was so incensed with the treatment he received and wanted to return to the Front. Well-known local footballer J.T. Hales, who was captured early in the war, wrote about their food consisting of 6oz of black bread each for ten men, coffee without milk, stringy beans and a tiny piece of sausage or cheese. On the strength of this they were expected to carry out hard manual labour for many hours. News that a group of German POWs in a local camp had gone on strike over the level of pay they were receiving for work they did in the community was greeted with hostility.

The camp at Frith Hill between Frimley and Deepcut held German aliens as well as POWs. George Kenner was one of the aliens deemed to be from hostile countries swept up by the authorities following the sinking of the Lusitania in 1915. He had moved to London from Bavaria in 1910 and was working as an artist. Kenner painted a series of pictures and kept a diary depicting life in the camp. Breakouts took place and one highlighted the discontent that existed about the conditions those in the tents and temporary huts experienced. Kenner was later moved to another camp at Alexander Palace, and then to the Isle of Man.

In the middle of the year a commentator claimed that interest in women's suffrage had been allowed to drop. This seemed against the evidence of the increasing role women were already playing in the life of the town and camp. The growing number of women teachers in the schools were demanding equal pay to the men they were replacing. Women bus conductors appeared on the Aldershot Traction Company buses. The essential role women would have to occupy was highlighted by a severe shortage of nurses already developing for Cambridge and Connaught Hospitals. On 26 June, the town's first postwoman was observed delivering letters. However, in July Mr Hoffman from the Shop Workers' Union was making disparaging remarks about the competence of the women now replacing men behind the counters in the town. 'They have not the slightest experience of the work,' he said. The home secretary denied driving licences to women on the basis that 'they would not be trusted by the general public'.

Meanwhile, the seventy-strong team of ladies supporting the Seaforth Highlanders outlined the prodigious amount of clothing and goods they had produced in support of the regiment. Their record shows 9,000 pairs of socks, 2,248 shirts, 321 vests, 1,231 belts, 890 handkerchiefs, 895 scarves, 2,901 gloves/mittens, 609 cardigans, seven bales of blankets, 2,000 towels. As well as these, 4,500 pipes, 100,500 cigarettes and 2,850lb of tobacco were donated.

However, the class lines dividing middle- and working-class women's experience of the war were becoming very apparent. Because of the rising cost of living more and more women were forced out to work. At the magistrates court on 6 August, Nellie Smith was charged with loitering on army land, an euphemism for soliciting for sex. Because of the scrutiny the police in the town took to check all arrivals, offenders such a Lucy Dudney, who took rooms in the Royal Hotel dressed as a nurse and entertained men she claimed were friends, were tracked down and brought before the court. Again on 4 September, four young women were brought before the court charged with loitering on war department land. On 24 September, charges against older women soliciting in the town refer to 'indecency'.

In the second year of the war a number of Aldershot families were identified as making major sacrifices. For instance R.H. Dell with four sons serving received a letter from the king congratulating his family for their contribution towards the war. Congratulations from the king for his eight serving sons was also received by Mr Williams. C. Farrow of the Coldstream Guards from St George's Road in Aldershot, presently in Egypt with the army, had five sons serving – Edward with the Royal Garrison Artillery, William with the navy on torpedo boats, Edwin, also with the Royal Garrison Artillery, Harold with the E Company of the Hampshire Regiment, and Victor with the 3rd Coldstream Guards. The Rolfe family of West View, Farnborough, had Alfred serving in France, Gary with the Medical Corps also in France, William serving with the 1st Yorkshire/Lancashire Regiment and Philip serving with the St Helen's Regiment. Mrs Pettys of St Michael's Road in Aldershot had sent six sons. Alfred, who was on HMS *Foxglove*, Herbert with the Royal Surrey Regiment, Ernest with the Royal Fusiliers, Harry on HMS *Excellent*. Unfortunately, one of her sons Ernest is reported missing. In June Mrs Soffe of Queen's Road had the dreaded news that a second son had been killed.

Aldershot Operatic Society production.

Training in the Aldershot Gymnasium.

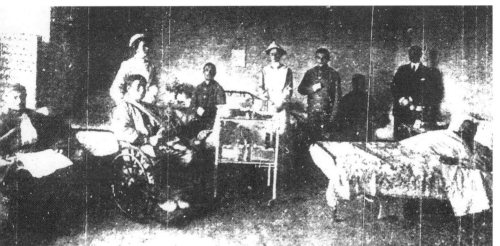

Hospital care for the wounded from Belgium early in the war.

A leading local politician.

Kitchener volunteers training with sticks. Early 1915.

Wilfred Owen, poet, in Aldershot in 1915.

German POWs arriving at Frimley Railway Station on the way to Frith Hill Internment Camp.

Parade in Queens Avenue, 1915.

The P.O.W. camp at Frith Hill.

Army Service Corps practising loading horses at Fleet Pond.

Inside Aldershot Gym.

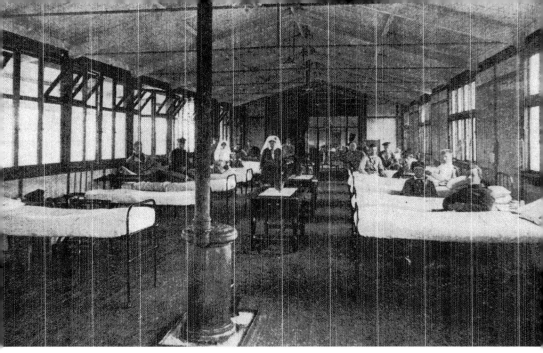

Inside an Aldershot Military Hospital 1915.

Kenner painting of Panorama of Frith Hill P.O.W. camp 1914.

Kenner painting of hand soccer being played at Frith Hill P.O.W. Camp1915.

Kenner painting of playing croquet at Frith Hill P.O.W. camp.

Kenner painting of kitchen at Frith Hill camp.

Kenner painting of a rainy day in a leaky tent at Frith Hill.

Workshop in the Aircraft Factory.

Aldershot Parish Hall during WW1 1915.

The Commander and founder of the Aircraft Factory, Mervyn O'Gorman (FAST).

CHAPTER 3

1916

The third year of the war opened with a meeting at the St Michael's Institute where the Bishop of Winchester and the Vicar of Aldershot sought to answer the question of how a Christian could interpret the war. The role of a soldier was atrocious and bitter and it could not be denied that it changed men. Indeed, it changed England because it could not leave England as it found it. Christians should seek to find a synthesis between the fact that the war had produced two extremes of men – the militarist and the pacifist men that matched the fact of the noble cause they were fighting for. This meant that the man who voluntarily left his wife and children to fight should be honoured. During this year, with the advent of conscription in Aldershot, situations such as this would be tried and tested. Both clergymen expressed concern at falls in church attendance despite having to respond to the German's 'ruthless and barbaric practices'. Later, in January, the town's MP, Clavell-Salter, was quoting the statistics of the war that had already resulted in 500,000 killed, wounded or taken prisoner and was costing the country £38,000 every ten minutes. He was certain that the Germans had not given up their confidence in victory.

It was a year that would bring discomfort, darkness, increased demands on those left behind, heavier taxation and increasing prices of scarce food and clothing. On the other hand, it would witness Aldershot seeking to respond to the demands placed on it as the centre for the British Army. Money to expand the capacity of the town's power station had to be found in order to keep the lights on in the camp. Increased military traffic meant that the dangerously congested Newport Road had to be widened. Although the war dominated everything, the council was seeking to discuss industrial development with Farnham and Farnborough councils without marked success. There was a lack of co-ordinated housing policy. Aldershot sought financial support for housing development in Sandford and Brighton Roads. However, just how acute the problem was is revealed by environment inspectors finding seven people crammed into a single room in Cove near Farnborough. In a similar way, attempts to improve the transport infrastructure for the town through schemes to construct a rail link between Aldershot and Farnborough failed because of lack of enthusiasm from Farnborough.

In March, the performance of the Aldershot and District Traction Company in providing an effective bus service for the area drew strong criticism. Its manager, T. Foster, in apologising, explained the grave difficulties in maintaining the service due to the release of so many men for service abroad. The company had attempted to replace these men with women and with men who were ineligible for service in the forces. Collins, a leading councillor, accepted that the company was under stress but suggested the solution might be to run fewer buses providing they ran on time. The buses ran at irregular times and, seemingly, to suit themselves. 'Buses are timed to run every quarter-of-an-hour, but you are lucky if you see them at intervals of half- or three-quarters-of-an-hour,' he said. 'They are continually breaking down and no reliance can be placed on them.'

Problems continued with the supply of water to the camp. Apart from contractors used by the army who offered bulk washing, a large amount of washing was carried out by wives and widows in their own houses. The test case brought before the magistrates was the case against a widow who was in arrears of over £5 to the water company. The court ruled that the widow had no right to use water for domestic purposes to wash clothes for the army. Despite the support of the council for her case, the widow was fined 30 shillings by the court.

In June the council moved to cut its fire service from twenty-three men to twelve. In response, the firemen wrote to the council resigning *en masse*. Resignations took place because the council had refused to support the firemen's case for exemption from military service. The council accepted their resignation and then proceeded to reinstate the service using volunteers. Councillor Ainger pointed out that there was an overlap between members serving on the fire brigade committee of the council and the military appeals tribunal. However, Councillor Calvert reported that the committee had already entered into discussions with the firemen who were prepared to continue to work. They would not talk to the eleven other firemen who had resigned because they were no longer serving firemen.

There was also serious debate in the education committee about the allowances that should be offered to teachers on active service. Two teachers, Southgate and Hand, now serving, requested that they be paid on the same basis as teachers who had previously enlisted. Councillor Calvert said there was a difference between men who had volunteered and those who had been conscripted. He sympathised with the young men who had sacrificed everything to join at the beginning of the war. It was disheartening to these men that they might be just receiving their army pay while next to them were men who were receiving an additional allowance. The clerk of the committee pointed out that in the case of Hand he had originally sought to enlist but been rejected because of poor eyesight. With regard to Southgate, he had delayed enlistment because his father was dying. The committee supported Rev'd Hawkes' proposal to allow the allowance for both men.

Both Smith-Dorrien and Haig had seen playing sport an invaluable role in preparing men for service in the army. However, the immediate consequence of the rush to the colours was to limit the amount of sport in Aldershot and the command area. Initially there were few sporting facilities available to greet the new army on their arrival. However, by early 1916, systems of sports training had been incorporated into military training. A large reservoir of talent was developed through both the Southern Counties Cross Country Association and the Aldershot Athletic Command. Activities were worked out, blending things like bayonet-fighting, bomb-throwing, gas-helmet-exercises and trench-digging with cross-country running, relay racing, weight throwing and miniature rifle shooting. These activities took in Ewshot (the New Zealanders), Bramshott (the Canadians), Blackdown and Witney. For major sports, like football, rugby and cricket, Aldershot became the centre for sport of national significance.

As well as the deaths of those serving overseas usually reported through lists arriving at the railway station, a feature of the year would be the deaths through accident and suicide reported to the Aldershot coroner from the camp. One such death was that of driver Joseph

Radcliffe of the 115th Army Service Corps, who prior to committing suicide in the guard room had complained of being persecuted by those claiming he had VD. Private John Smith was found dead in the town's reservoir. He had cut his own throat. At the following inquest, a letter to his wife stated how he hoped his wife would be able to do the best for their children. He had been sent home from the Front suffering from 'nerves'. In May, an inquest was held into the death of a 34-year-old mechanic, Thomas Benyon. He too had cut his own throat only a week after joining up in London. On 16 June, Edward Bean from the Lincolnshire Yeomanry, was killed in bayonet practice. On 21 July, Private William Mason of the 2/5th Kings Liverpool Regiment was found shot in a tent. He had enrolled on 22 February 1915 and had served in France. Mention was made of his effeminate ways and his having been seen dressed in women's clothes in Dover. In October, the death of James McKinin of the Army Service Corps was reported. He was a married man with six children from Belfast. Previously he had been granted leave to visit his family. His decomposed body was only discovered some time after he was assumed to have left on leave. Deaths from accidents to members of the Royal Flying Corps continued. Lieutenant J.S. Reed had been flying in an aeroplane piloted by Lieutenant Burden when the machine plunged from 200 feet causing him serious injuries from which he died. The crash, which occurred on Laffan's Plain, was attributed to pilot error due to the pilot's lapse in attention having seen another plane and allowing the plane to lose speed. Lieutenant Reed was 19 and a graduate of Sandhurst. In August, Lieutenant Humphrey Pearson was killed in training after crashing into a tree. At the inquest his father complained as a new machine was being used his son should have been offered training before being allowed to fly. One of the most serious deaths was that of Major Frank Goodon, who Mervyn O'Gorman, the aircraft factory superintendent, had appointed as one of his test pilots three days after the commencement of the war. Born in 1889, he received his pilot's licence in 1913. Reports were received that the new FE8 aeroplanes were likely to spin out of control. He carried out a series of exercises putting the plane in a spin and managing to correct the spin. However, on 22 September, flying the prototype SE5, the material on the aircraft's wing ripped, the plane crashed and he was killed.

After the opening of the Somme campaign in July, the Cambridge and Connaught Hospitals struggled to cope with the numbers coming off the hospital trains from Southampton. Annexe hospitals were opened attached to the camps at Ewshot and Bramshott. Many of the men were horribly disfigured as the result of high explosives. In the trenches, the head was more exposed than any other part of the body and soldiers' faces were often shattered beyond recognition. The New Zealander Harold Gillies arrived at Cambridge Hospital, with a small unit, who would seek to pioneer a new method of rebuilding faces by taking tissue from other parts of the body. Gillies' background marked him out as possessing considerable aesthetic ability, exhibiting paintings in London as well as being a master surgeon. A colleague observing in the operating theatre at the Cambridge commented: 'In many hours spent assisting or in watching Gillies I never once saw him perform a rough movement. All the actions of his hands were consistently gentle, accurate and deft.' He pioneered the practices of ensuring that soldiers with jaw and mouth wounds were placed face down on stretchers, bone grafting and close working with dentists.

Gillies was 32 when war broke out and, anticipating he would soon be drafted, joined the Red Cross. He was commissioned and sent to Belgium. However, on the way he had a chance meeting with Auguste Valadier, who had set up a special unit dealing with jaw wounds through grafting tissue from other parts of the body. 'I realised that I had struck a branch of surgery that was of intense interest to me. My first inspiration for plastic work came from a few pictures in a German book,' he stated. He followed this up by applying to the War Office to set up a plastic surgery unit based on those he had observed at Boulogne, Étaples, Amiens and Paris.

On 11 January 1916, Gillies was ordered to report to the Cambridge Military Hospital 'for special duty in connection with plastic surgery'. He was charged with getting the unit up and running. Ever practical, he paid £10 out of his own pocket for labels directing all the wounded with injuries to the jaw and face to himself and arranged that the labels be sent to France to the field hospitals where they would be pinned to wounded soldiers' uniforms.

At the Royal Army Dental Corps Museum in Aldershot, evidence of Gillies' work can be found in sixty-nine pastel drawings. In addition, Gillies spent at least an hour before each operation seeking to visualise what would be the result of his work on the soldier's face. He could be seen in the corridors of the Cambridge in a world of his own pacing up and down then cutting out pieces of paper and fitting them together in a jigsaw representing a face. Part of his work involved creating a plaster model of what the face would look like. What was unique about Gillies was the way in which he introduced an aesthetic element into the creation of the faces he was rebuilding. Later he worked with another artist/surgeon, Henry Tonks, to create an artistic record of this pioneering work. His cousin, Archibald McIndoe, carried on his work, particularly with severely burnt pilots in World War Two.

On 7 July, Wilfred Owen, probably one of Britain's greatest war poets, arrived at Talavera Barracks with the Middlesex Regiment. He was scheduled to do a musketry course based at Mytchett. He described arriving at Aldershot as 'representing his transformation into a soldier', in a letter to his mother. He complained bitterly about having to share his room with a high church divinity student, who he described as 'dogmatic, pig-headed, preachifying, and domineering'. He gave instruction to his servant to move his belongings to another room he had found in the barracks. Owen's detestation of the man is reflected in this aphorism about the clerical gentleman: 'A parson is a lamb in a drawing room, but a lion in the vestry,' said Keats. 'In a bedroom and arrayed as an officer, he is an ass in lion's clothing.'

He described his work as a company commander of B Company of the 25th Middlesex, taking parades and acting as fire officer when there were two scrub fires nearby. He suspected he may be appointed as a gas officer as well. He claimed to be 'well up' in gas warfare as a result of the course he had been attending. He talked about designing a new gas helmet and then cautioned himself about disclosing secret information. He complains about the concert party in their mess refusing to leave until well after midnight, when they had to march to their firing range at 7 am. His company staged a practise attack on an area with a lake behind it so his men were able to swim afterwards. The brigade musketry officer was displeased with how well he was marking his soldiers' firing in the butts. He had to give his men two hours extra training because they were scheduled for guard duty and most had not fixed a bayonet in their lives. He felt under pressure from his men to perform exceptionally well on the rifle range and was able to fire off five rounds in thirty seconds, scoring three bulls and two inners, registering seventeen points out of twenty.

Owen complained that most of his men were second-class and some third-class, with some suffering from defective eyesight.

In the surrounding countryside, a desperate shortage of labour meant that more women were being employed in work previously reserved for men. It was slowly being recognised that if the nation hoped to feed itself, Aldershot Council would have to give as much publicity as possible to the necessity of employing women. A leading councillor, Mr Calvert, questioned whether a woman earning 25 shillings a week in Aldershot would go to Ash to dig potatoes. He went on to criticise the 'fancy work' done between ten and eleven in the morning and three and four in the afternoon. The chairman of the committee considering farm employment, Mr Attfield, chipped in saying that his experience of women workers was 'very unfortunate'. In some cases, farmers only agreed to employ women in short shifts. Advertisements begin to appear seeking hundreds of women to work in areas such as the camp's kitchens.

In all this it was being belatedly recognised that there needed to be positive action to support women and children if they were to play the important role now expected of them. At the annual meeting of the town's Women's Refuge held in the parish hall on 16 February, the Bishop of Winchester complained about the monstrous forms of vice that could be found in Aldershot and how this should arouse militant indignation in all Christians. Reacting to the steep increase in VD, the call for sex education advanced by a recent royal commission was supported. Presenting a report on the work of the refuge, Mrs Kitchen said they had struggled with the surge in new cases they had dealt with. This had been due to the numbers of wives and relatives who had followed their husbands to the town and needed shelter. The supervisor of the refuge might be woken four times a night. In one case a wife arrived from Canada with five children. Help had come from Mrs Fetley, who provided a hostel at the Church of England's Soldiers' Institute for soldiers' relatives paying a small sum for a night's lodging. Miss Avery attended hearings at the magistrates court and had come to the assistance of fifty-five women, many of whom had arrived in Aldershot with only flimsy information about the whereabouts of the men they sought. As many of those seeking help at the refuge came from surrounding villages, it was felt they should make a contribution towards their welfare. The soldiers who brought women wandering the streets in the town to the refuge were commended. The superintendent urged donations towards the refuge supply club, who provided women in need of clothing.

The magistrates court hearing of 23 June revealed the nature of the problem of women following the army. Twenty-two-year-olds Daisy Turner and Hilde Heath were found in officers' quarters partially undressed and although already being dealt with under military law, were brought before the magistrate. They claimed they were filling in time before they caught the last train out of Aldershot at 11.45 pm. A complaint was heard about Turner's 'immoral life' and the way she was seen in the frequent company of officers. Her father was at the Front and her mother now disowned her. Both were fined £12. There then followed charges against four women found illegally on army land or sleeping rough.

The physical manifestations of vice in Aldershot are revealed by a prosecution against Mary Moody, Ada Wilkinson and Mary Allwright, who were observed entertaining officers and NCOs at a house in Grosvenor Road. On 9 November, a policeman arrived at the house only to have the door slammed in his face. He managed to enter the house and was able to observe what was happening in the bedrooms. In her defence Moody is reported as saying: 'It's my husband's fault. He put me on the streets before I was 16. If you give me a chance I'll go straight back to Leeds.' She was sentenced to two months in prison with hard labour. The final act in the life of a lady of the streets might be to be found dead in the front garden of a house in Alexander Road in late November, as was Annie Potts. The coroner felt there was no need for a post mortem.

Rev'd Hawkes believed that the group likely to suffer most during the war were children. For many weeks schools had been closed and this was likely to continue. Many children were now being sent out to work when they ought to be at school. Coupled to this he identified the adverse consequence of not having a father present. He claimed he knew many families with admirable mothers but whose characters had been undermined by the absence of a father to run up against and in this way learn obedience. He said: 'Every woman who has been a little lax should remember that she has to be both father and mother, and be strong and strict as well as loving.' However, on 17 March, Aldershot Council refused to increase the provision for child welfare despite a request from the Local Government Board for them to do so. Councillor Harland criticised this action in the face of real problems of the care of children arising in the town. Councillor Ainger spoke in his support and urged that further childcare provision be put in place. In response, Councillor Calvert stated that Aldershot had been the first council to appoint a doctor placed in schools to monitor children's health. Were they proposing that councillors go out and nurse the babies themselves like old Mother Hubbard? An attempt by Councillors Ainger and Harland to refer the matter back to the council's health committee was rejected. However, on May 16· Mrs Fullbrook is reported as writing to the council criticising Councillor Calvert's remarks and demanding to know why the council had refused to comply with the instructions of the Local Government Board. Aldershot's poor record in childcare was exemplified by the fact that, although there were 1,014 births registered in 1914, the health visitor was recorded as having made only 1,070 visits to mother and child. Councillor Ainger wanted the letter taken very seriously and moved that its contents be referred to the health committee.

On 30 June, Rev'd Hawkes spoke in favour of awarding certified teachers an extra 3 shillings a week due to an increase of 60 per cent in the cost of living. However, the *Sheldrake Military Gazette* criticised the award citing the payment of just 5 shillings to old age pensioners and suggested that if Aldershot teachers were experiencing hardship this should be dealt with as individual cases not through a lump sum award.

The passing of the Military Services Act, bringing in conscription, would throw a sharp focus on the commitment and attitudes to the war throughout the Aldershot community. Appeals Tribunals were set up at Aldershot and Farnborough, and by late February, 200 appeals had been lodged. From late February onwards, the acute labour situation faced by Aldershot and the surrounding area was revealed. Fred Cook, a farm worker, stated that his three brothers were already serving and his call-up would cause the family farm acute difficulties. Among a plethora of individual cases, appeals by essential services like transport, water and gas stand out. The Aldershot and District Traction Company complained that the enlistment of fitters would seriously diminish the company's ability to operate. They stated to the tribunal that if they were given time to train replacement engineers, they might be able to manage. Women were not capable of doing the work and they were likely to be left with a single fitter who was over 60. The company also applied for an exemption for the company's secretary. They claimed his work was indispensable for the carrying on of their business because only he had the financial and business details that enabled the company to operate. He was given a three months' postponement.

A similar request was made on behalf of an assistant at the sewerage works by the council and achieved only a month's extension despite the fact that there had been a 60 per cent increase in its operation since the start of the war and that an advertisement for a replacement had not produced a single reply. Signs that the Aldershot Gas, Water and District Lighting Company were finding great difficulty operating with a shortage of technical staff is evidenced by its appeal on behalf of one of the two electrical engineers in their employ. A feature of the tribunals was the appeals of skilled men working in the aircraft factory. John Garland was working on contract at the factory putting in electrical installations in new workshops. His foreman stated that without him the completion of the work would be very difficult. A month's extension was granted. However, a similar application from a 19-year-old technician was turned down. A dairyman of 33 applied for absolute exemption and when asked about a woman replacing him said that a woman would not be able to lift the milk churns. When questioned about getting an over-age man for his work, he stated that no one would do the work because of the long hours involved. He was granted a temporary exemption for six months when the tribunal would review his case.

When the applicant cited religious and philosophical arguments about enlistment, the argument became much more heated. Ernest Athorn, a toolmaker and machine-tool fitter from the aircraft factory, stated that he did not believe in any kind of warfare. 'You mean you would let others fight for you,' responded the committee chairman, Herbert Robinson. 'I didn't ask them to go,' Athorn replied. 'It's disgraceful that any man working for a government department won't go to war,' Robinson replied, dismissing his appeal. At another hearing the chairman, G.W. Collins, exploded when Albert Hires, another aircraft factory employee, stated that he refused to sign-up because he refused to commit murder and that every man was his brother. 'What if someone came over here and outraged your mother?' Collins demanded. 'I don't know because it hasn't happened yet,' Hires replied. Conscientious objectors were given a rough time by the tribunals as W.F. Jeffrey, an elementary school teacher who taught at East End School, discovered. 'Taking up arms is disobeying the will of God,' the 22-year-old Jeffrey said. 'If anyone assaults you, what attitude would you take?' asked Chairman Collins. 'I regard all men as my brothers. War is the consummation of everything inhuman, unjust and a betrayal in man.' Collins continued: 'In the event of someone assaulting your father what would be your action?' 'I cannot say,' Jeffrey replied. At this the chairman retorted angrily, 'Dear me – you are qualifying for the lunatic asylum.' In the end Jeffrey reluctantly agreed to a non-combatant role in the army.

Chairman Collins was not alone in questioning why all the young skilled workers O'Gorman had recruited for the aircraft factory were not in the army. The local papers questioned this as well. Perhaps this may have been a reason why the War Office replaced O'Gorman with Henry Fowler to manage a factory with 5,000 employees.

What happened to conscientious objectors following these hearings must be found in the memoirs of those involved. In 1916, Mark Haylor was arrested and taken to the guardroom in one of the Aldershot barracks. He was asked to put on a uniform but he refused. A whole range of inducements were employed, but he still refused. He was then taken to Farnborough to a tent where he refused to help with washing up in the mess. He was then court-martialled, this taking place at the Royal Pavilion in Aldershot. Haylor was receiving support from the No Conscription Fellowship led by Fenner Brockway, later MP for Dagenham. His argument was that he could not follow military orders because he was a civilian and therefore had not broken military law. As this was the first hearing of this kind, the press were in attendance and so the army had to tread very carefully. Two days after the court-martial, the whole battalion where he was located were paraded and his sentence to Wandsworth Prison was read out. Leonard Percy was also brought to Aldershot after refusing to serve at a tribunal. He was prepared to carry out limited non-military duties, such as supplying coal to the officers' mess. Quite remarkably he was given a rail pass for Watford for leave over Christmas.

In nearby Camberley in September, a Colonel Ponsonby-Potts decided to increase the rate of recruitment for the command in the town. A circus had arrived in the town and between 3,000 and 4,000 people were in attendance at the big top. Ponsonby-Potts formed up members of the police and reserves in a nearby road and surrounded the tent. They entered the tent and began to work through the papers of all the men. Suddenly the lights went out accompanied by shrieks and cries of distress, particularly from women and children. In the confusion one of the generators caught fire. Finally, when the lights came on, the audience was observed to be considerably reduced. Nevertheless, Ponsonby-Potts used the opportunity of lecturing those present about how they should do their duty and support the war.

Newsreel pictures from the war show troops being taken forward to the Front in seventy-five London buses. A letter from a member of the transport section of the Army Service Corps based in Aldershot provided an interesting insight into what happened to the buses in France. Twenty fitters worked night and day to keep them in operation working out of a mobile repair unit. As the British line extended, the original wheels on their vehicles proved useless. They were equipped with pulleys and tackle in order to rescue not only buses but also trucks, which had fallen into shell holes and ditches, the last of these being one of the original buses, which had fallen into a canal in 1914.

Reports continued to arrive in the town about the poor treatment of British POWs. Due to funds raised by groups such as the aircraft factory, the Co-operative Society and Solomon Brothers, weekly parcels were dispatched to POWs. There were forty local men who were currently POWs. The diet they were receiving was calculated to keep them alive and nothing more. In many cases the relatives of these men were too poor to do anything to offer assistance. Nevertheless, they were making great sacrifice to send the occasional parcel. It was reported that because the parcels might take up to five weeks to arrive the bread when it arrived finally was inedible. Arrangements had been made to substitute wholemeal biscuits for the bread and the parcels now included cheese, fruit, biscuits, chocolate, condensed milk, tea, soap and cake. POWs arriving in the area in August were observed disembarking surrounded by soldiers with fixed bayonets. They were seen to be of lesser physique than the soldiers of Kitchener's army with: 'small eyes set close together and bullet heads. They had puny receding foreheads and chins.' Based on this appraisal of the enemy the country had little to fear. They were wearing grey-green uniforms and peakless caps. However poor their physical make-up, some escaped from Frith Hill, where their camp was located, and managed to get as far as Ascot.

Frith Hill Camp was a mixture of a prisoner-of-war camp and a concentration camp. At one time there was talk of expanding the camp from under 2,000 to 10,000. Many of the original captives were prisoners taken at the battles of the Marne and Aisne. They arrived in Frimley on two special trains. They were then marched to Frith Hill, except for one man who was suffering from a leg injury. He was taken to the camp on regimental transport, which arrived to take the luggage. Before rules of fraternisation were brought in the prisoners were showered with gifts of cigarettes, cakes, fruit and ginger beer. Such were the numbers arriving one of the officers described it as being worse than directing traffic at Ascot.

When a tradesman was delivering goods to the camp one of the Germans remarked, 'I see you can't make do without things German,' pointing to the Bosch Magneto on his motorbike. In October, another 200 prisoners arrived and the crowd that had gathered to witness their arrival was amazed at how young they were. A correspondent from the *Camberley News* pondered whether any of these men had witnessed the treatment metered out to English prisoners and compared it to the treatment they were receiving.

On 27 July, almost four weeks after the opening of the Somme offensive and convinced the British forces were moving forward, Aldershot District Council wrote to General Haig congratulating him on the 'splendid achievements of our army'. This message was dispatched in a telegram from the council.

In August, Mervyn O'Gorman, the genius behind the creation of the aircraft factory, failed to have his contract renewed by the War Office. After seven years at the helm of the RAF he was replaced by Sir Henry Fowler, director of Southern Railway. O'Gorman's departure was followed by that of Fred Green, the factory's chief engineer, Henry Folland, de Havilland's chief draughtsman, Major Heckstall-Smith and Henry Hall, who were managers of the factory's engineering department. They all obtained employment with private aeronautical firms.

Kiwi ghosts at Ewshot

At one time between 1916 and 1918 there were 5,000 New Zealand soldiers at Ewshot. They were part of the artillery regiment but virtually all traces of their existence have disappeared.

Modern Ewshot is a brand new parish of 281 homes, some farms, St Mary's Church, a haulage company and a pub, The Windmill. The settlement is grouped around St Mary's, which would have played a sad part in the lives of the Kiwis there for the funerals for the men who died in the hospital that was located there after 1916. It's about 3 miles to the south of the town of Fleet and 3 miles to the north-east of Farnham in Surrey.

Original Ewshot in ancient records referred to the Manor of Itchel, which took in a large area of land to the north and west of the present village. It became a village as the result of the parson of St Mary's opening a school in 1844/5 and the building of St Mary's in 1876. It has been suggested that the name originates from the Anglo Saxon for grove.

From its establishment in 1854, the military camp at nearby Aldershot began to spread its tentacles into the neighbouring hinterland. The countryside provided invaluable space for army manoeuvres, a process that accelerated as war approached in the early part of the last century. An artillery base was in existence in 1914 as part of the regular army. The New Zealand government paying for bases for New Zealand troops arriving in Britain from late 1915 hired the camp from the British government for its Artillery Regiment. From August 1917, New Zealand troops took over a permanent camp with associate comforts certainly superior to the occupation of a bell tent. Troops travelled to the camp via Waterloo Station in London alighting at the nearby Fleet Station. As they approached the camp along tree-lined roads they would see the extensive playing fields surrounding the camp, the result of the former commander of Aldershot General Haig's belief in games as an essential part of soldiering.

Only spoken in a low voice was the fact that the camp's original name was Leipzig Barracks, given to it at the time of the kaiser's visit to Aldershot before the war. The camp the arriving New Zealanders found was of 30 acres and well-designed. It could accommodate 1,500 soldiers of all ranks and 1,000 horses, still a vital part of the British Army. As well as the Artillery Regiment, the New Zealand Medical Corps were located there. In late 1917, as a result of the Passchendaele disaster and subsequent fighting, 21,000 New Zealand soldiers were treated in a hospital here.

Having deposited their kit in one of the barracks, the Kiwi soldiers would look out on to headquarters buildings and the inevitable square for their square bashing. They would see the 18-pounder gun sheds and the stables with the draught horses that did most of the pulling of the guns during the war. Their quarters extended into streets behind these stables and they would look with some envy at the prestigious buildings allocated to the officers. Some of the more fortunate artillerists were given the barracks previously occupied by the married men of the regular British Army. Compared with other camps, like Sling Camp on Salisbury Plain, Ewshot boasted a luxurious plunge bath and hot water in its bath houses. Unlike the bleak Salisbury Plain in Wiltshire, they had pleasant villages to explore on leave as well as the fleshpots of nearby Aldershot. There was a good canteen, well-stocked even when rationing was introduced – although local court cases indicate a certain amount of horse trading to achieve plentiful supplies. At this time the camp boasted its own gardens to supply fresh vegetables. The Wesleyan Church from its base in Aldershot provided a reading library and a place for writing letters home. All indication is that a YMCA building was also popular with the New Zealanders. However, some New Zealand married officers whose wives had followed them to England sought out rented accommodation in Farnborough. Here they believed were better schools for their children. There was a general criticism of Aldershot schools at this time for their lack of training in basic skills for science and technology.

The course offered at Ewshot was a smartening-up of training that had occurred previously in New Zealand. To be effective on the Western Front, speed was of the essence. They were able to take advantage of the concentration on cavalry activities, a feature of Aldershot's fox hunting commanders like Smith-Dorrien, to further develop their riding skills. Backing all this up was a small army of tradesman from the Army Service Corps providing essential shoeing and saddling support. The camp and Aldershot also boasted excellent veterinary services.

The crucial part of an effective artillery operation is observation and here the proximity of the original balloon factory, now the Royal aircraft factory, with its work on signalling and wireless technology provided vital skills for the artillerists. Simulations testing the accuracy with the aid of Avith signallers laying wires between huts over an imaginary landscape provided vital indication of necessary skills for the Front. Successful firing was indicated by puffs of smoke from the sheds.

The role of the New Zealand Medical Corps was to support the New Zealand Hospitals that had been established at Brockenhurst, in the New Forest and Walton upon Thames. As well as these there was the medical aid offered on hospital ships and the support of the hospital at Ewshot itself. The training given the corps consisted of courses in dealing with gas poisoning, water supplies (a real problem when rapid advance took place from April 1918), and general hospital orderly duties. A trench system had been constructed where the work in advanced dressing stations could be practised. Apart from failure at Passchendaele when the ground was such a quagmire making stability impossible, the New Zealand gunners had achieved a reputation as being among the best on the Western Front.

Ewshot boasted its own paper similar to *New Zealand at the Front*, written by soldiers in France. It was called *Youshot* and portrayed a strong kindred spirit among all Kiwis there, whether they were there for training or in the iron bungalow hospital with its cluster of brick chimneys.

However, it was through rugby that the New Zealanders at Ewshot stamped their reputation on Aldershot and the surrounding area. A report of a game at Queen's Parade in Aldershot refers to the great 'Invincibles' of 1905 who 'carried all before them'. Charlie Seeling, who was the coach of the Ewshot team, had been one of 'The Invincibles'. The New Zealand Artillery played the New Zealand Engineers in what must have been an exhibition game for rugby supporters. English observers were struck by the backline formation of the Kiwi team – three quarters, two five-eights and one half in comparison with the domestic formation of four three-quarters and two halves. There were seven forwards and one flying winger designed to pick up opportunist balls.

Both teams contained players of note in New Zealand who were provincial reps while a previous encounter in Christchurch (Hampshire) had resulted in a narrow victory for the Engineers eight to three. A weakened Engineers' side was defeated by twenty-four points to eight in front of a good crowd drawn from the resident artillerymen. Following the game, the commander of the Aldershot command, Major-General Sir Archibald Murray, listened to the Artillery Band play a wide range of music. The game was refereed by H. Young, chaplain to the New Zealand forces.

The victorious path of the artillery team continued with a victory over a side of Canadian Mounties by sixteen points to nil and in a follow up game at Queen's Park in Aldershot by twenty-two points to nil. Charlie Seeling refereed this game on 21 November 1917. There was another easy victory at Ewshot against a side drawn from the newly formed RAF side boasting a previous victory against the Australians, by forty-eight to three. Another game played at the aircraft factory resulted in a narrower win of 8 points to nil. New Zealanders were in an Aldershot command side, which defeated an Australian Headquarters side by eight points to three. The side included two Internationals, Captain Bull from England and Lieutenant R.T. Gabe from Wales.

The success of these New Zealand rugby players paled into insignificance alongside the deaths and wounding taking place in France. Gunner Johnson's parents received the following note from his commanding officer after they were notified of his death:

> Your son was always a conscientious and thorough gunner and his loss is deeply regretted by the battery. You have the consolation of knowing he was on his job on the guns at the time and a chance shot happened to land adjacent to the pit. His death was instantaneous and he suffered nothing. Please accept my heartfelt sympathy.

Many of the letters from the Front drafted in this way speak of 'instant death', leaving no genuine doubt that the intention of the writer was to lessen the grief of the soldier's family by indicating that death came without suffering.

Gunner Johnson's Church of England chaplain wrote:

> I am the Church of England Chaplain with the New Zealand Field Artillery, so it fell to my lot to conduct the funeral service for your son, who was killed in action on the night of 29th December 1917. I know how futile words are at a time like this, but I am just writing to you to give what scanty information I can, in the hope

that it might give you some slight comfort to know where your boy rests and that his grave will be cared for. Gunner Johnson was in the gun pit of one of the guns of the battery on the evening of the 29th, when a German shell exploded, a fragment striking him on the head and killing him instantaneously. His mates brought his body down from the guns, and he now lies in the Divisional Military Cemetery at Dickebuch Road, Belgium, where so many of our brave New Zealand artillery boys are lying.

He then goes on to describe the scene of Johnson's burial:

The twilight of the short winter day was falling as I stood at the head of the grave and took the beautiful service – so full of the certain hope of the resurrection to life eternal. At the foot of the grave stood his battery major and grouped around it in the snow were Gunner Johnson's mates from the Brigade. At the end of the service, and just before the Last Post we added a prayer for all those upon whom sorrow had fallen through his bereavement – that God himself in His love, would comfort them, even though their sorrow would bring them nearer to Him.

Johnson's mother also received messages of condolence from the governor general of New Zealand and the minister of defence in the New Zealand government. Arriving as well was a letter from one of his mates who felt the loss deeply of a closely bonded friend.

When autumn comes along among the orange hues of tree-dotted hedgerows, which almost 100 years ago echoed to the cries from the rugby field, who now remembers the hundreds of Kiwis who lived out the crucial part of their lives at Ewshot?

Finally, two rather jaundiced views from 'down under'. In 1917, Gunner Laing criticised the 'bull' and seemingly needless spit and polish associated with army life in the camp. 'Strikes one things are pretty easy here called the Old Man's home; all they seem to worry about is that you keep things clean especially buttons and boots. You might as well hit a colonel in the eye as having a dirty button.' Gunner Watson uses a quaint expression about his liaisons with prostitutes in the town. 'Had some sport with Aldershot 1 and 2 don't know their names but they were splendid value.'

The Canadians in Bramshott

Canadian troops first arrived at Bramshott on 10 October 1915, taking over a small hutted camp originally occupied by British troops. This began a historical connection with the Aldershot command, which would continue throughout the war. Although the original Canadian troops had gone straight to France, Canadian commanders now demanded training from the new drafts arriving. The original mixing of troops from all parts of Canada changed in 1917 where troops from particular areas of the dominion were put in appropriate regiments related to the areas of their origin.

Bramshott became known as 'Mudsplosh' Camp because of the almost perpetual mud encountered at the camp. Sometimes arrangements for billeting groups, such as the Canadian Grenadier Guards, broke down badly. When they arrived at Bramshott from Liphook station no arrangements had been made for their arrival and no food was available. The slate-roofed huts were ramshackle affairs and had to be replaced. When they were more comfortably housed and were able to enjoy the countryside, the Canadians described their time at Bramshott as the happiest in their division's history. Training was run by outstanding Canadian officers and NCOs with experience from France, bayonet fighting, bombing, wiring and entrenching being industriously practised. This was from five in the morning to nine at night. Coaching them in bayonet fighting was a cockney NCO who shouted 'Fink it's yer muvver-in-law'.

After the Battle of the Somme, Bramshott witnessed battalions that had been decimated replaced with new recruits from Canada. The camp was a collection of hurriedly erected iron huts running along the London to Portsmouth Road. There were church huts, shops, cafés, a YMCA, a post office and a bank. Strong relationships developed between café owners like Mrs Edwards, who was protected when Canadian troops, unhappy about delays in going home, rioted in Liphook in 1919. A large hut was turned into a three-penny cinema and then rebuilt as a garrison theatre. Bramshott was a vast camp and inevitably local girls married Canadians following dances arranged in the camp.

A 630-bed hospital opened in November 1915 to take advantage of the 'mountain air'. However, mortality rates were low at 3.75 deaths per month until the Spanish influenza epidemic of September

1918. The pandemic hit the camp with twelve funerals on 8 November alone. Drivers would hurriedly deliver goods and drive off as quickly as they could. The last Canadian burial here was that of Private J. Lawrence of the 3rd Canadian Division, who died on 15 July 1919.

'Their name liveth forevermore' is the sentiment on innumerable memorials to the dead throughout the English speaking world. At The Beeches in Cargate Avenue, Aldershot, tangible proof exists that this was more than a pious hope. David Strong, the present resident, speaks of sensing Second Lieutenant Harold Jaye walking down the stairs of the house for the last time on the way to France and the Somme in 1916. Mr Strong's wife, Gill, and his mother-in-law – when she stayed with the family – speak of seeing a young army officer on the stairs.

Just 24, Harold Jaye was a sensitive talented young man, the youngest in the family and a promising pianist. He was educated at the Collegiate School Aldershot followed by Farnham Grammar School. He joined the London University Training Corps in March 1915. After being gazetted as an officer serving with the 3rd Battalion of the North Yorkshire Regiment, he left for France in May 1916. He was seriously wounded during one of the attacks on the Somme on 5 July and died in hospital a few days later on 9th July 1916.

2nd Lieutenant Harold Conway Jaye, West Gloucestershire Regt. Wounded on 5 July on the Somme and died on 9 July 1916.

Connaught Hospital 1916.

*Councillor John
May, leading
Councillor.*

The King and Queen and Aldershot Commanding Officers at the Royal Pavilion.

Aldershot football team drawn from volunteers.

Recruits from Aldershot for the Hampshire Regiment 1916.

Councillor Harland, Council Leader and Secretary of Workers' Union.

Panorama of Bramshott camp.

Sir Harold Gillies, pioneer of plastic surgery at The Cambridge Hospital, Aldershot.

Camp of the Argyle & Sutherland Highlanders at Scrogg's Bottom, Aldershot.

Royal Flying 'Boys' in uniform wearing cadet officers' white bands whilst on leave.

Presbyterian Hall in Aldershot being prepared for letter writing by the troops.

Kitchener's 'Boys' enjoying tea and musical entertainment in the Presbyterian Hall.

Aldershot Traction buses used during the war.

Corunna Barracks Officers' Mess.

CHAPTER 4

1917

This was the year that witnessed fundamental changes in Aldershot. Events thousands of miles away in Russia brought with them recognition that there were limitations to the sacrifices working people could be asked to make in supporting the war. They brought with them questions about what sort of society they were being asked to live in, in the light of their present privations. In recognition of this situation, working-class organisations like trades councils came in from a cold atmosphere of indifference and hostility to be part of serious discussions about how the affairs of Aldershot and Farnborough should be managed. Acute problems arose over managing wages and salaries for those in public employment in a time of high inflation. There was a shortage of men, not only for the army but maintaining the economic fabric of the town, which not even the bringing in of female labour could rectify. Clavell-Salter, the town's MP, was swapped for Auckland Geddies in an uncontested election and Sir Archibald Murray took over leadership of the camp. The focus of camp and town in the war was shown by the prominence given to war savings and attempts to boost pensions for the army through the Aldershot Patriotic Fund.

There was resentment that this fund had been organised for the whole of Hampshire rather than Aldershot itself because Aldershot was aware of the hardship caused by inadequate pensions for the many in the town who had served. A feeling that the people in power were out of touch with the circumstances people now found themselves in came to a head in discussions at the town's local food control committee. Further disillusion arose through the decision of the War Office to take away Aldershot's role as the recruiting centre for the Aldershot command and appeared to confirm the perception that the War Office paid little attention to the concerns of Aldershot. The recruiting office was to be closed completely together with its operation in Basingstoke. This was only reversed following a protest by the town's Chamber of Commerce. They complained that these changes removing the focus away from the centre of the nation's army and incurred additional expenses for telephone fees and railway fares. In reply the army claimed that it was necessary to centralise its recruitment activity in a new centre at Hartley Wintney. Finally the War Office agreed to maintain a small office in Aldershot and it apologised for not giving Aldershot Council prior warning that it intended to move most of its recruitment activity out of town.

Councillor Calvert complained that it was 'An extraordinary situation where Aldershot known all over the world as the centre of the British Army should not be central for recruiting'. The recruiting office in Hartley Wintney was not even based in the town and was some distance from the railway station. However, the council had to reluctantly accept the army's decision and made a room available in its offices for army recruitment.

As with 1916, the Aldershot Traction Company was straining to maintain an adequate service as evidenced by a letter received by the council on 18 December from the company chairman, W.E. Foster. He sent to the council a report on the struggles the company was experiencing because of the war due to be submitted to the company's shareholders on 21 December. Quoting from the report, he blamed the company's unsatisfactory service on its loss of skilled labour and the difficulty experienced in getting spare parts. This was the reason a large number of buses were sitting idle. Coupled to this was a great escalation in the cost of materials and labour. Unless the company was able to obtain skilled mechanics and drivers it would not be able to maintain the level of service it currently offered. Despite the pressure on them, the bus company insisted that in the interest of the safety of the travelling public only those competent and fit to drive a bus would be allowed to do so. Mr Foster requested that the council represent the company's case for retaining skilled workers to the military tribunal presently hearing appeals against enlistment. By the end of the war the company was limited to a ratio of three employees for every bus.

In an environment in which death was being continually reported, the terrible murder of the quartermaster at the Isolation Hospital was still able to dominate the January headlines. A boy walking over trenches used by soldiers for training near the Marlborough Lines discovered the body of William Watterton, quartermaster of the Royal Army Medical Corps, lying in one of the trenches. Watterton had left the Isolation Hospital the previous day to go to the Connaught Hospital. He was found to have severe head wounds. Watterton was 49 and had enlisted in the Royal Army Medical Corps in 1887 retiring from the service in 1908. However, in 1915 he re-joined the army as a quartermaster with the rank of lieutenant.

The discovery of Watterton's body led to the immediate arrest of a 28-year-old Irish sergeant called Leo O'Donnell, who was attached to the Royal Army Medical Corps. O'Donnell had been walking out with Watterton's daughter, who was reported as being devastated at the violent death of her father. It emerged that O'Donnell had unsuccessfully been seeking someone who could replace him following his orders to go the Front, due to happen within days. He was planning to desert and needed the money he knew was in Watterton's safe at Connaught Hospital in order to finance him whilst on the run. O'Donnell had used a toilet brush to batter Watterton to death before carrying his body to the trench, where he was discovered the following day. Right up almost to the day of his execution, O'Donnell sought to find contacts to bribe so he could produce an alibi proving he could not have committed the crime, despite the fact that blood was found on his boots. He even claimed he was with a girl he had picked up in The Avenue. Unfortunately, he had been witnessed carrying the murder weapon into Watterton's office. The blood-stained bank notes O'Donnell had been found in possession of could not rationally be said to be in that condition when they were placed in Watterton's safe.

At the Assize Court in Winchester on 17 February, Leo O'Donnell was found guilty of murdering William Frederick Watterton in order to get the keys to his safe. After being found guilty by the jury in just seven minutes, in response to the clerk of the Assize's question if he had anything to say, O'Donnell said: 'I am innocent – that's all.' The judge, commenting that he had committed a cruel and heartless murder, donned the black cap and passed the sentence of death. Miss Watterton, who sat in the next dock behind the prisoner, buried her face in her hands when sentence was passed and left the court in tears. Right up to the time of his execution, O'Donnell was writing to friends such as 'My Dearest Jenny' offering £250, and even £500 to a warder at Winchester Prison to give him an alibi for an appeal. After his death, commentators puzzled about O'Donnell and what the background was of this charming, handsome, Irishman before his arrival in Aldershot.

The third anniversary of the war was marked by a united service of thanksgiving and intercession in the Municipal Gardens. The service was very simple but made a deep impression. The *Last Post* preceded the *Lord's Prayer* and the singing of *O God our help in ages past*. Leaflets listing the names of the fallen since the outbreak of the war were distributed.

As in previous years the cycle of deaths of those testing planes for the Royal Flying Corps continued. On 24 February, a 22-year-old pilot, Second-Lieutenant Frederick Evans, was killed. At 12.30 pm he left the aerodrome alone, testing an RE 8 machine. When he reached 500 feet his machine was observed to make a spinning nose-dive into the ground and burst into flames. Although a certified pilot, Evans had only had forty hours flying experience. His death was caused by severe injuries to his head but his body was also badly burnt when his engine exploded.

As food supplies diminished, Aldershot was required to create a food control committee of twelve members. At least one of these was to be a woman and there should a representative from labour. It is indicative of the changes happening as war progressed that the council voted that the local Women's Suffrage Group be asked to nominate a representative. However, an issue was to arise about who would represent labour. Councillor Calvert stated that as he was the president of the largest union, The Workers Union, he was eminently suitable therefore to take this responsibility. Calvert was an existing councillor. However, a letter appeared in the press shortly afterwards, seriously questioning Councillor Calvert's claim to represent labour and stating that only someone directly elected from a labour organisation could claim that position. The letter accused the council as being a self-appointed clique representing no one but itself. A short time later Calvert took the opportunity of a meeting of The Workers' Union in Aldershot to justify his presence on the committee as a labour representative. He had been an active trade unionist since working in Australia in 1892 as a railway porter. In 1900, after a short time in the town, he had put up for the council stating that he was in favour of the trade union rate for the job. A meeting of the Aldershot and District Trades Council was called to dispute the way the labour representative had been selected, as he was not from among active supporters of the labour movement. Its chairman, J.R. Noble, quoted a statement from the minister that food control committees should include at least one labour representative and that the fullest consideration should be given to appointing representatives from trades and labour councils. It was pointed out that three of the men appointed were food traders and therefore had a vested interest in how available food might be rationed. Further, the chairman challenged his audience to nominate any present member of Aldershot Council who directly represented labour. In reply, Calvert claimed his organisation represented 4,000 workers in Aldershot and was being ignored. In contrast, Farnborough Council invited their local trades council to nominate two members to its food control council, as had Farnham Council. The operation of the war economy had changed the basis on which councillors had been originally elected. A committee of this kind required to be more represented was a new feature of local government.

As the crisis in food supply deepened, the decisions of the committee drastically affected people's lives. On 9 November, for instance, the controlled price of potatoes was a £1 a ton, but in an open market the price asked might be as high as £6. All the problems associated with rationing seemed to occur in the town's shops. The committee heard reports that grocers were demanding sugar coupons when people bought tea, as it sought to monitor maximum prices for meat and bread set by the government. There were bitter comments about what they regarded as irresponsible purchasing by serving soldiers, who already enjoyed army rations purchasing food supplies for the camp. Butter had now become a luxury. Concern was expressed that the aircraft factory was selling some food at 1s 6d above the approved price. Bad spring weather with snow, hail and rain prevented allotment holders producing food to make up the shortfall from national sources. Showing his usual practical sense, F.O.T. Hawkes, the Aldershot vicar, proposed the establishment of a central canteen where nutritious food could be purchased by anyone on low income. In May of the following year, the *Aldershot News* was able to comment positively on the quality of the fish cakes and fish pies being served by the central canteen. On 26 October, no chink of light was shown in the rationing regime that existed in the town revealed by the food control committee's refusal to sanction the ingredients required for Christmas cakes being taken off rationing.

By June the trades council was complaining to the food control committee that profiteers would be rejoicing at the recent sinking of four cargo ships carrying food to the country. They noted that the sinking of a Canadian boat carrying grain had resulted in an immediate escalation of the price of bread in shops. Increasingly, bread was required to be made from potatoes. There were complaints as well of rotten potatoes being sold in the town. Claims were made by the trades council that profiteers were allowing food to rot in order to increase prices. Warnings that the country might struggle to feed itself began to be published from April, and appeals for thrift in its consumption appeared in both the *Aldershot News* and the *Sheldrake Military Gazette*. An emphasis was placed on the provision of allotments so that as many people as possible in Aldershot could grow their own food. From this time on, large sections of both papers would be devoted to advice about effective horticulture. For this reason reports of a shortage of seed potatoes in March was bad news and the inclement weather in April limited the amount of work that allotment holders could do.

There was well-justified recognition of the work carried out by the Aldershot War Hospital Department, who were responsible for supplying splints, padding, bandages and other appliances for the hundreds of soldiers arriving at the Cambridge and Connaught Hospitals. Women who were not engaged in this work were busy producing garments and other things for hospitalised soldiers. It was now becoming evident that there was even a shortage of female labour available for this work. Requests for surgical dressings were often made with a few hours notice, and the production of articles often ran into millions of items. A continual stream of casualties covered in blood, filth and mud arrived each day. Wounds were washed after cutting off mud spattered clothing as speed was of the essence. Fresh dressings were put on the wounds and the men sent to a ward in the hospital. After boots and socks were removed with some difficulty, the long woollen stockings knitted by the Medical Supplies Depot were put on the wounded, much to their appreciation and gratitude.

In February, criticism arose about the extent to which doctors based in Aldershot took their responsibility to the civilian population. Frederick Smith, the 3-year-old son of Private H.F. Smith of the Army Service Corps, became seriously ill. A civilian doctor was called for the child at 6.30 pm, but he refused to attend. Two hours later in desperation a call was made to the Cambridge Medical Hospital, but by that time the child was dead. There was some evidence that the doctor had previously had some difficulty in recovering his fees from the family. However, the coroner reviewing the case said that in a life or death situation a doctor should not refuse to attend a case. It appears that civilian doctors when uncertain of their fee were advising patients to seek help from military doctors.

Ernest Douglas was sent to the Cambridge Hospital for ten weeks to train as a stretcher-bearer. Part of it involved marching up Box Hill in nearby Surrey carrying a heavy load. Tall men were picked out to have responsibility for loading the top shelf of the ambulances with the stretchers. Any enthusiasm he had for getting to France in his new role was dampened by having to unload the trains bringing the wounded back from France. He also acted as a pall-bearer for soldiers who had died at the Cambridge.

That people in the town were looking ahead to a post-war world is indicated by a speech given by Mactavish, the secretary of the Workers' Education Association, to a meeting of the Railway Clerks' Association and the National Union of Railwaymen in the Aldershot Institute. He started by establishing a clear link between education and democracy. He pointed out that in rural Hampshire there were those who would deny an education to farm labourers, in this way denying the intellectual potential available to society. He demanded that farm labourers should be educated as far as their intellectual ability would take them. When the war was over, democracy would stand in a far different relationship to the government of the country than it had before the war. Men returning from overseas would have first-hand knowledge of foreign affairs. He stated that those who controlled land and capital had a monopoly on 'trained mental power'. He went on to speak about the social reconstruction of the country that must follow the war. 'The education of working-class women has always been regarded as being of no importance,' he said. He advocated the introduction of a leaving age of 15 with eight hours of part-time education continuing to 18. He pointed to the child labour still continuing in the area and how it undermined the well-being of the country, with children being forced into work in order to supplement the inadequate wages of their parents. He was critical of the present size of classes in local schools, which meant children could only be drilled and not educated. He was highly critical of the new Education Bill before the House of Commons, which the trade union movement would seek to change for the better.

The stream of accidents and related fatalities continued in the town and camp. On 20 August, there was a terrible explosion at a bomb store in Blackdown. As a result a number of soldiers from the Post Office Rifles lost their lives. The explosion took place in an area between Blackdown Barracks and Colony Gate when a group of Post Office Rifles were preparing hand grenades for training. They were in an enclosure putting a black powder from kegs into ball bombs made of tin. After this a fuse-head was placed on the bomb. At 3.20 pm an explosion occurred in the enclosure inside the building where the men were filling bombs. Unfortunately Kennedy, the man supervising the work, was also killed, so a full understanding of how the explosion came about involving fourteen men was difficult to establish. Such was the force of the explosion that it was heard for miles around, shattering nearby windows and completely destroying the bomb store itself. All roads in the vicinity were closed. Nine men, some terribly burnt, were brought from the store and placed in ambulances to be taken to the Cambridge and Connaught Hospitals. Overnight four died – Sergeant George Kennedy, who was married; Lance-Corporal Joseph Baugh; Lance-Corporal Arthur Draper; and Lance-Corporal Arthur Bradbury, all instructors with the Post Office Rifles. In addition, a number of men were seriously injured. Captain T. Dudley of the Reserve Battalion of the London Regiment reported that he assisted two men in unrecognisable condition out of the building after the first explosion. Ten minutes after, these flames in the timber and tin building reached the main store of grenades, producing an even greater explosion. Evidence was heard that when the kegs of gunpowder were partially full they were likely to explode. Sergeant Kennedy, the depot supervisor, was buried at Aldershot Military Cemetery with a full military funeral.

In June a military fete attended by the king and queen was held to lift the gloom of the war. Thousands of spectators attended a wide

variety of events in aid of military charities. Events held throughout
the town and camp included athletics, football, comedy shows, a wide
variety of military displays, a horticultural show, a baby show, an
exhibition of art and craft work produced by wounded soldiers,
wrestling on horseback and a whole range of activities to maintain the
interest of the crowd. The Royal Flying Corps sports ground provided
an excellent backdrop for the proceedings. It was noted that a very large
Stars and Stripes was hoisted in the king's enclosure, recognising the
entry of America into the war. The local paper underlines the light-
hearted nature of the occasion, referring to a ragtime band dressed as
clowns, 'niggers' and Pierrots. One of the highlights of the day was the
spirited wrestling on horseback between teams of eight from the Royal
Engineers and the Army Service Corps. The sappers took an early lead
by dismounting two of their opponents in quick succession and forced
their opponents off their horses without losing a man themselves. One
of the other highlights was a display by two hundred officers from the
Headquarters Gymnasium. Evidence that the Americans were here was
provided by an American tug-of-war team made up of railwaymen. A
guard of honour at the Royal Stand was provided by the New Zealand
Artillery from Ewshot.

Women were now playing a crucial part in the war effort, as
evidenced by the opening of a YWCA in the town devoted to providing
rest, recreation and refreshment for many women passing through, on
the way to France. The ground floor, which was originally a shop, was
transformed into a large refreshment room offering dinners from 12
until 2 pm, to be followed by light refreshments from 2 pm until 9.45
pm. The centre boasted two writing rooms and a library. The Aldershot
Institute offered dances on Thursday evenings. The local paper
acknowledged the increased freedom now available to working 'girls',
calling on them to develop 'self-control' in the concourse of the town
and camp. At the YWCA hostel, women residents were allowed to
bring in their men-friends for tea on Sundays. In opening the centre, a
Mrs. Ellison hoped that the YWCA's work would be extended to
Pirbright, Bisley, Bramshott and Brookwood, where there were now
as many as 3,000 girls employed by the Aldershot command.
Meanwhile, in April, there had been an urgent call for women to join
the local land army as milkers, ploughwomen, carters, fieldworkers,
cow women and market gardeners.

Evidence of growing discontent with soaring food prices came in the form of a packed meeting at the Aldershot Liberal Club, organised by the Workers' Union. Its president, Councillor Calvert, supported by Councillor Ainger, backed claims that war department wages were inadequate. At 29 shillings a week it was not a living wage. The meeting demanded that the rates of pay be increased to match the rising cost of living. Calvert noted that the aristocratic official managing the Field Stores Department received a decent wage, which was certainly not the case for other workers in that department. He went on to complain that since 1914 he had been in contact with the War Office about the chaos and confusion in the way civilian labour was employed in the camp. There was no co-ordination because one part of the Army would be paying one level of wage and in another, for comparable work, a different amount. He accused the War Office of hypocrisy in calling for contractors to keep strictly to good employment policies while conspicuously failing to do so themselves. The councillor called for a wages board to be set up in Aldershot tasked to ensure that an adequate living wage was available to all in the town and camp. 'I know that 10 per cent of the children in our schools here are away because they are undernourished and under-clothed because of low wages,' said Councillor Calvert.

Another councillor, Harry Ainger, said that labour was only just beginning to take their responsibilities in Aldershot. He now called for greater equality in income distribution and was critical of the way the coalition government had spent months debating whether a soldier should have a shilling a day more on their pay. They should rise up against this exploitation by organised capital. He went on to demand action on the housing crisis facing Aldershot. With people still flooding into the town there were no houses to rent for half a guinea a week, all that working people could afford. He estimated that there were more than a thousand people looking for a place to live in the town. 'Why is there money available for town gardens and not to build houses people can afford?' he asked. Councillor Ainger criticised the lack of planning for post-war Aldershot and the lack of support for both Farnborough and Aldershot from the government to build affordable homes.

During this year, John Ross talked of arriving as a cadet from Sheffield enlisted in the Royal Air Flying Corps in Farnborough and seeing row upon row of tents. A strong no-smoking regime was enforced by their corporal, forcing the cadets to hand over all the cigarettes they possessed. Nine boys shared each tent, each boy with three blankets. In the morning a bugle would sound and they were expected to be up with all their blankets and possessions neatly packed for inspection.

At the Deepcut base, Rev'd John Sellor experienced many of the trials and tribulations of army life at first hand. The base at this time was the home of the 9th Reserve London Regiment. He described the bulk of the men as 'decent' and welcoming him as their padre. On his arrival he was assigned to a cottage near the camp and given three blankets. On 2 December he began taking services for the men and on the 3rd took a service in Aldershot. On the 4th he visited a soldier in detention for saying obscene things to a corporal, and then was entertained in the officers' mess to a six course meal with champagne. It fell to his lot to minister to those in trouble with the army authorities. He saw Jewish and American deserters and a conscientious objector, whose wife, he reported, expressed disgust with her husband's stand. On Christmas Day it was his task to minister to those in the detention huts at the base. On Boxing Day, the NCOs expressed pleasure at the padre joining them in their mess and watched with approval as he downed a beer.

During this time Rev'd Sellor's diary reveals he was agonising whether he should ask a Miss Roberts to marry him. When he met her in Maidenhead on the 22nd, he expressed disappointment with her appearance and the fact that she was a non-conformist. Ultimately, however, he popped the question and his proposal was accepted.

The campaigning for temperance continued in earnest. On 29 June there was a youth rally at the Aldershot recreation ground where the Farnborough Boys' Band was playing. It was focused on moves to bring in prohibition, or at least temperance, and persuade as many young people as possible to shun alcohol. Addressing the young people, Councillor Ainger pointed to the wasting of precious resources in the manufacture of beer. He claimed that food supplies were so low the country was on the verge of starvation, and yet it was still giving permission to brew more beer. 'If it's a choice between the working man's beer and bread for his children I'm on the side of his children,' Ainger said. He introduced Tom Wing, member of parliament for Durham. The MP identified the squalor caused by overcrowding as being a prime cause for the scourge of drunkenness. At another meeting the Dean of St Paul's claimed that drunkenness in Britain had caused the Germans to believe that the country was a nation of 'muddlers', and encouraged them to attack. The state was urged to buy up the drink trade and should now play an active role in lessening intemperance.

On 12 October, the commander in charge of the Aldershot command, Sir Archibald Hunter, bid farewell to both the camp and town. In going he spoke of his regret that he had not been able to fight at the Front with the men he was responsible for training. Hundreds of thousands of men had passed through the camp since he took over from General Haig in 1914. He was being replaced by Archibald Murray. As with Lady Haig, Lady Hunter had played a leading role in a whole range of social causes in the camp since 1914. In his farewell speech Hunter talked of the dramatic changes that had occurred in the army since the outbreak of war. He now claimed that 'the army is the nation'. In discussing the transition from civilian to soldier, the general observed that the speed the transition had to take place required the greatest physical and mental fitness. Like Haig he put emphasis on the role competitive sport played in encouraging a spirit of 'playing up for one's side rather than for oneself'. In this context he spoke out against professionalism in sport and cited Ancient Rome, where a few well-trained gladiators were kept to 'amuse an effeminate people', so that the Roman Empire became soft and unable to defend itself. There was an urgent need for huts for the soldiers, both for accommodation and recreation. He claimed that the bringing together of people from all parts of the country by the army as well as from every trade would broaden realisation of working for the nation's interests. Harking back to 1914, Hunter said anyone there had been a witness to a miracle when the command changed from being in a state of chaos to one where first-class soldiers were turned out. In his farewell order he was at pains to praise the 'many ladies who have given their services', not only in nursing and social care but as substitutes allowing soldiers to be released to serve abroad.

In a letter to the *Aldershot News*, W.F. George from the Aldershot Central Savings Association called for Spartan denial in order to save towards the war effort. His letter appears to be confused because he starts out by talking about an 'honourable and lasting peace', but then goes on to advocate a victory. He calls for civilian mobilisation in Aldershot and chastises the general population for being selfish and pleasure-loving. Mr George claimed that most people had savings that should be placed in war savings. Those who were hoarding this money for a 'rainy day' were being selfish because Britain needed their 'pounds and pences'.

Sitting in Aldershot, the Hampshire Appeals Tribunal heard a constant stream of appeals against enlistment. Ernest Hobbs, a local taxi driver of 39, said his business would collapse bringing hardship to his wife and family if he was forced to serve. His appeal was dismissed. On the wider issue of public transport, the Aldershot and District Traction Company appealed against the call-up of its secretary, Alfred Webster, who was 31. Webster had been with the company since 1900 and possessed a unique intimate knowledge of the affairs of the company. The company identified the role it played by pointing to the buses it ran for munition workers. A letter from the company suggested public transport might collapse in the area if Webster was taken. Representations were received from the War Office indicating that they regarded it as being vital that public transport was maintained in the area. However, the appeals committee determined that the position of company secretary was not a reserved occupation and Webster's appeal was dismissed. The company then went on to appeal for James Chitty, one of their engine fitters. He was granted an exemption for six months with leave to appeal again. A former soldier, Charles Cox, who ran a grocery shop and off licence, was told to return to the colours by 1 June. As the call for more men was stepped up by the army so did the level of appeals against enlistment increase.

In June there was a serious case of espionage involving a breach of the Defence of the Realm Act. The accused were Peter Brown, a 29-year-old foreman from the Royal aircraft factory, Sergio Campo Fregoso and Herbert Mothersell, a garage proprietor from Brighton. Fregoso and Mothersell were charged that they had collected information in respect of aircraft that might be directly or indirectly of use to the enemy. The accusation against them was that they been passed twenty-four documents about two new aircraft that had not yet been put into service. Three documents taken from Fregoso at the time of his arrest were selected for the case. One was a letter written by Brown on Royal aircraft paper with the Royal aircraft factory letterhead crossed out and his own address superimposed. In that letter there was a full description of the two aeroplanes that concluded with the statement: 'What a pity we cannot see each other more often.' There was a letter purporting to be written from Mothersell to Brown found in Fregoso's possession with descriptions of the aircrafts' engines. 'Please let me know if there are any more particulars you are wanting and I will procure them if possible. The trouble is that if I go too often the same person gets suspicious.' The letters had been intercepted in Brighton. Smith was aware of the secret nature of the documents because he wrote: 'I am almost afraid to send these through the post because of their national importance.'

At the aircraft factory, Brown was confronted with the letters taken from Mothersell's house in Brighton. 'You have supplied these letters to a Mr Mothersell,' said the police inspector. 'That is quite right, Inspector,' Brown replied. 'I can explain everything. Mr Mothersell is about to apply for a commission in the Royal Flying Corps as an equipment officer and I have been assisting him over the last few weeks and have furnished him with these particulars. Mr Mothersell and Mr Fregoso are both engineers and have been engaged in inventing an engine for aeroplanes and have been in communication with the War Office. They had previously been interviewed by scientists and engineers from the factory but their design was considered too revolutionary.' 'I do not believe that,' stated the police inspector, and handed over letters Brown had written. Brown was then arrested and taken to Farnborough Police Station.

Fregoso's background was hardly that of a spy. He was the son of the Marquis Compo Fregoso, who was chief engineer for the city of Milan. He had come to England five years before to study engineering at Glasgow University. In Brighton he devoted most of his time to designing an engine with Mothersell. After a promise that proceedings would recommence in the New Year, details of what happened to Brown, Mothersell and Fregoso disappear from public view and what happened to these men remains a mystery.

Evidence that events in the war had radically shaped the character of Aldershot is provided by the two visits to the town by the leading labour figure George Lansbury, MP. On 8 March he was speaking at a packed meeting in the parish hall on social injustice, organised by F.O.T. Hawkes. In introducing the speaker he defined these as being related to intemperance, impurity and forgetfulness of God. In his speech Lansbury, who later became leader of the Labour Party, said he was there to speak about the message Christianity had for the Labour Party. The best element in the labour movement was that related to the Christian Socialist Charles Kingsley. It fell to him to interpret the first revolution in Russia in relation to the needs and aspirations of the working people in the town. The strength of the revolution lay in the determination of the revolutionaries to see liberty established in their country. The lesson that should be learnt in all countries was that workers must not shoot workers, as had happened in the revolution in Russia in 1905. When soldiers learnt not to shoot ordinary people, as they had done at Featherstone, Dublin and Liverpool, an important step forward had been made. If this message spread from Russia, the stupidity of war would become obvious. The finest thing was that from these revolutions there was no vengeance against those who had previously exploited them, but it should be remembered that many people in the country were living in conditions that the owners of race tracks would not expect their horses to live in. Lansbury said that he did not agree with those who claimed that drink caused poverty, but certainly drink accompanied poverty. He called for Factory Acts to improve working conditions citing the thirty-four deaths that occurred every week in the mines, and said that existing health and safety Acts were being ignored in order to improve production.

The meeting in the parish hall passed a resolution sending joyful congratulations to the democrats of Russia and urging the allied governments to follow the new Russian government's example in establishing industrial freedom, freedom of speech and of the press and immediate amnesty for religious and political offences and universal suffrage. Lansbury pointed to the value of trade unions shown by the government's retraction of an order to conscript doctors after protests from the British Medical Association. He said he was suspicious of secret police operating in the country and said it was vital to maintain civil liberties. There was evidence of *agent provocateurs* being active in the country. This reflected the fact that in modern warfare chivalry did not exist. The moral issue was that the rich in the country believed that the only thing that mattered was the possession of material goods. An economic system based on universal competition only produces universal beggary. In conclusion he claimed that the socialist motto 'From each according to his ability and to each according to his need', was a Christian one.

At the conclusion of the meeting Lady Hunter, the wife of the Aldershot commander, proposed that each member of the parish should make themselves aware of local housing, local wages and education with a view to making these adequate to the needs of the people. She was followed by Major H. Pidcock, JP, county councillor, who proposed the following resolution:

> That the Church people of this meeting, sincerely deploring the past silence of the Church in the face of crying social evils, expresses a hope that in the future the Church will be on the side of all efforts made for the bettering the conditions of life and labour.

Captain P.B.H. Lyon, MC described a whole series of cultural and intellectual activities in and around Aldershot after returning from convalescence in Weymouth after service in France. He reported cycling across to Farnham to act in a show his theatre group were doing there in a beautiful country house that had been turned into a hospital. In between his thespian activities he described seeking to fill his cadets with 'necessary book learning'. On 8 June, his group presented an outdoor show in Fleet. All this time he was trying to have his book of poetry published but receiving rejection letters from Blackwell and Heinemann. He described the organisation of a mock attack involving the newly arrived Americans in Aldershot that went badly wrong. On 22 July he reported complete exhaustion and a return of his knee injury after repeat performance of his shows in the area.

At the close of the year Rev'd Hawkes addressed himself to serving men in a Christmas message. He said many people in Aldershot had expressed the sentiment, 'One does not have the heart to enjoy oneself with so many away.' He alluded to the fact that to many overseas in the fourth year of the war the idea of goodwill and peace on earth seemed to be a hollow mockery. Despite this, history shows that despite grim times the Christian message had survived. His door was wide open on Sunday nights between 8 and 9.30 pm for anyone who wished to come and see him.

Councillor Harry Ainger,
Candidate for Liberal/ Labour
1918 Khaki Election.

Poster campaign in Aldershot to buy bonds to
support the war.

Hampshire volunteers from Aldershot.

Aldershot members of the Hampshire Regiment in Mesopotamia.

Queen Mary with the newly arrived Americans at a gymkhana in 1917.

King George V awarding the V.C. to a New Zealander.

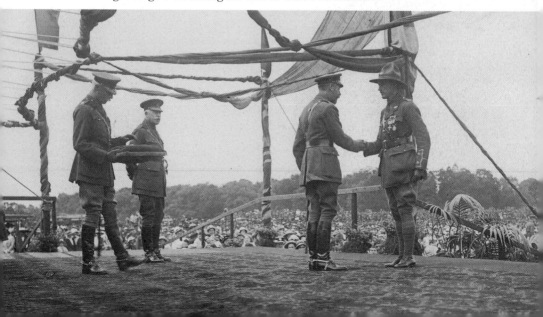

Cricket team drawn from serving officers in Aldershot 1917.

George Lansbury, future Labour leader, spoke twice in Aldershot in 1917.

The Parish Church Hall. Uniformed men in informal poses with Red Cross badges.

County High School Cadets in Aldershot, 1917.

Leading Aldershot figure, Councillor T.B. Jefferies, J.P.

The Canadian Army on parade at Bramshott 1917.

Shop fronts at Bramshott base along the A3.

Women workers at the Aircraft Factory in 1916 (FAST).

Inter-dominion boxing at Bramshott in 1917.

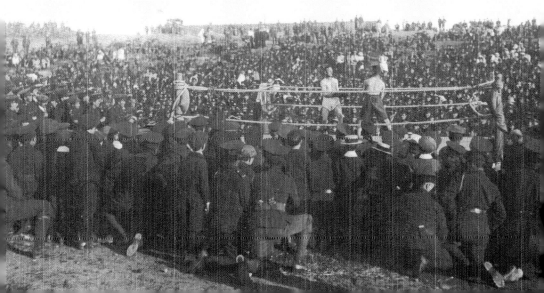

Women factory workers carrying out engineering tasks (FAST).

Women factory workers at the Aircraft Factory (FAST),

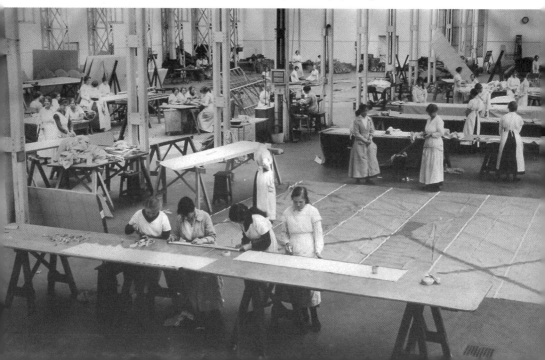

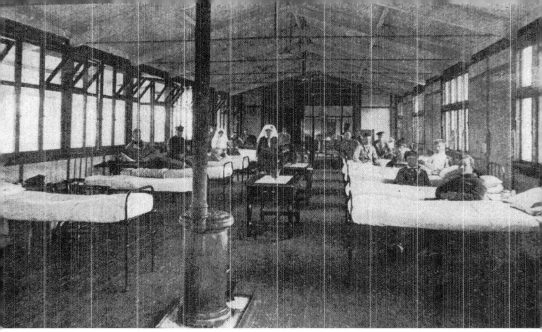

In the Canadian Military Hospital at Bramshott.

Pt Charles Arthur Ricketts of the Australian Imperial Army, who at 17 emigrated to Australia and joined the Australian army. He died of wounds in the Canadian Hospital in July 1917.

An Aldershot Military Hospital ward during the war.

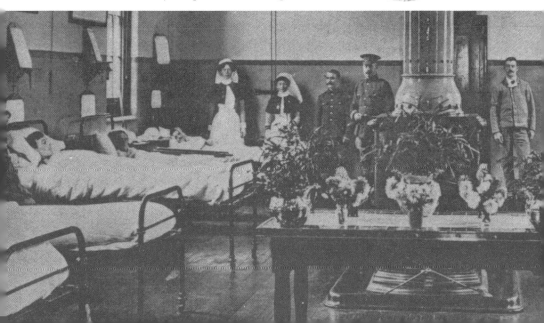

Soldiers drilling at the barracks.

The Parish Hall.

Recreation room at the New Zealand Artillery Camp at Ewshot

CHAPTER 5

1918

It is unrealistic to review Aldershot in 1918 as a chronological entity because the consequences of the war carried on from the 11th day of the 11th month of 1918, the day the armistice was signed. After the armistice, troops were being brought back from theatres of war and Aldershot adopted a demeanour of military tattoos and parades, many of which were attended by royalty driving over from Windsor. At the start of 1918, however, few people in the town thought the war would be over by the end of the year. On the home front Aldershot came to depend more and more on its womenfolk for survival.

> We women can do so much to support and strengthen the resolution and determination of the men of the empire who are fighting the greatest of all causes.
> *Lady Murray, wife of the camp commander.*

Perhaps a black comic attitude to the war is best summed up by a story appearing in the local press. They refer to a 'socialist agitator of the worst type' finding himself in khaki being an intolerable nuisance to his commanding officers by repeatedly claiming his 'rights'. He tried to do it with his drill sergeant and received the following reply: 'Look here sonny, the only right a British private has got these days is 6 feet of earth, and you've got to go to France to get that.'

If 1917 had seen the centre of gravity shifting for the town and camp, 1918 would mean coming to terms with what the changes meant for reconstruction after the war. During 1918, Aldershot, due to its link with the army, gave disproportionately of its manhood to the war.

Through the emphasis placed on the War Savings Campaign, it dug deep in its pockets to support the war financially. In just one week a campaign by businessmen produced £100,000. Many of its women were now employed in the armaments industry or working for organisations like the Red Cross. Despite the fact that thousands of soldiers walked the streets, the town was remarkably free from public disorder most of the time. The realisation that survival meant collective activity saw the communal kitchen for Aldershot being successfully brought to fruition due to the efforts of the town's vicar, F.O.T. Hawkes. Because of its success a branch was opened in the West End of the town. The Aldershot Trades Council was now to be recognised as playing an important part in the life of the town and the Chamber of Commerce was seeking to produce a blueprint for Aldershot's economic future once thousands of men departed the camp. Despite the fact the wartime government was placing more and more responsibility on the district council, much of its normal civilian activity was on hold. Rates for Aldershot increased even though no general improvements were made in the town. This was due to wage levels being pushed up because of increases in the cost of living. Against this the town's own electrical supply facility achieved a profit of £600 for the year as well as clearing off a £625 deficit from the previous year. By the end of the year some progress appeared to be have been made with the housing crisis for the town with the adoption of a scheme to build 100 new houses. The council dragged its feet on the provision of a clinic to cope with its very real problem of venereal disease, and although a building was rented by the end of the year, it still had not opened. In February, an approach to the army to assist with the scourge produced a negative response from the commander of the camp, Sir Archibald Murray. Councillor Harry Ainger stated that he found the army's position inexplicable and that no problems had been experienced in setting up clinics of this kind in Reading and Winchester.

At the Stanhope Concert Hall on a Saturday afternoon in January, 700 soldiers were treated to a pantomime *Cinderella* performed by a company made up of soldiers' wives and children. The wounded were guests of the town's Chamber of Commerce. The audience was drawn from the wounded at Cambridge and Connaught Hospitals who, during the interval, were presented with 3,000 cigarettes by the lady principals.

A gift of two bath chairs from the company was presented to Lady Murray for her hospital charity. It was reported that the wounded in their blue uniforms responded with three ringing cheers to the wife of the commander of the camp.

In February there was a large attendance at the Percy Illingworth Institute on Gun Hill to Rev'd A.A. Green's talk about the Jewish contribution to the war and about his religion in general. Rev'd B.G. Simmons said that the comradeship enjoyed by the men in the war had broken down many prejudices between Jews and those of other faiths.

> I am proud to say that when England asked for men, the Jews of this country did not fail to respond loyally and nobly. I am not a Zionist. I am an Englishman. When Jerusalem was captured by the British, I was asked when I was going back to Palestine. I responded by replying 'When are you going back to jail?' He looked at me in a puzzled way and replied. 'I've never been to jail,' he said. 'Neither have I been to Palestine,' I responded.

On 15 February, a letter from W.J. Hunt in the local newspaper illustrated the growing crisis in public transport. On 19 January, he had caught a bus from Aldershot Railway Station travelling to Netley Street in North Camp. Because of the acute shortage of buses at 10.30 pm, a great crowd surged around the only available bus. The Aldershot and District Bus Company was seeking to ration travel by forbidding particular services to stop between their stated destinations. In this case it was Farnborough station. The lady conductor ordered two soldiers travelling to one of the camps off the bus and they jumped off the fast moving bus at their stop. Two more soldiers did the same thing when the bus reached the Wellington Lines. The complainant was forced to travel on to Farnborough Station and had to get another bus back to his true destination.

In reply the company manager pleaded for understanding of the nightmare of trying to run an acceptable service when so many of his staff were conscripted. By the end of the war the company was operating with just eighteen employees for thirty-six lorries and twenty-six buses. At the tribunal hearing appeals against military service, an interesting debate was opened up over the question of women being allowed to drive local buses. The Aldershot and District Traction Company were opposing the enlistment of Henry East, a 37-year-old driver/foreman for the company. East himself appealed on the basis that his enlistment would bring financial hardship for his wife and family. In response to the company's appeal the military representative asked why women could not drive local buses. Mr E.G. Hawkins, for the company, stated that he could not take responsibility for women driving buses. 'Do you realise that women are driving cars?' the military representative questioned. 'Do you realise women are driving motor ambulances in France? I think the time has come when the point should be put to you very strongly.' 'This man repairs buses. Women couldn't crawl under a bus to repair a back axle,' Mr Hawkins replied. In the end Mr East and another employee of the company were given a one month final exemption for medical tests to be carried out.

We have seen that because parts of the empire were so recently settled by British immigrants, the war provided an occasion for their return to 'the old country'. On 15 February, the wife of a Canadian soldier, Margaret Gibbs, was in court for not having completed form ARE required of any non-Aldershot resident. She was living with a Sergeant Greenough and had travelled from Colchester where he had been previously based. She was waiting for a divorce from her previous husband, Gibbs, who had mistreated her. Initially she had left her husband and gone back to her original home in Glasgow, subsequently joining up with Sergeant Greenough in Colchester. She was fined 21 shillings with 2/6d witness fee.

As the war progressed, so too did the deaths reported to the coroner's court. A 51-year-old shoesmith, George Ravin, was recorded as 'dying of natural causes' after sleeping in a tent for three weeks in the bitter winter weather. Sergeant T.A. Condon was killed in an accident at the aircraft factory. The sad report of suicides continued on 22 February with the death of Private Joe Smith, whose body was found in the Basingstoke Canal. The hazards associated with horses were highlighted by the death of Harry Bingham of the Army Service Corps, who was fatally kicked in the head by a skittish horse. In March, Tom Clare, a mentally ill soldier in Connaught Hospital, blindfolded himself with a red handkerchief and jumped from the hospital's roof. Witnesses described him jumping as though he was diving into water with the result that he fractured his spine. News came that Rev'd McIlvaine, who had previously preached at St Michael's and the camp church, had died when the hospital ship bringing him back to Britain after having been gassed was torpedoed in the Bristol Channel. The sad death of Lieutenant Lutyens of the Royal Air Force (a merger of the Royal Flying Corps and the Royal Naval Air Service in 1918) was reported. He had been flying in the area with an observer carrying out a test on the aircraft. The body of the navigator had not been found at the time of the inquest. A further gruesome death was reported on 12 July when the body of Herbert Reeves of the Machine-Gun Corps was discovered on the line between Ash Junction and North Camp. Reeves had enlisted in 1916 and been seriously wounded. Because of this he had been in hospital for nearly fourteen months and suffering from depression. He was 23 years old.

The growing confidence of the labour movement is revealed by the response from W.W. Miller from Farnborough Labour Party to comments from the member of parliament for the area, Sir Auckland Geddes. Geddes had blamed seamen for a fall in output from shipping. 'Men are not working as though the life of the nation depends on their exertions,' he is quoted as saying. In reply Miller said that industrial disputes such as the one the MP complained about could only be dealt with through arbitration between the government and the workers. It was sinister to paint workers in this way and the MP revealed that he was of the same school as the employers. At the same meeting, Farnborough Labour Party was set up through the initiative of Farnborough Trades Council. The chairman of the meeting, N. Farley, emphasised the role of Labour was to gain representation on local committees such as the food control committee. There needed to be organisation towards the general election likely to be held that August and the need to increase the thirty-eight seats currently held in parliament by the Labour Party. On 1 May, the first May Day demonstration in Aldershot was held in appalling weather. Frank Watters, chairman of the trades council, addressed the question of wide-scale industrial unrest throughout the country. 'There would be no unrest if the workers had been treated and recognised in the manner they were entitled to,' he said. 'More than 60,000 men and women die of consumption every year according to medical officers as a direct result of living in houses not fit for habitation,' Councillor Pyle,

Labour's candidate for Petersfield in the coming election, told the May Day Rally.

Throughout the year the council made a number of positive steps to deal with the food emergency. Land was identified in the north of North Town and a piggery established using some of the kitchen waste from the camp. The council purchased seed potatoes to sell to allotment holders as well as arranging for four spraying machines for spraying potatoes being grown on its allotments. However, the absence of a motor fire tender was highlighted when the large Gale and Polden Works caught fire on 14 July. By the end of the year it still was not in service. However, as the food crisis deepened there were complaints heard in both Aldershot and Farnborough councils about the number of soldiers seen in queues for food when they were being fed by the army. The commander of the camp was approached on the matter, who replied that soldiers had a democratic right to seek food in this manner. However, he arranged for notices to be placed in all the camps suggesting to soldiers they should not seek additional food in this way. On 5 July, Nora O'Brien received cards at one address and then obtained more ration cards at another address under the name of Smith. She was severely fined by Aldershot magistrates.

The Wellington works of Gale and Polden were devastated by fire on 14 July. The company was both a major employer and the publisher of the *Aldershot News*. The fire started at 4.45 pm. People became aware of fire issuing from the premises on the corner of Birchett and Cavendish Roads. The strength of the fire was indicated by glass in the building smashing and falling on to the road. By five o'clock the volunteer fire brigade and the command brigade from the camp were in attendance. They began attacking the source, which was in a building packed with paper. As the fire was confined to the upper floors, staff were able to move into lower level offices and retrieve important company documents. One of the dominant features of Aldershot, the Gale and Polden clock, was destroyed and showers of burning paper, wood and ashes could be observed above Victoria Road. At this stage the walls of the building began to bulge, indicating a collapse might be imminent. The next event was the floor holding heavy machinery collapsing, sending the machines through into the lower floors. By six o'clock the great corner wall at The Grove parted from the main building with a crash. Exposure to the air made the flames even more intense. The main effort of the fire workers was to cut off the passage of the flames from the east and west sides of the building. Although some parts of the company's operation were saved, the editorial office of the *Aldershot News* was in ruins. Management immediately set in motion ways in which the company could continue to operate in the limited space available. The Aldershot Chamber of Commerce commented that the fire could not have occurred at a worse time in the light of a desperate shortage of building materials and labour. There would now be a grave difficulty in replacing the specialist machines that had been lost.

The largest communal events in Aldershot were those associated with the war. On 4 August, hundreds of people gathered in the Memorial Gardens to mark Remembrance Day in an inter-denominational service. The Bishop of Winchester unveiled a war shrine for all those in St Michael's Parish who had given their lives. On a happier note, F.O.T. Hawkes provided an eloquent address for an armistice service at the parish church. It had been preceded by a parade around Aldershot, which included girl guides and scouts, volunteers, cadets, the fire brigade, uniformed police and special police, trade unionists and members of friendly societies. Local freemason lodges were also prominent in a service of intercession at the All Saints' Garrison Church on 3 August.

At the end of August a Women's War Service fete and gymkhana raised £500 for the YWCA. As in 1917, the emphasis placed on the role of sport in military training meant 1918 featured a great deal of sporting activity. Boxers from the camp went to the Albert Hall and members of the army gymnastic staff carried off the King's Trophy at a gymnastic event. Another boxing event saw a contest in Aldershot when the Southern command swept the board by thirteen fights to one. Aldershot achieved distinction when the Aldershot command, represented by the 6th London Regiment (City of London Rifles), won the under-19 class in the novices team competition against the other army commands. They did equally well in the over-19 class. Unfortunately, because of the frequent removal of soldiers for active service, football in the command was limited to infrequent matches.

On the other hand, rugby in the town and camp could boast a successful season. The command achieved victories over the military college and Australian Headquarters. A command tournament was won by the New Zealand Artillery. Cricket was affected by the war, only three games were successfully completed by the command cricket club.

The *Aldershot News* commented on the year's khaki election for the town's constituency stating the 'the poll attracted but little interest' and 'no excitement'. Captain Lord Wolmer, representing the coalition government, defeated Harry Ainger, the Liberal/Labour candidate. However, the Farnborough Labour Party disputed whether Councillor Harry Ainger really did represent the labour interest because at national level Labour was determined to be seen as a party separate from the Liberals. Wolmer was educated at Winchester and University College Oxford, where he graduated in 1909. As a unionist candidate he fought the Newton seat in Lancashire, winning it in 1910. He was commissioned with the Hampshire Regiment in 1906 and became a captain in 1913. He was then turned down for war service on health grounds. During this time he decided to swap the seat he represented and was selected to contest the Aldershot Division close to his home in Bordon. His speeches for the coalition show a willingness to recognise that the workers had a right to a share of the control and management of British industry. He could offer little hope of the price of food falling because of the destruction of so much shipping during the war. He appeared to be in favour of the railways remaining in state hands at the end of the war. He was adamant that pensions should reflect the cost of living. He supported the 'dumping' of German aliens out of the country back into Germany when hostilities finished. Returning soldiers should be guaranteed employment for several years after they were demobilised. This turned out to be a pipe dream.

The Liberal/Labour candidate, Harry Ainger, was born in Dovercourt, Essex, in 1877. He was sent out to work when he was 9. From there he moved on to the clothing trade, arriving in Aldershot in 1894. After ten years he opened his own business. He played a major part in forming the local branch of the Shop Assistants' Union, the Workers' Union and the Trades Council. Since 1914 he had been a member of the Aldershot Urban District Council. Ainger had been a member of Aldershot Women's Suffrage Society since its inception. At his first meeting of the election the opinion was expressed that this was a rushed election that should have been delayed until all the troops were home and the dust of the war had settled. Labour supporters expressed the view that Harry Ainger's opinions were closest to their own and their support was because the election came so soon after the formation of the party in Aldershot and Farnborough that they could not mount an effective campaign. Ainger based his campaign on the fact he was a local man who knew both town and camp extremely well. He said there were questions about corrupt trading in the camp that should be answered prior to an election, but the coalition had rushed through the election. He raised questions about how much a peer of the realm had brought benefits to the lives of working people. He accused his opponents of using his lowly birth and lack of education against him. His was the university of experience of life and not of Oxford or Cambridge. Harry Ainger said he had tried to get changes in the trading arrangements for the camp and to improve sanitary arrangements there. He believed that the army and navy should be based on democratic lines and that commissions should not be reserved for the upper classes. He criticised the rates of pay being paid to army personnel. As far as women married to soldiers were concerned, they were often married to the washtub over which they had to labour in order to make ends meet. There had been a struggle to build affordable homes because of the price those who owned land demanded. Despite his campaign, Lord Wolmer was duly elected for the Aldershot seat.

At the beginning of the year complaints that the German POWs were enjoying a better diet than folk in Aldershot were being made. A correspondent complained about covering a meatless day by using fish paste and vegetables. In contrast, POWs were receiving meat five days a week with pickled beef on one of these days, salt-cured herring on two days, tea, coffee, sugar, salt, fresh vegetables, split peas or split beans, rice, margarine, oatmeal, margarine, jam, cheese, pepper and maize meals. In the middle of the grave food shortage being experienced throughout the country, the writer questioned the extent of the nation's generosity towards these men. In comparison with the 6oz meat or 10oz fish received by the POWs, the average family in Aldershot would be lucky to receive 2oz meat daily. 'Where is the justice in this?' the correspondent asked, 'when the poor are asked to fight for scraps of meat and fish? The public have a right to demand that the privations they are presently experiencing be borne on an equal basis.' He demanded the food provided to German POWs be the same as the limited diet given to British POWs in Germany.

Whatever the rights and wrongs of this the town's food control committee had the task of managing food rationing in Aldershot. They had earlier written to the Regional Food Control in Reading asking about a local butcher who in October had received 50 per cent (500lb) more meat than he was entitled to. The butcher was summoned to appear before the committee. The committee had received instructions about rationing butter, margarine and meat. Ration cards would be issued for a meat card and a general food card, which in the first instance would cover butter and margarine. The secretary of the committee had gone around the queues in the town for margarine and sugar and had observed soldiers standing in the line ahead of women and children.

Proof that the police monitored the waste of food is seen in a statement to the committee about a 10oz piece of meat being found amid tea leaves in a house in the town. The meat was pronounced fit for human consumption. After debate the committee voted against prosecuting the offender. During January and February a whole raft of rationing regulations came into force and ration cards were issued. Arrangements for prioritising babies and children were put in place with babies under 18 months being allowed 1½ pints of milk daily and children up to 5 years 1 pint. On 4 January, the committee struggled to agree an appropriate price for milk for the town, starting with 8d a quart and then reducing the price to 7d. The committee indicated that they would try and prevent retailers setting their own prices. On 8 February, Alton Police Court heard of a raid on 16 January from military stores at the nearby Bordon Camp. Supplies of tea and sugar had been discovered in the town by the police.

As meat became scarcer, so too did the temptation to sell condemned meat become greater as witnessed in court on 29 March, when a butcher was fined for selling diseased tongue. Farnborough food control committee, in a similar way to Aldershot, expressed exasperation at the excessive prices being charged by retailers for tea. But for both committees, the real challenge was to increase food production primarily by providing encouragement to allotment holders. As summer approached, an acute need for cold storage was identified. Councillor Ainger, in support of the proposal for cold storage provision, said that adults in the town would be prepared to go without milk themselves in order that sufficient milk could be given to babies and children. The food crisis added emphasis to F.O.T. Hawkes' call for a communal kitchen, both as a way of providing food for the poorest and to make limited supplies of food go further.

There was a new militancy among the women of the Women's Army Auxiliary Corps who had been called to Pirbright Camp as cooks for the army. At 9.15 am their forewoman cook called them together and asked why they were refusing to work in the cookhouse. They stated that they were refusing to work under her. Testifying at Aldershot Police Court, Mabel Gill, the officer in charge of the unit at Pirbright, said she asked the women individually why they were refusing to work and received that same answer about their opposition to their forewoman cook. It turned out that their key reason for their refusal to work was an order keeping them in their quarters after dark, which had come from command headquarters. This was combined with their refusal to work under Mrs Wells, the forewoman cook. The women were then threatened with being reported to the commanding officer for the camp if they did not return to work. They did not return to work that day or the following day.

Lieutenant-Colonel Villiers, commander of the 19th Officers' Cadet Battalion, then heard complaints of bullying against Mrs Wells and the order from headquarters forbidding the women to leave their barracks after dark. They had all signed an order to serve and would face charges if they disobeyed these orders. After retiring the chairman of the bench said the nature of the offence by the women should have resulted in prison sentences. However, as these were first offences they would each be fined £3. As their pay for the year was £26, it was agreed that a stoppage of 5 shillings a week be made towards the fine.

Attempts by a group of conscientious objectors called the non-combatants to take the question of justification for war onto the streets of Farnborough produced a violent response in May. The *Sheldrake Military Gazette* commented: 'The country is sick to death of shirkers and men who won't fight.' The previous Sunday night had seen hundreds of soldiers looking for 'conchies' after their meeting had been broken up with a view to violence. The Non-Combatant Corps had held a number of meetings in gospel halls but had made the mistake of seeking to take their message of peace onto the streets. One conchie was given a 'well-deserved mauling', according to the *Gazette*, which resulted in the loss of all his teeth. Another group of conchies on bikes were met with stones and missiles returning from a mission hall meeting in Cove.

Rev'd Hawkes led a deputation to the council. He pointed out that there was a recommendation from London in favour of establishing communal kitchens. He had visited similar kitchens in Reading and other members of the food control committee had visited Guildford and, as a result, believed that a kitchen of this nature would be beneficial to the town. They had located what they thought were suitable premises at the church room at Redan Hill. He was seeking the committee's support because there was a great deal of fitting-up required. He felt this would not cost more than £250. In other towns after the council had approved the scheme, they had put up half the cost of setting it up. In practice the kitchen paid for itself through fees charged for its meals. If the kitchen was successful, other kitchens of this nature could be opened in the town. Mrs Wright, one of the women on the delegation, pleaded for the kitchen on the basis of need by working women and their children. Meals would be available at a reasonable price. The kitchen opened its doors and proved a remarkable success.

The year saw a major meeting of the Leagues of Aldershot Freemasons. More than 600 masons and their relatives met at the All Saints' Garrison Church for a major act of intercession, remembrance and thanksgiving, despite the flu epidemic and wretched weather. A marquee had been built in the grounds of the church to facilitate the robing of those taking part. As the procession entered the church the Band of the Reserve Regiment of Dragoons played *Land of Hope and Glory*. A letter from the Duke of Connaught was read to the congregation by the presiding minister that urged donations to the Freemasons' War Hospital.

Frank Seddon from Bow in London described his work as a PT instructor during 1918. 'The emphasis was on sport with boxing and cross country but after France I wasn't a fit man,' he said. 'However, by the time the armistice came my health had returned. After I was demobbed I went back to my job in the Post Office at Bow moving up from a message boy to a postman. In my opinion the war was a waste of time. It got me and no one else anywhere.'

In September, W. Sydney Smith replaced Sir Henry Fowler at the aircraft factory. In June, the change of name from the Royal Aircraft factory to the Royal Aircraft Establishment had occurred. The change was necessary because the initials caused confusion with the flight arm of the air force.

> Two boys, Archie Bowman who was 11 and Edwin Knot who was 9, gained access to a stable at the Lille Barracks where the materials for making hand grenades were stored. They stole four ready-made grenades, black gunpowder and a tin containing other explosives. Outside and being discovered and pursued, they threw their bounty over a hedge causing a loud explosion. Both boys were brought before the magistrate at Aldershot. Archie was sentenced to nine lashes of the birch, and Edwin received four.

The return to Aldershot of influenza was not reported because reporting its consequence was banned under the Defence of the Realm Act on the grounds that it would lower morale. However, it must have been hard to disguise the virulent hold it had on the town and the camp. Overcrowding was so bad at the Cambridge and Connaught Hospitals that the hopeless cases had to be placed in annexes outside the hospitals. There had been an upsurge in cases coming across after the Battle of the Somme in 1916. It arrived back in 1918 in pandemic proportions. Lord Wolmer, who was to become Aldershot's MP, provided proof there was now a slow recognition that the conditions of overcrowding and poor sanitation shared with Étaples, the huge military base in France, were now recognised as being prime factors behind the pandemic. He asked the under secretary of state for war how many cases of influenza had been reported in the British Army in September/October. He criticised the lack of hospital accommodation in places like Aldershot to respond to it. The minister was unable to provide the figures for October but for September, 2,901 men were recorded with influenza and 381 with pneumonia. He admitted that because of the number of wounded the government could not make more beds available to deal with the pandemic. Wolmer went on to question the minister about whether he had received complaints about overcrowding at the Connaught and Cambridge Hospitals. In reply the military authorities said they were seeking to maintain a system of 60 cubic feet for each case and hoped to increase this amount. Using parliamentary privilege, he demanded a full report on how the government was dealing with the epidemic.

At a meeting of the council, alarmist stories that whole families were stricken with the virus were dismissed. There was only a small proportion of deaths in relation to the cases reported. Most of the deaths in Aldershot were occurring at the Connaught Hospital and were among soldiers who had been taken there from active service. All the elementary schools in the town were closed because so many of the children were suffering from colds. At one school, 67 per cent of teachers and children were absent. When the roll was called in one class there was no response. The board of governors at the Farnham Workhouse reported struggling to cope with patients arriving with septic influenza and not having the nursing space to deal with them.

On the streets of Aldershot, when news of the armistice arrived, there was uninhibited rejoicing. A soldier wearing a German helmet was seen being led through the streets with his hands above his head. Soldiers from the camp seemed to vie with each other for whom could make the most noise. A Royal Navy Division collected scores of flags as they marched round the town. The Foot Guards were led by a tiny drummer, who allowed everyone in sundry to beat his large drum. Every available car was taken over by joyriders. The sight of a soldier wearing a bonnet and pushing a pram caused considerable merriment. A lorry laden with beer and groceries was stripped bare, much to the distress of its driver, who appealed to its owner about what he could do. The advice he received was to drive to the police station, which he did. However, by the time he got there the culprits had jumped off. American soldiers in the town were led by a big 'Sammy' carrying a Stars and Stripes flag. He was followed by men beating iron plates and kitchen utensils and singing songs from the Deep South. In nearby Camberley, Sergeant Kenway at the police station received the news of the armistice on Monday morning and phoned the good tidings to the municipal buildings and to the staff college at Sandhurst. Various hooters around the town and a plane's hooter flying low gave ample indication that something was afoot. By eleven o'clock the High Street of the town was ablaze with colour. Despite the heavy drizzle, crowds assembled in the streets joined by boisterous cadets from the military college, together with youngsters beating any form of metal which would serve as a drum.

Again in Aldershot, in the parish church, the senior Wesleyan chaplain to the armed forces, E.P. Lowry, presided over a ceremony for all sections of the town's community. A special place in the congregation was reserved for uniformed bodies from within the town with over 500 assembling outside the drill hall on Redan Hill. From here the procession moved to the parish church led by the band of the 3rd Regiment Hussars. Behind them were the County School Cadet Company, cadets from the Hampshire Regiment, the volunteer fire brigade, police and special constables, the staff of the post office, trade unionists and members of friendly societies. Rev'd Hawkes said that never in the 500 years of the church's existence had a congregation been more thankful to God than they were that morning. Family love and love of men and women for each other had been broken by the war. 'But in the sound of many feet coming here, there were some who would not hear the footsteps of those they loved. We are not forgetful of the bereaved in our joy, which was chastened by their sorrow, and we pray for them.' He went on: 'For four-and-a-half years the story has been one of waste in human effort, human intellect, and human material. Those who had been in France have seen devastated towns and villages. Peace will mean they will now be rebuilt.'

After the service the procession proceeded to the recreation ground, where the chairman of Aldershot Urban District Council spoke of the way in which it was second to none in giving its sons to the forces. He went on to thank Sir Archibald Hunter, the general officer commanding the camp, for the relationship that existed between the town and the camp. He acknowledged the profound change in the role of women in Aldershot by singling them out for praise for their contribution during the war. The annual occasion of gifts to over 300 elderly in the town later took on a special significance because of the end of the war. It was held in the large hall of the West End Infants' School and for a short time memories of rationing were forgotten in the midst of tables laden with bread, butter and cake. Money to pay for the occasion had been raised through public subscription sponsored by Gale and Polden, a large part of whose premises had only recently been destroyed by fire. However, Rev'd Senior, attending the occasion, said fortunately he had kept details of the Old Folks' Fund himself and not at the Gale and Polden office.

In Farnborough, those celebrating still found time to donate to St Dunstan's Hostel for Blinded Soldiers. The hundreds of workers at the Royal Aircraft Establishment turned away from their vital war work to devise amusing floats and exhibitions, such as one labelled 'Hang Dora', a reference to the unpopular Defence of the Realm Act.

Aldershot on Armistice Day was packed with laughing jostling crowds. Mixing among them were processions such as the one with the gymnasium staff distinctive in their khaki tunics and blue trousers. They were followed by a group of guardsman with bugles and drums, to be followed by American soldiers playing tom toms. The hooter at the Wellington works was sounded for a prolonged period of ten minutes, and this intermingled with the sound of hooters from the railway station. Into the midst of all this were lorries packed with shouting troops.

However, a few weeks later all this joy appears to have evaporated:

A dismal night accompanied by a cold north-east wind wherein blew particles of sand, mixed with particles of street refuse against which we struggled manfully as we crawled along dark and deserted streets, talking low to each other and wondering what had become of everyone. It was scarcely 10.30 and this was New Year's Eve – the last day of the most wonderful year in the History of the World!

What was wrong with Aldershot? Is it the mud, is it the climate, is it a want of total energy or are its inhabitants naturally unsociable?

As I say, it was New Year's Eve. We tried despairingly to find what seemed in the darkness to be the main entrance of the principal hotel to get 'best suppers' but unfortunately on this occasion the fire had gone out and we departed supper less. Wandering round in quest of food and genial society we met no better success. As the night wore on we began to wonder whether there had been too much Armistice, and over rejoicing generally had turned the inhabitants' heads.

There are adventurous individuals who have made long pilgrimages from the civilised parts to see Aldershot and having seen it I believe they have gone away satisfied; and there are others!!! It must be confessed that Aldershot is not the happiest place on earth. A thoughtless traveller arriving in the town on a wet Wednesday afternoon, being early closing day, might reasonably imagine he had accidentally landed in the City of the Dead! For an important military centre it has one of the most uncomfortable railway stations in the country. I have stood in the station yard on a drizzly wet Sunday and watched the miserable plight of our visitors awaiting their train home. No one has raised the question of building a waiting room where tea and coffee might be purchased'.

The writer went on to say that as the station approach was covered in mud and coal dust, the idea of building memorial baths is a timely one. Charles Ross, the writer, said there was compensation to be had in Aldershot in the quality of military bands, yet remarkably there were no bandstands. Neither was there a free public library or a public bath. He criticised that 'get all you can today and never mind tomorrow' attitude to be found in Aldershot. He cited the criticism of many officers and men of the town for the treatment and discomfort they had experienced during their time in Aldershot. Due to this they had sought to find amusement in the camp to the general detriment of the town.

He concluded by saying it would be better to create a welcoming atmosphere for returning soldiers and their families rather than a drinking fountain that had been proposed.

Aldershot Cadets, assembled 1918.

Royal Garrison Church, Aldershot, with Memorial Window.

W.A.A.C.s marching past The Queen in Aldershot 1918.

The Aldershot Staff Command after the signing of the armistice 1918.

Church Parade 1918.

*Captain A.M. Toye, V.C.
wedding day.*

*Captain A.M.Toye, V.C.
being congratulated on
his award by his nurse.*

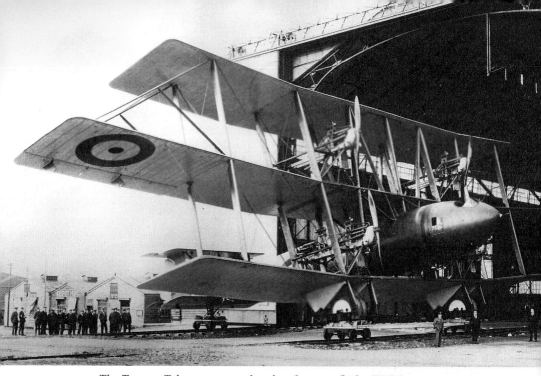

The Tarrant Tabor prototype bomber fore test flight (FAST).

Crashed plane after test flight, 26 May 1919. Pilots Capt. F.G. Dunn and P.T. Rawlings were killed like many other test pilots at Farnborough (FAST).

Canadian war graves at Bramshott.

The Chapel at Aldershot Military Cemetery.

WW1 graves at Aldershot Military Cemetery.

At the Royal Pavilion on 12 July 1918.

Canteen at the New Zealand Artillery Camp at Ewshot.

Roll of Honour

Alfred Maurice Toye, the eldest son of James R. Toye was born in D Terrace Stanhope Lines. He was Aldershot's only Victoria Cross winner in the war. Toye's father was a Christian Scientist and leader of a troop of boy scouts. Toye himself attended the garrison school and became a patrol leader in the scouts. At 15 he became a trumpeter in the Royal Engineers and went to Curragh to train. By his 18th birthday he was fighting in France and had applied to become an officer. He was sent to the cadet school at Blendecques near St Omer. He served with the Royal Engineers at Passchendaele, where he became an acting captain in command of a company in August of 1917.

Toye won his VC for his actions on 24 and 25 March 1918, serving with the 2nd Middlesex at the bridge south of Peronne. The Germans had crossed the Somme, but under instructions to fight to the end, Toye's men had lost the bridge three times and then regained it. Finally the Germans encircled the company. Toye determined to fight his way out, which he proceeded to do. He then gathered up seventy men from the 7th Durham Pioneers and successfully counterattacked the Germans, although Toye himself was quite severely wounded. Toye received his medal from the king in Queens Parade on 8 August 1918, and was presented with the freedom of Aldershot on 15 June. He married Flora Robertson, an army school teacher, who was the daughter of the bandmaster for the Royal Army Medical Corps. She received a silver pendant from the district council.

Captain Edward Bell, MC and Bar, Middlesex Regiment. Had been invested by the king. Regarded as a brilliant officer. He was a professional footballer who played for Portsmouth Blues. His first Military Cross was for repelling a German attack in 1916. The Bar to his Military Cross was for creating a forward ammunition dump in daylight, and in doing this he was killed on 24 March 1918.

Company Sergeant Major E. K. Elflett, Hampshire Regiment. Killed in Salonika on 25 April 1916. He served for six years in the Hampshires, was in the retreat from Mons and suffered frostbite in the Gallipoli campaign before being recommended for a commission. He had a brother who was a prisoner-of-war in Turkey who was a sergeant major in the Army Service Corps at Hounslow. Another brother also served for six years with the Hampshires and, after service in the Dardanelles, was a corporal attached to the gymnastic staff at Gosport. All were educated at the West End Schools.

Corporal S.W. Machin, Royal Flying Corps. Awarded the Italian Bronze Medal for bringing in a plane under fire in France. Before enlistment was employed by R. Dickeson and Co.

Sergeant H.T. Hills, Royal Scots. Joined the Territorials at 16. Wounded in 1915 and 1916. In June 1916 returned to the Front and won the Military Medal for conspicuous gallantry. He came from a military family and had two other brothers serving in the army.

Lance Corporal Munnings, Royal Berkshire Regiment. Received a parchment referring to his gallantry in July 1916 at Fermes Du Bois for repeatedly seeking to penetrate the German wire.

Sergeant A.H. Davis, 1st Kings Dragoon Guards, awarded the Croix de Guerre. Attended the Newport Road Schools.

Sergeant Major Drake, Military Mounted Regiment, previously a member of Frimley Urban District Council. Awarded the Distinguished Conduct Medal.

Postscript

It was sad to receive report of the deaths of Aldershot men after hostilities ceased.

Lance-Corporal G.H. Martin of the 4th King's Royal Corps from Upper Hale. His parents received formal notification of the death of their son, who had been missing since 18 October. He was with a small party holding an advance post when a shell burst among them. His body was not recovered for three weeks.

Lance-Corporal Martin was an enlisted man from 1911 who served in India before being transferred to France. He was severely wounded at Ypres and then transferred to Salonika.

Rifleman W.G. Dimpsey of the 1ˢᵗ King's Royal Rifle Corps had been a POW for over four years but died of influenza in Copenhagen on his way home.

Signaller R. Hardwick of the Royal Fusiliers is reported as dying from broncho-pneumonia in France. He was wounded and gassed on 9 November 1918. He was 24.

Private R. Driver of the Devon Regiment, whose parents lived in Victoria Road, were finally notified of their son's death. He had been missing since October. He had been wounded in 1916 and returned home suffering from trench foot but returned to the Front where he met his death on 26 October 1918.

Aldershot debated how it might remember its dead. A public meeting was held at the West End Schools and a committee formed to decide how to remember those who gave their lives. The choices before the committee were:

- a new town hall
- an extension to the Aldershot Hospital
- a free library
- children's homes for orphans of servicemen
- a special park with a monument and a monument in the Municipal Gardens.

The chairman of the district council, H. Baker, congratulated the town on the number of volunteers who came forward to fight in the war. Brigadier Harold Alexander and Major A.M. Toye had brought great credit to the town by their gallantry. Some, however, had made the greatest sacrifice of their lives. He believed that the town was unanimous in saying that money must be found for a memorial. Aldershot as a whole had done well out of the war and money was available to fund one. A resolution accepting this was passed.

The meeting became bogged down following a statement from Councillor Hawkins that money for the memorial should come from public subscription and not from the district council's rates. As far as an extension to the hospital was concerned would it then be administered by the council? However, Councillor A. Stroud said he believed that a new town hall should be financed through the rates. The recent influenza epidemic had proved that Aldershot Hospital did not have the capacity to deal with the needs of the town and recourse had to be made to Guildford Hospital. Mr Hutt spoke out in favour of extending the hospital because the war had brought suffering to the wives and children of soldiers and the town should offer them compensation. Mr Griffiths stated that what the hospital could offer was limited, although plans were underway to install an X-ray machine. The hospital should have an out-patients facility. The money available, £10,000-£15,000, might pay for a hospital extension, but would not finance a resident surgeon. The speaker also supported a town hall because of the almost total lack of public buildings in the town.

Clear evidence that among those who either volunteered or were conscripted that the contract was for defence of the realm and not domestic politics was provided in Aldershot in May 1919. On 6 May, some of the 9,000 Reservists recalled to the army for repression of the coal strike ran riot in Union Street, Wellington Street, Gordon Road and Victoria Road led by a soldier waving a red flag. Over sixty shops had their windows smashed and were looted, including the jewellers. Pockets were stuffed with diamonds and watches and the clocks were thrown at local traders. Local police in the town were unable to restore order, but this was finally achieved by loyalists among the Reservists wielding bayonets and pick handles.

In Memoriam

Are God and nature then at strife?
That nature lends such evil dreams?
So careful of the type she seems,
So careless of the single life.

Lord Alfred Tennyson

Please note that this is not a comprehensive list of those from Aldershot who lost their lives.

1917

Private H.G. Sherman, Royal Fusiliers. Worked as a baker in the town. He was killed by a shell while walking to a dressing station to receive attention for another wound.

Private W.R. Mills, Royal Warwick Regiment. Worked for Gale and Polden Ltd. Left a widow and two young sons.

Private E. Rix, Devon Regiment. Worked as a builder in the town. His company applied for exemption from military service because of his skills in drainlaying, but his appeal was denied. Left a widow and four young children.

Rifleman G.W. Waters, Rifle Brigade. Before being killed in action was wounded twice.

Corporal E.M. Coultas, The Yorkshire/Lancasters. First wounded at Ypres and mentioned in dispatches. Had been badly wounded and gassed in 1915.

Private Percy Cooper, Middlesex Regiment. Previously worked for T. White Ltd in ironmongery. He left a widow and child.

Private Kitchetts, serving with the Australians. Had previously emigrated to Australia after growing up in Aldershot and attending

Pte E. Rix   *Rifleman G.W. Waters*   *Cpl E.M. Coultas*   *Battery Sgt Maj G.E. Owen*

the East End School. His father owned a butcher's shop in North Camp.

Battery-Sergeant-Major G. Evan Owen, killed in action leaving a widow and five children. Killed in an accident in Salonika. He had completed twenty-two years' service with the army. Had been a member of the RA Mounted Band.

Able Seaman P.W. Rogers

Able Seaman P.W. Rogers, Royal Navy, 19 years old. Had joined the navy in 1915 after attending the West End Schools. Was in the water for two hours after the ship he was serving on was rammed by a German destroyer in the Atlantic. He was buried in the Aldershot Cemetery with full military honours.

Private R.F. White, 23rd London Regiment. He was 24 and educated at The Church of England School. Confirmed as dead after the Battle of the Somme.

Private F. Bone, Royal Fusiliers. 19 years old. Educated at West End Schools and worked as a junior at Army and Navy Stores prior to enlistment.

Private Applegate, Hampshire Regiment. When reported missing his parents advertised in the local paper seeking information about their son. His death in Mesopotamia was confirmed.

Sergeant G.T. Ross, Queen Victoria Rifles. Attended West End Schools and graduated from Aldershot Teachers' College. His brother Ray was killed in action in 1915 at the Battle of Loos.

Company-Sergeant-Major E. K. Elflett, 1st Hampshire Regiment. Killed in action in Salonika. Educated at West End Schools.

Private Thomas Goss, Hampshire Regiment. Worked as a painter after leaving school. Killed at Messines on 17 June 1917. He was married with no children.

Gunner H. Larby, Royal Garrison Artillery. He was 20 and one of four brothers serving in the army.

Pte F. Bone

CSM E.K. Elflett

Gnr H. Larby

Pte B.J.H. Mills

Private B.J.H. Mills, Hampshire Regiment. Killed in action on 23 April 1917. Educated at the Garrison School. Aged 25. Had been employed by Army and Navy prior to enlistment.

Private George Reynolds, Hampshire Regiment. Employed by Lewes Motor Works. Had previously been withdrawn from service at the front suffering from trench foot. An active member of Christ Church, St George's Road. In 1915 his brother was killed at Gallipoli.

Pte G. Reynolds

Sergeant Walliker, Army Service Corps. He was a regular soldier who had served with the South Wales Borderers since 1909. He was killed on 6 February at Kut.

Private H.C. Caws, Royal Berkshire Regiment. Had worked at Aldershot Post Office before enlistment.

Private S.S. Yeoman, Somerset Light Infantry. Aged 19. Had worked at the Royal aircraft factory. Killed on 18 June on the Western Front.

Private Harry C. Burke, Motor Machine-Gun Corps. In business in Victoria Road prior to enlistment.

Lance-Corporal Charles Taylor, Queens Royal West Surrey Regiment. Killed on the Western Front, 31 July 1917. A well-known footballer and athlete.

Lieutenant George Hounsom, London Regiment. Died in Devonport after a fortnight's illness. Had served in the Army Service Corps before being commissioned. A popular officer who was greatly missed by his battalion. This was the family's loss of a second son.

Corporal H. Turner, Royal Regiment of Artillery. Educated at the East End Schools. Enlisted at the beginning of the war.

Private C.A. Ricketts, Australians. Emigrated to Australia four years before but enlisted in the Australian Army when he was 17. Saw service in Gallipoli and went through the Somme after transferring to France in April 1916. Died of a gunshot wound to the chest in the Canadian casualty clearing station. He had two brothers serving in France.

Private Harry Burke, Motor Machine-Gun Corps. Was in business in the town.

Signaller A. P. Jolly, London Regiment. He enlisted with the Devons in 1917 and then transferred to the Artists Rifles. He was killed by a shell on 24 September 1917. He was from an Aldershot family with a long history of army service.

Private W.A. Jarrett, Royal Engineers. He was 19. Died of wounds on

8 September 1917. Educated at the West End Schools. He had worked in the Royal aircraft factory and had been on the Western Front for three weeks.

1918

Captain Edward Bell, MC and Bar, Middlesex Regiment. Had been invested by the king. Regarded as a brilliant officer. Killed on 24 March 1918.

Signaller A.P. Jolly

Corporal Elflett, Hampshire Regiment. He was wounded at Gallipoli in 1915. On his recovery he was sent to France with the 13th Hampshire Regiment. One of his brothers, Company-Sergeant-Major E. K. Elflett, was killed at Salonika. A further brother was a POW in Turkey.

Sergeant-Major W.H. May, 3rd Canadian Regiment. He had been wounded seven times in the course of his army service. After emigrating to Canada he enlisted in the Canadian Army in 1914. He had been a student at the East End schools and was awarded the Military Medal. His brother was serving with the American Army.

R.E. Pinkney had been a teacher in Aldershot before his enlistment. He was 36 when he was killed. Previously he was seriously wounded in his lung and back. He subsequently died of influenza.

Capt E. Bell

Second-Lieutenant H.L. Mepham, Royal Fusiliers. Killed in action on 11 April 1918. He was 23. A talented musician, he was the organist at the Wesleyan Church in the town.

Private C.S. Maries, Hampshire Regiment. Educated at West End Schools. He was a research chemist at the Gas Company and had been doing important work in chemistry for the government.

Lance-Corporal S. Porter, Northumberland Fusiliers. He was 36. Educated at the West End Schools. Had spent time with the army in India. Was called up from the Reserves for service.

Private F. C. Chick, 16th Lancers. He was 33. Had been in the retreat

CSM W.H. May   *2Lt H.L. Mepham*   *Pte C.S. Maries*   *L/Cpl S. Porter*

from Mons. Employed at the local post office. Died of the influenza.

Lance-Corporal F.T. Miller, West Yorkshire Regiment. Prior to enlistment worked for Army and Navy Stores.

Lance Corporal Travers Thomas. He was educated at St Joseph's School. He was 19 when he died after a long illness.

Private J.W. Diaper, 2nd Suffolk Regiment. Killed on the Western Front on 17 February 1918. Enlisted with the Army Service Corps but moved to the 2nd Suffolks.

Pte F.C. Chick

Private Albert Styles. Killed by a sniper on the Western Front on 11th April 1918. Had been a member of the local cadets. Worked for Gale and Polden prior to enlistment. A member of the Wesleyan Church Congregation. He was 19.

Private W.A.Jarrett, Royal Engineers. Killed on the Western Front on 12 September. Educated at West End schools. Had been in France for three weeks. He was 19.

Sapper T.C. Tye, Signal Service. Worked for the post office prior to the war. Educated at West End schools. Died of influenza while serving on 9 November.

Lance-Corporal A.W. Major, Z Company 2nd Royal Fusiliers. Reported missing since 14 April but confirmed dead. Was with the Army Pay Corps before transferring to the infantry.

Private P.J. Orange, Hampshire Regiment. Died of influenza in France. Worked as a newspaper photographer in Aldershot. He was 27.

Private W.A.Childs, Worcester Regiment. Killed in action in France aged 19.

Gunner Charles Adams, RGA. He served seven years with the Royal Marines. Worked at Borden Camp. Left a widow and small son.

Pte W.A. Childs

L/Cpl F.T. Miller

L/Cpl Thomas

Pte J.W. Diaper

Pte A. Styles

A number of churches in Aldershot contain lists of the fallen during the Great War:

St Michael's C of E Church

Frederick H.L. Applin; Arthur P. Archer; Albert G. Austin; Charles Bentley; Henry Berry; Herbert N. Bills; Maurice A. Black; Berthold F. Bradley; Lawrence B. Bradley; Ernest Bree; Harold V. Bresser; William Bridge; George W. Brookes; Charles Browning; Horace E. Bunting; Henry P. Chaffey; Frederick Chandler; William A. Childs; Arthur Chittenden; Robert E. Chown; Albert R. Clarke; Eric W.G. Barrett; Alfred Clements; Henry G. Collar; Frank Collinson; Harold W. Collyar; Leslie L. Cooke; George W. Cooper; Sydney J. Cooper; Theophilus Cooper; Thomas O.V. Cox; Arthur F. Curry; Thomas R. Dalziel; Alexander J.C. Duncan; Walter Eden; Claude F. Elliott; John T. Ellis; Richard Evans; Alexander Evetts; Harold C. Farrow; Henry J. Ford; John Ford; William Ford; William Fowler; Reginald T. Franklin; Frederick G. Fuller; Frederick G. Ganter; Douglas V. Gayleard; William McD. Green; Alfred W. Hall; Frederick Hawthorne; William Head; Joseph P. Herrington; Harry T. Hobbs; Daniel W. Holland, Edward Hounsom; Arthur Huggins; Charles A. Hutton; Oliver G. Izzard; Percival G. Gasser; Harold C. Jaye; Michael P. Jennings; William G. Johnson; Arthur P. Jolly; Peter T. Jones; Edward D. Kay; Walter A. Kent; John King; James Kirkpatrick; Robert C. Levett; Albert S. Lingard; H. Edward Lloyd; William G. Lugg; Thomas McGowran; George W. McKenzie; Alfred MacLean; James MacLean; Patrick J. Martin; Victor L. Martin; Horace L. Mepham; Cecil P. Mills; Robert H. Mills; George Newcome; Arthur Pockington; James Nolan; John P. Oak; Charles Oakham; George E. Owen; William P. Owens; Roger Palmer; Samuel F. Palmer; Victor J. Powell; Charles Raymond; George E.T. Reynolds; Herbert F. Richardson; John W. Robinson; Alfred Rossiter; Joseph E. Salisbury; Charles W. Shanks; John Smith; Walter Smith; Colin D.M.C. Tocher; John Soffe; Frank Stovey; Arthur Suter; Sidney Terry; George Titmus; Jesse W. Turner; Alexander G. Wallace; Arthur G. Warner; William Warrilow; Frank Way; Richard F. White; Thomas Wilkinson; Charles Williams; Walter F. Williams; William J.A. Willson; Joseph Wilmot; Arthur Wiseman; Ernest Withers; Gordon B. Woollford; Harry Younger.

St Andrew's Church of Scotland
A. Alfred Andrews; C. Richard Hampson; Henry Kelk; Harry Leat; C. Stewart Maries; James Newell; Keith Watts Reavell; Rev'd R. Arthur Stewart.

St Joseph's Roman Catholic Church
Henry Ayres; James Russell Carver; Leslie Cook; Charles Cooper; George Denham; Joseph Dunn; William Dunn; William Dunn; Albert Griffiths; Frederick Barnett; John Henry Ingram; Charles Breary; Albert Burdett; George Burnham; Michael Joseph Johnson; Leo Berans; Thomas Lawrence; Edward Mahoney; Francis Joseph Murray; John O'Connor; Walter Smith; Joseph Patrick Spiller; John Tate; John Townsend; Arthur Wallcher; Ernest Green; Water Goodrich; William Parkes.

Holy Trinity Church (1914-1919)
P.G. Anson, AB; J.W. Barnett, Pte; J.R. Blackler, Pte; C.D. Bricknell, SWO; H.C. Caws, Pte; A.G. Cullen, CSM; R. Driver, Pte; W.E.F. Goodrich, Pte; T.E. Goss, Pte; C. Grainger, Pte; W. Grainger, Pte; C.J. Hart, Pte; F. Hill, Driver; F.W. Hunt, Corp; H.C. Jaye, Lt; G. Johnson, Gunner; C.G. Lawes, Lt; R.C. Marsh, Lt; F.H. Mills, Sgt; B.J.H. Mills, Pte; W.H. Mills, Pte; G.A. Pickles, Cpl; P.W. Rogers, AB; C.L. Ross, Sgt; R.M. Ross, Pte; E.E.W. Singleton, Pte; S.P. Smith, Capt; H. Stokes, Pte; H.T. Turvill, Cpl; H.H. Thompson, Capt; W. Urpeth, Cpl; F. Willis, RFM; J.H. Woolger, Pte.

Kemal Ataturk the legendary leader of Turkey, said of the fallen from the British Empire after Gallipoli that they are now our sons. In the same way, the people of Aldershot wish to record the names of the fallen in the Aldershot Military Cemetery.

For those wishing to see a list of the men buried in the Aldershot First World War Military Cemetery, the full list can be viewed by typing the following URL into your web browser on a PC, Mac or Tablet: http://www.pen-and-sword.co.uk/aldershot-military-cemetery

Alternatively, for those with smart phones the same list can be viewed by scanning the QR code here:

Aldershot Deaths

Please note that these lists do not include officers.

Sort Order : Surname, Christian Name(s)

SURNAME,Christian Name(s),Born,Enlisted,Residence,Number,RANK,Cause,Place,Date of Death,ADDITIONAL TEXT,Regiment,Battalion

ABBOTT, Alfred A., b. Aldershot, Hants, e. Templemore, Co. Tipperary , r. Bruff, Co. Limerick, 8076, C.S.M., Died of wounds, France & Flanders, 18/06/15, Royal Scots Fusiliers, 2nd Battalion.

ABBOTT, Percy Ducan, b. Aldershot, Hants, e. Perth, 1343, CPL., Died, Home, 14/11/15, Royal Army Pay Corps.

ADAMS, James, b. Aldershot, e. Aldershot, 307679, PRIVATE, Killed in action, France & Flanders, 08/08/18, FORMERLY 59693, ROYAL FLYING CORPS., Tank Corps.

ADAMS, William, b. Aldershot, e. Dumbarton, 225, GUNNER, Killed in action, France & Flanders, 23/09/16, Royal Garrison Artillery, Clyde. [RGA - (TF)]

ALDEN, Frederick William, b. Aldershot, e. Aldershot , r. Gosport, 9862, C.S.M., Died, France & Flanders, 09/08/16, King's (Liverpool Regiment), 1st Battalion.

ANDREWS, Edward James, b. Aldershot, e. Dover , r. Westbury, Wilts, 54810, PRIVATE, Killed in action, France & Flanders, 28/07/17, Welsh Regiment, 15th Battalion.

ANDREWS, Thomas Henry, b. Aldershot, Hants, e. Newcastle-on-Tyne, Northumberland, 70323, L/CPL., Died of wounds, France & Flanders, 19/09/17, FORMERLY 5258, LEICESTERSHIRE REGT., Sherwood Foresters (Nottinghamshire and Derbyshire Regiment), 17th Battalion.

APPLEGATE, Sydney, b. Aldershot, Hants, e. Bustard Camp, Hants , r. Aldershot, Hants, 200821, PRIVATE, Killed in action, Mesopotamia, 24/02/17, Hampshire Regiment, 1/4th (T.F.) Battalion.

ARTHUR, Louis Henry, b. Aldershot, Hants, e. Winchester , r. Aldershot, Hants, 26952, PRIVATE, Died of wounds, France & Flanders, 24/08/18, Hampshire Regiment, 15th (Service) Battalion.

ASHMAN, Frederick Edward, b. Aldershot, e. London , r. Stoke Newington, 373690, RIFLEMAN, Killed in action, France & Flanders, 08/08/18, London Regiment, 8th (City of London) Battalion (Post Office Rifles).

ASPINALL, Reginald Clarence, b. Aldershot, e. Aldershot , r. Portsmouth, Hants, 8052, L/CPL, Killed in action, France & Flanders, 07/11/14, Hampshire Regiment, 1st Battalion.

BAILEY, Arthur Charles, b. Aldershot, e. Hounslow , r. Hounslow, 16816, C.S.M., Died of wounds, France & Flanders, 30/08/18, Royal Fusiliers (City of London Regiment), 11th Battalion.

BAIRD, David Eugene, b. Aldershot, Hants, e. Woolwich, Kent , r. Berris, Co. Carlow, 7516, C.S.M., Died of wounds, France & Flanders, 06/07/16, Border Regiment, 1st Battalion.

BAKER, George Henry, b. Aldershot, e. Camberwell , r. W. Norwood, 701925, PRIVATE, Killed in action, France & Flanders, 16/09/16, London Regiment, 23rd (County of London) Battalion.

BAKER, Henry Alfred, b. Aldershot, e. London , r. Ashton-Under-Lyne, 7234, RIFLEMAN, Killed in action, France & Flanders, 15/10/14, King's Royal Rifle Corps, 1st Battalion.

BALDRY, Alfred Mitford Walter, b. Aldershot, Hants, e. Winchester, Hants , r. Aldershot, 20759, PRIVATE, Killed in action, France & Flanders, 06/08/18, Dorsetshire Regiment, 6th Battalion.

BALDWIN, James Hamilton, b. Aldershot, e. Whitehall, Middlesex, 30122, PRIVATE, Died of wounds, France & Flanders, 09/08/16, FORMERLY 27944, DUKE OF CORNWALL'S LIGHT INFANTRY., Prince Albert's (Somerset Light Infantry), 1st Battalion.

BANKS, John Thomas, b. Aldershot, Hants, e. London , r. Chelsea, Middx., 47362, RIFLEMAN, Died of wounds, Home, 12/01/18, FORMERLY 7337, R.A.S.C., Royal Irish Rifles, 1st Battalion.

BANNISTER, Sidney, b. Aldershot, Hants, e. Maidstone , r. Chatham, 67988, GUNNER, Died of wounds, France & Flanders, 09/04/17, Royal Garrison Artillery.

BANTING, Henry Harry, b. Aldershot, Hants, e. Folkestone, Kent , r. Folkestone, Kent, G/22702, PRIVATE, Killed in action, France & Flanders, 12/10/17, Buffs (East Kent Regiment), 7th Battalion.

BARKER, Gilbert, b. Aldershot, Hants, e. Edinburgh , r. Long Wittenham, Berkshire, 25078, PRIVATE, Killed in action, France & Flanders, 01/07/16, Royal Scots (Lothian Regiment), 16th Battalion.

BARNETT, Percy, b. Aldershot, e. Aldershot, 9018, L/CPL, Died, France & Flanders, 25/02/15, Royal Welsh Fusiliers, 1st Battalion.

BARNETT, Walter Edward, b. Aldershot, Hants, e. Aldershot, 13584, PRIVATE, Killed in action, France & Flanders, 07/07/16, FORMERLY 20777, HUSSARS., Dorsetshire Regiment, 6th Battalion.

BARRELL, Arthur William Joseph, b. Aldershot, e. Hammersmith, Middlesex, 21572, L/CPL., Killed in action, France & Flanders, 25/08/16, Prince Albert's (Somerset Light Infantry), 1st Battalion.

Sort Order : Surname, Christian Name(s)

SURNAME,Christian Name(s),Born,Enlisted,Residence,Number,RANK,Cause,Place,Date of Death,ADDITIONAL TEXT,Regiment,Battalion

BARTLETT, Harry Henry, b. Aldershot, Hants, e. Bodmin, Cornwall , r. East Finchley, Middx., 9337, PRIVATE, Killed in action, France & Flanders, 14/03/15, Duke of Cornwall's Light Infantry, 2nd Battalion.

BARTLETT, John William. b. Aldershot, e. Finchley , r. Finchley, 51483, PRIVATE, Killed in action, France & Flanders, 10/04/17, FORMERLY 32927, MIDDX. REGT., Royal Fusiliers (City of London Regiment), 13th Battalion.

BARTON, William, b. Aldershot, e. Kingston-on-Thames, Surrey , r. New Malden, Surrey, 4322, RIFLEMAN, Killed in action, France & Flanders, 23/10/16, Rifle Brigade (The Prince Consort's Own), 1st Battalion.

BASHFORD, William, b. Aldershot, e. Wimbledon, Surrey, 3065, GUNNER, Killed in action, Salonika, 26/11/16, Royal Horse Artillery and Royal Field Artillery.

BEAL, Frederick, b. Aldershot, e. Woolwich , r. Blackheath, T/24526, A/C.S.M., Died, Egypt, 13/10/18, Royal Army Service Corps.

BEATTIE, Robert, b. Aldershot, Hants, e. Blackburn, Lancs, G/8782, PRIVATE, Killed in action, France & Flanders, 22/07/16, Queen's Own (Royal West Kent Regiment), 1st Battalion.

BEETON, Arthur, b. Aldershot, Hants, e. Guildford, Surrey , r. Borden Hants, S/643, PRIVATE, Killed in action, France & Flanders, 16/05/15, Queen's (Royal West Surrey Regiment), 2nd Battalion.

BELLINGHAM, Bertram Charles, b. Aldershot, Hants, e. Maidstone, Kent , r. Snodland, Kent, 33686, PRIVATE, Killed in action, France & Flanders, 15/08/17, East Surrey Regiment, 7th Battalion.

BENEWITH, Alfred, b. Aldershot, e. Poplar, Middx. , r. Stockton-on-Tees, Durham, 11072, L/SGT, Killed in action, Italy, 29/10/18, Border Regiment, 2nd Battalion.

BENNETT, Arthur, b. Aldershot, e. Devizes, Wilts , r. Portsmouth, 9057, L/CPL, Died of wounds, Home, 01/06/15, Duke of Edinburgh's (Wiltshire Regiment), 1st Battalion.

BENNETT, Thomas, b. Aldershot, Hants, e. Aldershot, Hants, 9994, PRIVATE, Killed in action, France & Flanders, 25/02/15, Prince of Wales's Leinster Regiment (Royal Canadians), 1st Battalion.

BERRY, Harold, b. Aldershot, Hants, e. Aldershot, 10926, PRIVATE, Died of wounds, France & Flanders, 19/09/14, Highland Light Infantry, 2nd Battalion.

BERRY, William, b. Aldershot, Hants, e. Hartley Wintney, Hants , r. Aldershot, Hants, 17445, PRIVATE, Killed in action, Gallipoli, 06/08/15, Hampshire Regiment, 2nd Battalion.

BICKNELL, Joseph, b. Aldershot, Hants, e. Dumbarton , r. Dumbarton, 7893, C.S.M., Killed in action, France & Flanders, 25/09/15, King's Own Scottish Borderers, 8th Battalion.

BISCOE, Frederick, b. Aldershot, e. Winchester, 37375, PRIVATE, Died of wounds, Home, 31/07/17, Gloucestershire Regiment, 8th Service Battalion.

BISHOP, Alexander, b. Aldershot, e. Dublin , r. Belfast, 10824, DRUMMER, Killed in action, France & Flanders, 18/07/16, Welsh Regiment, 2nd Battalion.

BISHOP, William, b. Aldershot, Hants, e. Winchester, Hants , r. Aldershot, 37379, L/CPL, Killed in action, France & Flanders, 22/10/17, Manchester Regiment, 23rd Battalion.

BISSETT, Samuel, b. Aldershot, Hants, e. Edinburgh, Midlothian , r. Kirkcaldy, Fife, 7479, L/SGT, Killed in action, France & Flanders, 25/09/15, King's Own Scottish Borderers, 6th Battalion.

BLAKE, Edward Mitchell, b. Aldershot, Hants, e. Woolwich, Kent , r. Plumstead, Kent, S/6171, PRIVATE, Died of wounds, France & Flanders, 02/12/14, Queen's (Royal West Surrey Regiment), 2nd Battalion.

BLAKE, George, b. Aldershot, Hants, e. Camberwell, London, 3/4793, CPL., Died of wounds, At Sea, 19/07/15, Hampshire Regiment, 2nd Battalion.

BLOOMFIELD, James, b. Aldershot, Hants, e. Canterbury, Kent , r. Hythe, Kent, L/8917, SERGT., Died of wounds, France & Flanders, 29/08/18, M.M., Buffs (East Kent Regiment), 6th Battalion.

BONE, Frank James, b. Aldershot, Hants, e. Aldershot, 25145, PRIVATE, Killed in action, France & Flanders, 10/08/17, FORMERLY 24951, Y. HASSARS OF THE LINE., 8th Battalion.

BOON, Herbert Victor, b. Aldershot, Hants, e. Maidstone, Kent , r. Chatham, Kent, G/14405, PRIVATE, Killed in action, France & Flanders, 18/09/18, Buffs (East Kent Regiment), 7th Battalion.

BOSWORTHICK, William Ernest, b. Aldershot, e. Southampton , r. Southampton, 9907, RIFLEMAN, Killed in action, France & Flanders, 27/04/15, Rifle Brigade (The Prince Consort's Own), 1st Battalion.

Sort Order : Surname, Christian Name(s)

SURNAME,Christian Name(s),Born,Enlisted,Residence,Number,RANK,Cause,Place,Date of Death,ADDITIONAL TEXT,Regiment,Battalion

BOWERS, Archibald Francis, b. Aldershot, e. Guildford, Surrey, 55798, PRIVATE, Killed in action, France & Flanders, 04/11/18, FORMERLY 7289, EAST SURREY REGT., Northumberland Fusiliers, 2nd Battalion.

BOWERS, Edward, b. Aldershot, e. Winchester, 241729, PRIVATE, Died, France & Flanders, 16/08/16, Gloucestershire Regiment, 1/5th Battalion (Territorial).

BOWYER, Alfred, b. Aldershot, Hants, e. Derby, 7043, RFN. (L/CORP.), Killed in action, France & Flanders, 25/09/15, King's Royal Rifle Corps, 2nd Battalion.

BOWYER, James Arthur, b. Aldershot, e. London , r. Highbury, Middx., 8941, CPL., Died of wounds, Gallipoli, 26/04/15, Royal Munster Fusiliers, 1st Battalion.

BOXALL, Percy John, b. Aldershot, e. London , r. Hammersmith, E/775, PRIVATE, Killed in action, France & Flanders, 02/04/18, Royal Fusiliers (City of London Regiment), 17th Battalion.

BOYER, Ernest Earl, b. Aldershot, e. Aldershot, Hants, 33284, GUNNER, Died, Turkey, 31/10/16, Royal Horse Artillery and Royal Field Artillery.

BRADY, James, b. Aldershot, Hants, e. Birkenhead, Cheshire, 9715, SERGT., Died of wounds, France & Flanders, 06/11/17, FORMERLY 9428, SOUTH LANCASHIRE REGIMENT., Prince of Wales's Leinster Regiment (Royal Canadians), 2nd Battalion.

BRANT, William, b. Aldershot, e. Aldershot , r. Cove, 995, A/CPL., Died, Home, 09/06/16, Corps of Military Police, Foot Branch.

BRAZIER, Leonard Arthur, b. Aldershot, Hants, e. Hove, Sussex , r. Steyning, Sunnex, G/4416, PRIVATE, Killed in action, France & Flanders, 18/11/16, Queen's (Royal West Surrey Regiment), 7th Battalion.

BREWER, Herbert, b. Aldershot, e. Newbury, Berks , r. Hungerford, Berks, 129127, PIONEER, Killed in action, France & Flanders, 23/06/18, (NO. 1 SPEC. COY., R.E.), Corps of Royal Engineers.

BRIERS, John, b. Aldershot, Hants, e. Dorchester, Dorset , r. Wareham, Dorset, 5833, SERGT., Killed in action, France & Flanders, 12/04/17, Dorsetshire Regiment, 6th Battalion.

BRIGHTY, James Henry, b. Aldershot, Hants, e. Dover, Kent, 8218, DRUMMER, Died, Mesopotamia, 15/10/16, Norfolk Regiment, 2nd Battalion.

BRIMSON, Arthur Ernest, b. Aldershot, e. Holloway , r. Islington, 77731, PRIVATE, Died of wounds, France & Flanders, 08/10/18, FORMERLY 685501, LONDON REGT., Royal Fusiliers (City of London Regiment), 17th Battalion.

BROWN, Francis Anthony, b. Aldershot, Hants, e. Aldershot , r. King's Lynn, Norfolk, 92322, PRIVATE, Killed in action, France & Flanders, 20/09/17, FORMERLY T/90322, R.A.S.C., Sherwood Foresters (Nottinghamshire and Derbyshire Regiment), 16th Battalion.

BROWN, Joseph Samuel, b. Aldershot, Hants, e. London, 7130, SERGT., Killed in action, France & Flanders, 04/10/17, East Surrey Regiment, 1st Battalion.

BROWN, Lawrence Arthur, b. Aldershot, Hants, e. Nottingham, 40485, CPL., Died of wounds, France & Flanders, 29/07/17, Royal Horse Artillery and Royal Field Artillery.

BROWN, Thomas, b. Aldershot, Hants, e. Bury, Lancs, 1606, PRIVATE, Killed in action, Gallipoli, 07/08/15, Lancashire Fusiliers, 1/5 Battalion (T.F.).

BRYANT, George, b. Aldershot, Hants, e. London, 52984, GUNNER, Died, Mesopotamia, 14/05/16, Royal Horse Artillery and Royal Field Artillery.

BRYANT, John Francis, b. Aldershot, Hants, e. Worcester , r. Salisbury, 4481, L/CPL, Killed in action, France & Flanders, 05/11/14, Household Cavalry and Cavalry of the Line (incl. Yeomanry and Imperial Camel Corps), 16th Lancers (The Queen's).

BUDD, Leonard, b. Aldershot, Hants, e. Lewes, Sussex , r. Frimley, Surrey, 454, L/SGT, Died of wounds, France & Flanders, 21/08/18, FORMERLY 16341, COLDSTREAM GUARDS., Guards Machine Gun Regiment, 4th Battalion.

BUDD, Sidney Louis, b. Aldershot, Hants, e. Grimsby , r. Frimley, Surrey, 652, L/SGT, Killed in action, France & Flanders, 28/04/17, Lincolnshire Regiment, 10th Battalion.

BUDGEN, John, b. Aldershot, e. Brighton, SD/890, PRIVATE, Died of wounds, British Expeditionary Force, 30/06/16, Royal Sussex Regiment, 11th Battalion.

BURGAR, Albert, b. Aldershot, e. Ashton-Under-Lyne , r. Broughton, Manchester, 53075, GUNNER, Died of wounds, France & Flanders, 19/03/16, Royal Garrison Artillery.

Sort Order : Surname, Christian Name(s)

SURNAME,Christian Name(s),Born,Enlisted,Residence,Number,RANK,Cause,Place,Date of Death,ADDITIONAL TEXT,Regiment,Battalion

BURLONG, Sydney Frank, b. Aldershot, e. Chelmsford , r. Braintree, 12300, SERGT., Killed in action, France & Flanders, 23/03/16, Essex Regiment, 9th Battalion.

BURRELL, Oswald, b. Aldershot, e. Bunhill Row, E.C. , r. Hackney, 652730, RIFLEMAN, Killed in action, Balkans, 12/05/17, London Regiment, 21st (County of London) Battalion (1st Surrey Rifles).

BUSWELL, Frederick Henry, b. Aldershot, Hants, e. Guildford, Surrey , r. Farnham, Surrey, L/9285, PRIVATE, Died of wounds, France & Flanders, 10/11/14, Queen's (Royal West Surrey Regiment), 2nd Battalion.

BUXTON, Albert Edward, b. Aldershot, Hants, e. Chesterfield, Derbyshire, 19774, PRIVATE, Killed in action, France & Flanders, 04/10/17, FORMERLY 14348, LEICESTERSHIRE REGT., M.M., Sherwood Foresters (Nottinghamshire and Derbyshire Regiment), 9th Battalion.

CAHILL, William, b. Aldershot, e. Warley, Essex , r. Colchester, 4800, C.Q.M.S., Died of wounds, Egypt, 12/05/15, Essex Regiment, 1st Battalion.

CAMERON, Duncan, b. Aldershot, Hants, e. Whiteinch, Glasgow, Lanarkshire , r. Partick, Glasgow, S/10068, SERGT., Killed in action, France & Flanders, 31/07/17, Queen's Own Cameron Highlanders, 6th Battalion.

CAMERON, James, b. Aldershot, Hants, e. Edinburgh, Midlothian , r. Leith, Midlothian, 11261, PRIVATE, Killed in action, France & Flanders, 28/10/18, Princess Louise's (Argyll & Sutherland Highlanders), 1/7th Battalion.

CAMPBELL, Alan George, b. Aldershot, Hants, e. Aldershot, 3/7124, R.S.M., Killed in action, France & Flanders, 25/09/15, Gordon Highlanders, 8th Battalion.

CAMPBELL, William John, b. Aldershot, e. Devonport, 38384, PRIVATE, Died, France & Flanders, 29/04/18, FORMERLY 9393, 1ST SOMERSET LIGHT INFANTRY., Gloucestershire Regiment, 2/5th Battalion (Territorial).

CANEY, James Elias David, b. Aldershot, Hants, e. Shepherd's Bush, Middx. , r. Lambeth, Surrey, 10773, PRIVATE, Killed in action, France & Flanders, 16/06/15, Bedfordshire Regiment, 2nd Battalion.

CARPENTER, Sidney Mark, b. Aldershot, Hants, e. Kingston-on-Thames, Surrey, 10741, L/CPL, Killed in action, France & Flanders, 28/10/17, East Surrey Regiment, 1st Battalion.

CARR, Charles Thomas, b. Aldershot, Hants, e. Camberwell, Surrey , r. Penge, Kent, G/3663, L/CPL, Killed in action, France & Flanders, 03/05/17, Buffs (East Kent Regiment), 7th Battalion.

CARTER, Edward, b. Aldershot, Hants, e. Portsmouth, 15853, PRIVATE, Killed in action, France & Flanders, 27/01/17, Hampshire Regiment, 2nd Battalion.

CARVER, Frederick John, b. Aldershot, Hants, e. Aldershot, Hants, 200422, PRIVATE, Died, Egypt, 03/08/17, Hampshire Regiment, 2/5th (T.F.) Battalion.

CASTLETON, G. P. L., b. Aldershot, Hants, e. Cavan, 27899, E.C.Q.M.S., Killed in action, France & Flanders, 15/09/14, (23RD FIELD COY., R.E.), Corps of Royal Engineers.

CHALK, Archibald, b. Aldershot, e. Winchester , r. Winchester, 9905, RIFLEMAN, Killed in action, France & Flanders, 26/08/14, FORMERLY 5847, R. SUSSEX REGT., Rifle Brigade (The Prince Consort's Own), 1st Battalion.

CHAMBERLAIN, H., b. Aldershot, Hants, e. Portsmouth , r. Greatham, Hants, 1211, SPR., Died, Salonika, 24/07/16, (1/7TH HANTS FIELD, COY., R.E.)., Corps of Royal Engineers.

CHAPMAN, Harold Vincent, b. Aldershot, Hants, e. Brighton, Sussex , r. Brighton, Sussex, G/6681, L/CPL, Killed in action, France & Flanders, 18/03/16, Buffs (East Kent Regiment), 6th Battalion.

CHASE, Jack, b. Aldershot, e. Blackdown, Hants , r. Aldershot, 9641, SERGT., Killed in action, France & Flanders, 25/09/16, York and Lancaster Regiment, 2nd Battalion.

CHESTERTON, Charles Thomas, b. Aldershot, Hants, e. London, 1527, E.C.Q.M.S., Killed in action, France & Flanders, 14/09/14, (5TH FIELD COY., R.E.), Corps of Royal Engineers.

CHISHOLM, Charles, b. Aldershot, e. Northampton, 8745, L/CPL, Killed in action, France & Flanders, 22/07/15, Scots Guards.

CHRISTIE, David, b. Aldershot, Hants, e. Galashiels, Selkirkshire , r. Paisley, 18097, PRIVATE, Died, France & Flanders, 16/06/15, Royal Scots Fusiliers, 2nd Battalion.

CHRISTMAS, William, b. Aldershot, e. London , r. Fulham, 473428, RIFLEMAN, Killed in action, France & Flanders, 28/01/17, London Regiment, 12th (County of London) Battalion (The Rangers).

CHURCHILL, William James, b. Aldershot, Hants, e. Norwich, Norfolk, 6276, SERGT., Died of wounds, Home, 22/05/15, Norfolk Regiment, 1st Battalion.

Sort Order : Surname, Christian Name(s)

SURNAME,Christian Name(s),Born,Enlisted,Residence,Number,RANK,Cause,Place,Date of Death,ADDITIONAL TEXT,Regiment,Battalion

CHURCHMAN, William, b. Aldershot, Hants, e. Axminster, Devon , r. Ottery St. Mary, Devon, 27697, PRIVATE, Killed in action, France & Flanders, 16/09/16, FORMERLY 24101, SOMERSET L.I., Duke of Cornwall's Light Infantry, 6th Battalion.

CLARIDGE, Ernest J., b. Aldershot, Hants, e. Edinburgh, 39851, PRIVATE, Killed in action, France & Flanders, 06/12/17, Highland Light Infantry, 2nd Battalion.

CLARK, Thomas, b. Aldershot, e. Southwark , r. Walworth, 12185, PRIVATE, Killed in action, France & Flanders, 10/08/16, Royal Fusiliers (City of London Regiment), 11th Battalion.

CLARKE, Herbert James, b. Aldershot, Hants, e. South Farnborough, Hants , r. Aldershot, L/11789, PRIVATE, Died of wounds, France & Flanders, 08/04/18, FORMERLY 64176, R.A.F., Queen's (Royal West Surrey Regiment), 1/24th Battalion.

CLARKE, Urbane Hall, b. Aldershot, e. Whitehall , r. Weston-Super-Mare, DM2/223838, PRIVATE, Died of wounds, France & Flanders, 21/03/18, Royal Army Service Corps.

CLARKE, William Patrick, b. Aldershot, Hants, e. Liverpool , r. Rock Ferry, Cheshire, 28627, CPL., Killed in action, France & Flanders, 10/07/17, FORMERLY 20883, THE KING'S LIVERPOOL REGT., Border Regiment, 11th Battalion.

CLIFTON, Percy H., b. Aldershot, Hants, e. Bristol, 8938, L/CPL, Killed in action, France & Flanders, 25/09/15, Royal Scots Fusiliers, 1st Battalion.

COLDICOTT, Thomas, b. Aldershot, Hants, e. Warwick , r. Hampton-in-Arden, Warwicks, 2119, PRIVATE, Killed in action, France & Flanders, 13/10/14, Royal Warwickshire Regiment, 1st Battalion.

COLE, Reginald James Leslie, b. Aldershot, Hants, e. Winchester , r. Aldershot, Hants, 14337, L/CPL, Killed in action, France & Flanders, 09/08/18, Hampshire Regiment, 15th (Service) Battalion.

COLLINS, Timothy, b. Aldershot, Hants, r. Aldershot, T.F.242241, PRIVATE, Died of wounds, France & Flanders, 29/08/18, Duke of Cambridge's Own (Middlesex Regiment), 1/8th (T.F.) Battalion.

COMFORT, George Henry Harding, b. Aldershot, e. Aldershot, 33296, PRIVATE, Died of wounds, France & Flanders, 08/12/17, Princess Charlotte of Wales's (Royal Berkshire Regiment), 1st Battalion.

CONNOLLY, William Henry, b. Aldershot, Hants, e. Winchester , r. Aldershot, Hants, 9309, PRIVATE, Killed in action, Gallipoli, 13/10/15, Hampshire Regiment, 2nd Battalion.

COOK, Frederick William Thomas, b. Aldershot, e. New Cross, Surrey , r. Vauxhall, Surrey, 765, RIFLEMAN, Killed in action, France & Flanders, 25/09/14, Rifle Brigade (The Prince Consort's Own), 3rd Battalion.

COOK, Robert, b. Aldershot, Hampshire, e. Stirling , r. Stirling, 35479, PRIVATE, Killed in action, France & Flanders, 02/12/16, Royal Scots (Lothian Regiment), 2nd Battalion.

COOKE, Frank, b. Aldershot, e. Stockton-on-Tees, 9281, DRUMMER, Died of wounds, Mesopotamia, 05/10/17, King's Own (Royal Lancaster Regiment), 6th Battalion.

COOPER, Arthur James, b. Aldershot, Hants, e. Hartley Wintney, 68157, PRIVATE, Died of wounds, France & Flanders, 22/10/17, Royal Army Medical Corps.

COPPLESTONE, Frank, b. Aldershot, e. Aldershot , r. Barnstaple, Devon, 5844, L/CPL, Killed in action, France & Flanders, 30/08/15, Worcestershire Regiment, 3rd Battalion.

COSTELLO, Maurice Henry, b. Aldershot, e. Exeter , r. Devizes, 8256, PRIVATE, Killed in action, France & Flanders, 01/07/16, Devonshire Regiment, 8th (Service) Battalion.

COX, Eugene, b. Aldershot, Hants, e. Shrewsbury, Wilts, 11519, PRIVATE, Died of wounds, France & Flanders, 15/12/17, Irish Guards, 2nd. Battalion.

COX, Frederick James, b. Aldershot, Hants, e. Southampton, Hants, 12774, RIFLEMAN, Killed in action, France & Flanders, 24/12/16, King's Royal Rifle Corps, 13th Battalion.

COX, Harry, b. Aldershot, Hants, e. Aldershot, 20286, PRIVATE, Killed in action, France & Flanders, 15/11/16, Gloucestershire Regiment, 1/5th Battalion (Territorial).

COX, Harry, b. Aldershot, Hants, e. Aldershot, 200214, PRIVATE, Killed in action, Mesopotamia, 23/02/17, Hampshire Regiment, 1/4th (T.F.) Battalion.

COX, John Frederick, b. Aldershot, e. Finsbury, Middx. , r. Aldershot, 4471, L/CPL, Killed in action, Gallipoli, 16/08/15, FORMERLY 12738, WILTS REGT., Royal Munster Fusiliers, 6th Battalion.

Sort Order : Surname, Christian Name(s)

SURNAME,Christian Name(s),Born,Enlisted,Residence,Number,RANK,Cause,Place,Date of Death,ADDITIONAL TEXT,Regiment,Battalion

COX, Joseph, b. Aldershot, Hants, e. Aldershot , r. Frimley, Hants, 9240, PRIVATE, Killed in action, Mesopotamia, 31/12/16, Dorsetshire Regiment, 2nd Battalion.

CRAFT, Edward George, b. Aldershot, Hants, e. Norwich , r. Walsoken, Norfolk, 40229, PRIVATE, Killed in action, France & Flanders, 28/03/18, FORMERLY 5235, NORFOLK REGT., Bedfordshire Regiment, 2nd Battalion.

CRAWSHAW, John Andrew, b. Aldershot, Hants, e. Wandsworth , r. Southfields, 4581, PRIVATE, Died of wounds, Egypt, 08/12/17, Household Cavalry and Cavalry of the Line (incl. Yeomanry and Imperial Camel Corps), City of London Yeomanry.

CREED, Frederick, b. Aldershot, Hants, e. Winchester, 19524, PRIVATE, Killed in action, France & Flanders, 21/11/17, Hampshire Regiment, 2nd Battalion.

CROWSON, Walter, b. Aldershot, Hants, e. Bolton, 16447, PRIVATE, Killed in action, France & Flanders, 15/11/16, Loyal North Lancashire Regiment, 10th Battalion.

CRUMPLIN, William James, b. Aldershot, Hants, e. Hounslow , r. Harlesden, 6557, L/CPL, Killed in action, France & Flanders, 28/09/15, Royal Fusiliers (City of London Regiment), 12th Battalion.

CULLEN, James Ernest, b. Aldershot, Hants, e. London, 4707, PRIVATE, Killed in action, France & Flanders, 30/09/16, East Surrey Regiment, 8th Battalion.

CURRAN, William Michael, b. Aldershot, e. Colchester, 8498, A/CPL., Killed in action, France & Flanders, 10/03/15, Devonshire Regiment, 2nd Battalion.

CUTHILL, William John, b. Aldershot, e. Liverpool, 14694, L/CPL, Killed in action, France & Flanders, 02/03/16, King's Own (Royal Lancaster Regiment), 8th Battalion.

DALLAS, Stanley, b. Aldershot, e. Aldershot , r. Aldershot, P/1975, A/SGT., Killed in action, France & Flanders, 23/03/18, Corps of Military Police, Foot Branch.

DALLY, George Thomas, b. Aldershot, e. Devizes, Wilts , r. Devizes, Wilts, 9236, L/SGT, Killed in action, France & Flanders, 02/07/16, Duke of Edinburgh's (Wiltshire Regiment), 6th Battalion.

DALY, Francis, b. Aldershot, Hants, e. Belfast, Co. Antrim, S/21893, PRIVATE, Died, Italy, 03/11/18, FORMERLY 1808, LEINSTER REGT., Seaforth Highlanders (Ross-shire Buffs, the Duke of Albany's), 1st Garrison Battalion.

DANCE, Frederick Richard, b. Aldershot, e. Wimbledon , r. Leytonstone, M2/081393, A/M.S.S., Died, At Sea, 09/01/16, Royal Army Service Corps.

DARCH, Frederick, b. Aldershot, e. Reading, 21905, PRIVATE, Killed in action, France & Flanders, 14/09/16, Princess Charlotte of Wales's (Royal Berkshire Regiment), 2nd Battalion.

DAVIES, James, b. Aldershot, e. Sunderland, 8861, COL./SGT., Died of wounds, France & Flanders, 23/03/18, Durham Light Infantry, 1/6th Battalion.

DAVIS, Albert, b. Aldershot, Hants, e. Winchester , r. Aldershot, Hants, 27062, PRIVATE, Killed in action, France & Flanders, 20/04/17, Hampshire Regiment, 15th (Service) Battalion.

DAVIS, Henry Ernest, b. Aldershot, e. Llanelly, 60708, PRIVATE, Killed in action, France & Flanders, 08/10/18, Welsh Regiment, 14th Battalion.

DAVIS, John Benjamin, b. Aldershot, Hants, e. Woolwich, London , r. Plumstead, Kent, 25871, PRIVATE, Killed in action, France & Flanders, 20/09/17, Hampshire Regiment, 15th (Service) Battalion.

DAVIS, Thomas William, b. Aldershot, Hants, e. Woolwich, S.E., 95485, DVR., Killed in action, France & Flanders, 08/11/16, Royal Horse Artillery and Royal Field Artillery.

DAVIS, Walter John, b. Aldershot, Hants, e. Southampton , r. Shirley, Hants, 3/4465, SERGT., Died of wounds, Home, 26/08/15, Hampshire Regiment, 10th Battalion.

DELANEY, Charles, b. Aldershot, Hants, e. Aldershot, 10312, PRIVATE, Killed in action, France & Flanders, 26/08/14, Royal Inniskilling Fusiliers, 2nd Battalion.

DENNIS, Percy, b. Aldershot, e. Croydon, Surrey, 3934, PRIVATE, Killed in action, France & Flanders, 31/12/17, Northumberland Fusiliers, 1/7th Battalion (Territorials).

DENNY, William John Edward, b. Aldershot, e. Armoury House , r. Highbury, 10739, PRIVATE, Killed in action, France & Flanders, 09/10/17, Honourable Artillery Company, (Infantry).

DIAPER, John William, b. Aldershot, Hants, e. Bath, 52105, PRIVATE, Killed in action, France & Flanders, 13/04/18, FORMERLY T/254904, R.A.S.C., Suffolk Regiment, 2nd Battalion.

Sort Order : Surname, Christian Name(s)

SURNAME,Christian Name(s),Born,Enlisted,Residence,Number,RANK,Cause,Place,Date of Death,ADDITIONAL TEXT,Regiment,Battalion

DICKINSON, Alwyn, b. Aldershot, e. Guildford, Surrey, 3448, BGLR, Died of wounds, France & Flanders, 23/01/15, King's Royal Rifle Corps, 4th Battalion.

DODD, Archie, b. Aldershot, e. Aldershot, 10087, PRIVATE, Died, France & Flanders, 05/09/18, Worcestershire Regiment, 2nd Battalion.

DOLBY, Frank, b. Aldershot, Hants, e. Reading, 52487, GUNNER, Died of wounds, France & Flanders, 20/05/16, Royal Horse Artillery and Royal Field Artillery.

DONALDSON, Alexander, b. Aldershot, Hants, e. Edinburgh , r. Leith, 3638, PRIVATE, Killed in action, France & Flanders, 10/03/15, Royal Scots (Lothian Regiment), 1st Battalion.

DONOVAN, Cornelius, b. Aldershot, e. Dublin, 10903, SERGT., Killed in action, Gallipoli, 16/08/15, Royal Dublin Fusiliers, 7th Battalion.

DOWALL, William, b. Aldershot, Hants, e. Govan, Lanark , r. Govan, Lanark, 14525, PRIVATE, Died of wounds, France & Flanders, 28/08/16, King's Own Scottish Borderers, 7/8th Battalion.

DRENNEN, John Henry, b. Aldershot, e. Houghton-le-Spring, Durham , r. Bebside, Northumberland, 16192, PRIVATE, Killed in action, France & Flanders, 27/09/15, Prince of Wales's Own (West Yorkshire Regiment), 12th Battalion.

DRUMMOND, William George, b. Aldershot, Hants, e. Kingston-on-Thames, Surrey , r. Tooting, Surrey, 801, PRIVATE, Died of wounds, France & Flanders, 23/10/15, East Surrey Regiment, 7th Battalion.

DUNLOP, Francis Gerlad, b. Aldershot, Hants, e. London , r. Hampstead, N.W., 5808, BANDSMAN, Died of wounds, France & Flanders, 22/10/14, Household Cavalry and Cavalry of the Line (incl. Yeomanry and Imperial Camel Corps), 2nd Dragoons (Scots Greys).

DUNN, Edward, b. Aldershot, Hants, e. Aldershot, Hants, 25038, L/CPL, Killed in action, France & Flanders, 11/04/17, Hampshire Regiment, 1st Battalion.

DUNN, George, b. Aldershot, Hants, e. Winchester , r. Aldershot, Hants, 3/4122, PRIVATE, Killed in action, Gallipoli, 06/08/15, Hampshire Regiment, 2nd Battalion.

DUNNE, Albert, b. Aldershot, e. Howth, Co. Dublin , r. Dublin, 23117, L/CPL, Died of wounds, France & Flanders, 16/03/17, Royal Dublin Fusiliers, 2nd Battalion.

DURRANT, Frederick Arthur, b. Aldershot, Hants, e. Woolwich, S.E., 57430, GUNNER, Killed in action, France & Flanders, 29/09/18, Royal Horse Artillery and Royal Field Artillery.

DYMES, Arthur Stanley, b. Aldershot, Hants, e. London , r. Alperton, Midlesex, P.S.1560, L/CPL, Killed in action, France & Flanders, 19/04/17, Duke of Cambridge's Own (Middlesex Regiment), 16th Battalion.

EARL, Weldon, b. Aldershot, Hants, e. Camberley, Surrey , r. Farnham, Surrey, 32361, PRIVATE, Died of wounds, France & Flanders, 29/01/18, Prince of Wales's Volunteers (South Lancashire Regiment), 2/5th Battalion.

EDMUNDS, Arthur, b. Aldershot, e. Marylebone, London , r. Hertford, 9571, PRIVATE, Died of wounds, Mesopotamia, 12/05/16, Duke of Edinburgh's (Wiltshire Regiment), 5th Battalion.

EDWARDS, Frederick James, b. Aldershot, Hants, e. Aldershot, Hants , r. Alresford, Hants, 10031, PRIVATE, Killed in action, France & Flanders, 20/10/16, Hampshire Regiment, 2nd Battalion.

ELFLETT, Andrews, b. Aldershot, Hants, e. Aldershot, Hants, 8877, L/CPL, Killed in action, France & Flanders, 02/10/18, Hampshire Regiment, 15th (Service) Battalion.

ELFLETT, Edward Kitchen, b. Aldershot, Hants, e. Gosport , r. Aldershot, Hants, 8900, C.S.M., Killed in action, Balkans, 25/04/17, Hampshire Regiment, 12th (Service) Battalion.

ELPHICK, Frank, b. Aldershot, Hants, e. Leeds, 265296, PRIVATE, Died, France & Flanders, 08/11/18, Prince of Wales's Own (West Yorkshire Regiment), 1/8th Battalion.

EWIN, William John, b. Aldershot, Hants, e. Norwich, Norfolk, 4507, C.S.M., Killed in action, Mesopotamia, 14/04/15, Norfolk Regiment, 2nd Battalion.

EYNON, John Richard, b. Aldershot, Hants, e. Warley, Essex, 10660, B.S.M., Died of wounds, France & Flanders, 24/07/16, Royal Horse Artillery and Royal Field Artillery.

FAITHFUL, Percy Reginald, b. Aldershot, e. Aldershot , r. Alton, 267050, CPL., Killed in action, France & Flanders, 28/08/17, Gloucestershire Regiment, 2/6th Battalion (Territorials).

FEATHERSTONE, Edward George, b. Aldershot, Hants, e. London , r. Lonndon, F/1153, PRIVATE, Died of wounds, France & Flanders, 23/06/16, Duke of Cambridge's Own (Middlesex Regiment), 23rd Battalion.

Sort Order : Surname, Christian Name(s)

SURNAME,Christian Name(s),Born,Enlisted,Residence,Number,RANK,Cause,Place,Date of Death,ADDITIONAL TEXT,Regiment,Battalion

FINCH, Arthur, b. Aldershot, e. Aldershot, 31478, PRIVATE, Killed in action, France & Flanders, 26/09/17, Hampshire Regiment, 14th (Service) Battalion.

FINCHER, Frank Walter, b. Aldershot, Hants, e. Stratford-on-Avon, Warwicks , r. Shottery, Stratford-on-Avon, 203600, L/CPL, Killed in action, France & Flanders, 10/10/17, Royal Warwickshire Regiment, 2nd Battalion.

FISHER, George, b. Aldershot, e. Aldershot, 267049, L/CPL, Killed in action, France & Flanders, 19/08/17, Gloucestershire Regiment, 2/6th Battalion (Territorials).

FISHER, Harry Albert, b. Aldershot, e. Guildford, G/4683, PRIVATE, Killed in action, British Expeditionary Force, 30/07/16, Royal Sussex Regiment, 9th Battalion.

FLEET, Arthur James, b. Aldershot, e. Chichester, L/9077, PRIVATE, Died, British Expeditionary Force, 07/11/14, Royal Sussex Regiment, 2nd Battalion.

FOOTE, Randolph, b. Aldershot, Hants, e. Guildford, Surrey , r. Aldershot, L/9370, PRIVATE, Killed in action, France & Flanders, 19/10/14, Queen's (Royal West Surrey Regiment), 2nd Battalion.

FOSTER, Arthur William, b. Aldershot, e. Longmore Camp, 10729, DRUMMER, Killed in action, France & Flanders, 31/10/14, D.C.M., South Wales Borderers, 1st Battalion.

FOSTER, Percy Victor, b. Aldershot, Hants, e. Chatham, Kent , r. Gillingham, Kent, 22339, SPR., Killed in action, France & Flanders, 02/09/16, (59TH FIELD COY., R.E.)., Corps of Royal Engineers.

FOXON, Alfred George, b. Aldershot, Hants, e. Winchester , r. Aldershot, Hants, 7720, PRIVATE, Died of wounds, France & Flanders, 26/07/16, Hampshire Regiment, 2nd Battalion.

FOY, Henry, b. Aldershot, e. Guildford, Surrey, 1769, PRIVATE, Died, France & Flanders, 24/04/15, Northumberland Fusiliers, 2nd Battalion.

FRANKLIN, Albert, b. Aldershot, e. Aldershot , r. Aldershot, 1919, RIFLEMAN, Died, France & Flanders, 03/04/15, Rifle Brigade (The Prince Consort's Own), 1st Battalion.

FRANKS, John, b. Aldershot, Hamps, e. Guildford, Surrey , r. Ash Vale, Surrey, L/9783, L/CPL, Died of wounds, France & Flanders, 25/10/14, Queen's (Royal West Surrey Regiment), 1st Battalion.

FREE, Charles Alpha, b. Aldershot, Hants, e. Stratford, Essex , r. Poplar, Middx., 11216, PRIVATE, Died of wounds, France & Flanders, 10/07/15, FORMERLY 11623, HUSSARS., Royal Irish Regiment, 1st Battalion.

FREESTON, Walter, b. Aldershot, e. Belfast , r. Exeter, 5549, PRIVATE, Killed in action, France & Flanders, 19/09/16, FORMERLY 68516, R.A.M.C., London Regiment, 23rd (County of London) Battalion.

FRENCH, William Patrick, b. Aldershot, e. Dublin , r. Hounslow, 4558, PRIVATE, Killed in action, France & Flanders, 20/05/17, Household Cavalry and Cavalry of the Line (incl. Yeomanry and Imperial Camel Corps), 19th (Queen Alexandra's Own Royal) Hussars.

GALE, George, b. Aldershot, e. London , r. Lambeth, 452661, RIFLEMAN, Killed in action, France & Flanders, 25/08/18, London Regiment, 11th (County of London) Battalion (Finsbury Rifles).

GALLAGHER, Patrick Wilfred, b. Aldershot, Hants, e. Dublin, 9617, A/R.S.M., Died of wounds, France & Flanders, 06/05/17, Royal Garrison Artillery.

GALLIVAN, John Joseph Patrick, b. Aldershot, Hants, e. Newport, Mon., 7592, CPL., Died, At Sea, 10/10/18, FORMERLY 27146, R. DUB. FUS., Royal Irish Regiment, 4th Battalion.

GARDNER, William George Sylvester, b. Aldershot, e. Aldershot , r. Liphook, Hants, 9194, PRIVATE, Died of wounds, France & Flanders, 26/11/14, Devonshire Regiment, 1st Battalion.

GARNETT, John Edward, b. Aldershot, e. Aldershot, 12646, L/SGT, Killed in action, France & Flanders, 26/09/16, Grenadier Guards, 2nd Battalion

GARVEY, Patrick, b. Aldershot, e. Chichester, 27802, PRIVATE, Died of wounds, France & Flanders, 02/10/18, FORMERLY 22248, T.R. BATTN., King's (Shropshire Light Infantry), 7th Battalion.

GATES, George Charles, b. Aldershot, Hants, e. Camberley, Surrey , r. Bagshot Lea, Surrey, L/11065, PRIVATE, Killed in action, France & Flanders, 15/07/16, Queen's (Royal West Surrey Regiment), 1st Battalion.

GDANITZ, Francis Obree, b. Aldershot, Hants, e. London , r. Aldersgate Street, Middlesex, G/35346, PRIVATE, Died, Home, 02/01/17, Duke of Cambridge's Own (Middlesex Regiment), 30th Battalion.

GIBBONS, Albert John, b. Aldershot, Hants, e. Belfast, 42854, PRIVATE, Killed in action, France & Flanders, 22/08/18, Royal Inniskilling Fusiliers, 1st Battalion.

Sort Order : Surname, Christian Name(s)

SURNAME,Christian Name(s),Born,Enlisted,Residence,Number,RANK,Cause,Place,Date of Death,ADDITIONAL TEXT,Regiment,Battalion

GIBBS, Edward William, b. Aldershot, Hants, e. Lambeth, Surrey , r. Kennington, Surrey, S/16766, RIFLEMAN, Killed in action, France & Flanders, 05/03/18, Rifle Brigade (The Prince Consort's Own), 13th Battalion.

GILDING, Edward Guelph, b. Aldershot, Hants, e. Aldershot, 8456, SERGT., Killed in action, France & Flanders, 31/07/17, Northamptonshire Regiment, 2nd Battalion.

GILHAM, Henry James, b. Aldershot, Hants, e. Westminster, Middx. , r. Earlsfield, Surrey, 15374, C.Q.M.S., Died of wounds, France & Flanders, 17/08/17, Bedfordshire Regiment, 7th Battalion.

GILL, Alfred Charles, b. Aldershot, e. Aldershot , r. Eastleigh, Hants, M/27685, A/CPL., Died, France & Flanders, 20/02/16, Royal Army Service Corps.

GILLESPIE, George, b. Aldershot, Hants, e. Manchester , r. Peel Green, Manchester, 11905, PRIVATE, Killed in action, France & Flanders, 01/07/16, Border Regiment, 1st Battalion.

GLEDHILL, Henry, b. Aldershot, Hants, e. Winchester , r. Aldershot, Hants, 8396, SERGT., Killed in action, France & Flanders, 01/07/16, Hampshire Regiment, 1st Battalion.

GLEESON, Thomas, b. Aldershot, Hants, e. London , r. Aldershot, 37375, PRIVATE, Died of wounds, France & Flanders, 10/11/17, Manchester Regiment, 12th Battalion.

GODDARD, Harry, b. Aldershot, Hants, e. Aldershot, Hants, 8671, CPL., Killed in action, France & Flanders, 26/08/14, Hampshire Regiment, 1st Battalion.

GODDARD, Percy William, b. Aldershot, e. Norwich, G/5404, PRIVATE, Killed in action, British Expeditionary Force, 07/07/16, Royal Sussex Regiment, 7th Battalion.

GORMAN, Charles, b. Aldershot, e. Dublin, 9631, PRIVATE, Killed in action, France & Flanders, 08/07/16, Alexandra, Princess of Wales's Own (Yorkshire Regiment), 2nd Battalion.

GORMAN, Frederick Thomas, b. Aldershot, Hants, e. Naas, Co. Kildare , r. Wicklow, 17542, PRIVATE, Died, At Sea, 13/08/15, Hampshire Regiment, 2nd Battalion.

GORMAN, Thomas, b. Aldershot, e. Aldershot , r. Alton, 8835, SERGT., Killed in action, France & Flanders, 02/04/17, Alexandra, Princess of Wales's Own (Yorkshire Regiment), 2nd Battalion.

GOSS, Thomas Edward, b. Aldershot, Hants, e. Winchester , r. Aldershot, Hants, 21539, PRIVATE, Killed in action, France & Flanders, 07/06/17, Hampshire Regiment, 15th (Service) Battalion.

GOULD, George William, b. Aldershot, Hants, e. Chatham, Kent, 22554, DVR., Died, Italy, 01/11/18, (54TH FIELD COY., R.E.), Corps of Royal Engineers.

GOULD, William, b. Aldershot, Hants, e. Brighton, Sussex, 21177, L/CPL., Killed in action, France & Flanders, 23/08/18, FORMERLY 5005, ROYAL SUSSEX REGIMENT., Hampshire Regiment, 2nd Battalion.

GOVIER, Harry John, b. Aldershot, e. London , r. Finsbury, Middx., 6/473, RIFLEMAN, Died of wounds, France & Flanders, 17/04/17, Rifle Brigade (The Prince Consort's Own), 3rd Battalion.

GOWER, Vivian, b. Aldershot, e. Manchester , r. Longsight, Manchester, 34137, PRIVATE, Killed in action, France & Flanders, 22/08/18, FORMERLY 2/10892, BORDER REGT., King's (Shropshire Light Infantry), 10th Battalion.

GRAHAM, John, b. Aldershot, Hants, e. Athlone, Co. Westmeath , r. Wavertree, Lancs, 6482, PRIVATE, Died of wounds, France & Flanders, 04/09/16, Connaught Rangers, 6th Battalion.

GRAHAM, Ronald Leonard, b. Aldershot, e. Aldershot , r. Potterslane, Surrey, 10698, PRIVATE, Killed in action, Gallipoli, 30/04/15, Royal Dublin Fusiliers, 1st Battalion.

GRAY, George Benjamin, b. Aldershot, e. Woolwich , r. Chiswick, 19898, PRIVATE, Killed in action, France & Flanders, 10/10/16, Royal Fusiliers (City of London Regiment), 26th Battalion.

GRAY, William Andrew, b. Aldershot, Hants, e. South Farnborough, Hants , r. South Farnborough, Hants, L/11783, PRIVATE, Killed in action, France & Flanders, 22/08/18, FORMERLY 67699, R.F.C., Queen's (Royal West Surrey Regiment), 1/24th Battalion.

GREEN, John, b. Aldershot, Hants, e. Aldershot, 19844, A/Q.M.S., Died, France & Flanders, 10/05/17, Royal Army Medical Corps.

GREEN, Joseph, b. Aldershot, Hants, e. Guildford, Surrey , r. Shorncliffe, Kent, L/8270, PRIVATE, Killed in action, France & Flanders, 24/08/16, Queen's (Royal West Surrey Regiment), 1st Battalion.

GREENWOOD, Robert William Brecknell, b. Aldershot, Hants, e. Rotherham, 15378, PRIVATE, Killed in action, France & Flanders, 25/07/18, York and Lancaster Regiment, 6th (Service) Battalion.

Sort Order : Surname, Christian Name(s)

SURNAME,Christian Name(s),Born,Enlisted,Residence,Number,RANK,Cause,Place,Date of Death,ADDITIONAL TEXT,Regiment,Battalion

GREGORY, Frederick Gent, b. Aldershot, Hants, e. Londonderry , r. Aldershot, Hants, 40538, SPR., Killed in action, France & Flanders, 19/07/15, (62ND FIELD COY., R.E.)., Corps of Royal Engineers.

GREGORY, William Alexander, b. Aldershot, Hants, e. Aldershot, Hants, 7535, SPR , Died, France & Flanders, 15/10/18, (350TH E. & M. COY., R.E.)., Corps of Royal Engineers.

GRIFFIN, William, b. Aldershot, e. Hounslow , r. Watford, L/13838, CPL., Killed in action, France & Flanders, 10/09/14, Royal Fusiliers (City of London Regiment), 4th Battalion.

GRIFFITHS, Basil Gwynne, b. Aldershot, Hants, e. Brecon, 41567, SERGT., Killed in action, France & Flanders, 04/11/14, Royal Horse Artillery and Royal Field Artillery.

GRIGG, Joseph, b. Aldershot, Hants, e. Edinburgh, 201509, PRIVATE, Killed in action, France & Flanders, 22/08/17, Royal Scots (Lothian Regiment), 13th Battalion.

GRIZZELL, Richard, b. Aldershot, e. Woolwich , r. Lewisham, 911, PRIVATE, Killed in action, France & Flanders, 25/06/17, Household Cavalry and Cavalry of the Line (incl. Yeomanry and Imperial Camel Corps), 1st Dragoons (Royals).

HALEY, John Severan, b. Aldershot, e. Mill Hill, Middx., 64055, PRIVATE, Died, Home, 03/12/18, Suffolk Regiment, 1st Reserve Garrison Battalion.

HALL, Alfred William, b. Aldershot, Hants, e. Aldershot, Han Ts, 331266, RIFLEMAN, Killed in action, Palestine, 19/04/17, Hampshire Regiment, 1/8th (T.F.) Battalion.

HALL, Arthur, b. Aldershot, e. Hull, 12/747, PRIVATE, Died, Home, 05/02/15, East Yorkshire Regiment, 12th Battalion.

HALL, John, b. Aldershot, e. Bodmin, 301055, GUNNER, Died, Balkans, 25/02/17, Royal Garrison Artillery, 4th Highland (Mountain) Brigade. [RGA - (TF)]

HAMILTON, Douglas S., b. Aldershot, Hants, e. Edinburgh , r. Edinburgh, 59414, L/CPL, Killed in action, France & Flanders, 25/04/18, FORMERLY 2/9982, T.R. BATTN., 56977, H.L.I., Royal Scots (Lothian Regiment), 11th Battalion.

HAMMOND, Arthur Dudley, b. Aldershot, Hants, e. Portsmouth, Hants , r. Southsea, Hants, 18776, PRIVATE, Killed in action, France & Flanders, 13/04/18, FORMERLY 24476, SOM. L.I., Royal Warwickshire Regiment, 14th Battalion.

HAMMOND, Thomas Jacob, b. Aldershot, e. Salford, Lancs, 32328, PRIVATE, Killed in action, France & Flanders, 03/10/17, Border Regiment, 2nd Battalion.

HANDFORD, Frederick John, b. Aldershot, Surrey, e. Cardiff , r. Aldershot, 48912, PRIVATE, Killed in action, France & Flanders, 07/11/18, FORMERLY 9912, WELSH REGIMENT., Royal Inniskilling Fusiliers, 6th Battalion.

HANKINS, James, b. Aldershot, e. Reading , r. Aldershot, 20059, PRIVATE, Killed in action, France & Flanders, 12/10/17, Princess Charlotte of Wales's (Royal Berkshire Regiment), 6th Battalion.

HANLON, James, b. Aldershot, Hants, e. Guildford, Surrey , r. Reading, Berks, G/21, PRIVATE, Killed in action, France & Flanders, 15/07/16, Queen's (Royal West Surrey Regiment), 1st Battalion.

HARDING, Edwin John, b. Aldershot, e. Preston , r. Southsea, 5345, CSM., Killed in action, France & Flanders, 02/11/14, Connaught Rangers, 1st Battalion.

HARDING, Ferdinando Welch Smithers, b. Aldershot, e. Lambeth , r. Upper Norwood, 514713, PRIVATE, Died of wounds, France & Flanders, 17/08/17, London Regiment, 14th (County of London) Battalion (London Scottish).

HARDY, Cyril Victor, b. Aldershot, Hants, e. Southampton , r. Dartford, Kent, 241335, SERGT., Killed in action, Egypt, 19/09/18, Hampshire Regiment, 2/5th (T.F.) Battalion.

HARPER, William Francis, b. Aldershot, e. Oxford , r. Reading, 21011, PRIVATE, Died of wounds, France & Flanders, 02/08/17, Princess Charlotte of Wales's (Royal Berkshire Regiment), 6th Battalion.

HARRINGTON, Robert George, b. Aldershot, e. Guildford , r. Camberley, 5074, PRIVATE, Died of wounds, Home, 10/11/14, Household Cavalry and Cavalry of the Line (incl. Yeomanry and Imperial Camel Corps), 2nd Dragoon Guards (Queen's Bays).

HARRIS, Albert Edward, b. Aldershot, Hants, e. Halifax, Yorks , r. Brighouse, Yorks, 191962, PIONEER, Died, At Sea, 04/05/17, (R.E. SIGNALS)., Corps of Royal Engineers.

HART, Albert, b. Aldershot, e. Aldershot , r. Ash Vale, Surrey, 19834, CPL., Killed in action, Mesopotamia, 09/03/17, FORMERLY 10971, WORCS REGT. (72ND FIELD COY., R.E.)., Corps of Royal Engineers.

HASSALL, Joseph William, b. Aldershot, Hants, e. Lydd , r. Chatham, 10621, L/CPL, Died of wounds, Gallipoli, 29/06/15, South Wales Borderers, 2nd Battalion.

Sort Order : Surname, Christian Name(s)

SURNAME,Christian Name(s),Born,Enlisted,Residence,Number,RANK,Cause,Place,Date of Death,ADDITIONAL TEXT,Regiment,Battalion

HAVERON, Thomas, b. Aldershot, e. Newcastle, r. Newcastle, 9936, SERGT., Died, France & Flanders, 10/11/18, Rifle Brigade (The Prince Consort's Own), 1st Battalion.

HAYDON, Thomas, b. Aldershot, Hants, e. Devonport, 25882, PRIVATE, Died, Home, 16/06/17, Royal Army Medical Corps.

HAYES, Joseph, b. Aldershot, Hampshire, e. Edinburgh, S/9675, CPL., Killed in action, France & Flanders, 03/09/16, Black Watch (Royal Highlanders), 1st Battalion.

HAYWOOD, William George, b. Aldershot, Hants, e. Woldingham, Surrey, r. Croydon, Surrey, P.S.2479, PRIVATE, Died of wounds, France & Flanders, 03/08/16, Duke of Cambridge's Own (Middlesex Regiment), 16th Battalion.

HEALEY, William, b. Aldershot, e. Bury, Lancs, r. Manchester, 1581, PRIVATE, Killed in action, Gallipoli, 04/06/15, Lancashire Fusiliers, 1st Battalion

HEATH, Ernest Alfred, b. Aldershot, Hants, e. Southampton, Hants, r. Salisbury, Wilts, L/9093, PRIVATE, Died of wounds, France & Flanders, 26/09/14, FORMERLY 7718, DORSET REGT., Queen's (Royal West Surrey Regiment), 1st Battalion.

HEATH, William James Henry, b. Aldershot, Hants, e. Aldershot, Hants, 14681, SPR., Killed in action, France & Flanders, 05/03/17, (15TH FIELD COY., R.E.)., Corps of Royal Engineers.

HERRINGTON, Walter George, b. Aldershot, e. Leamington, r. Farnham, Surrey, T4/071729, DVR., Died, Mesopotamia, 14/07/17, Royal Army Service Corps.

HEWITT, Daniel Matthew, b. Aldershot, e. Berkhampstead, r. Watford, Herts, 5684, L/SGT, Killed in action, France & Flanders, 20/10/14, Household Cavalry and Cavalry of the Line (incl. Yeomanry and Imperial Camel Corps), 1st Dragoons (Royals).

HILL, Lawrence Carmon, b. Aldershot, e. Dover, 8189, DRUMMER, Killed in action, France & Flanders, 26/08/14, Suffolk Regiment, 2nd Battalion.

HILL, Percy, b. Aldershot, e. Birmingham, 11840, PRIVATE, Died, At Sea, 13/08/15, FORMERLY 12850, DUKE OF CORNWALL'S LIGHT INFANTRY., Hampshire Regiment, 2nd Battalion.

HINDRY, Herbert, b. Aldershot, e. Bury St. Edmunds, 2099, CPL., Died of wounds, Gallipoli, 21/08/15, Suffolk Regiment, 5th Battalion.

HOBBS, William, b. Aldershot, e. Guildford, Surrey, r. Lee, Kent, 9690, PRIVATE, Killed in action, France & Flanders, 09/05/15, FORMERLY 9123, R.W. SURREY REGT., Lincolnshire Regiment, 2nd Battalion.

HOLDEN, Archie, b. Aldershot, Hants, e. Tooting, Surrey, 38249, PRIVATE, Killed in action, France & Flanders, 03/04/18, FORMERLY 30272, EAST SURREY REGT., Lancashire Fusiliers, 16th Battalion.

HOLLANDS, Charles Stephen, b. Aldershot, Hants, e. Canterbury, Kent, r. Cookham Rise, Berks, L/9041, SERGT., Killed in action, France & Flanders, 28/09/15, Buffs (East Kent Regiment), 2nd Battalion.

HOLLEY, Frederick Henry, b. Aldershot, e. Birmingham, 28405, SPR., Killed in action, France & Flanders, 16/09/16, (6TH SIGNAL COY., R.E.)., Corps of Royal Engineers.

HOOK, Allan Charles, b. Aldershot, Hants, e. Winchester, r. Aldershot, Hants, 19148, PRIVATE, Killed in action, France & Flanders, 01/07/16, Hampshire Regiment, 1st Battalion.

HOOKER, Walter, b. Aldershot, Hampshire, e. Doncaster, Yorks, r. Uxbridge, Middx., 10013, PRIVATE, Died, France & Flanders, 14/09/14, Coldstream Guards.

HOPPITT, Charles, b. Aldershot, Hants, e. Aldershot, 23106, PRIVATE, Killed in action, France & Flanders, 23/10/16, Hampshire Regiment, 1st Battalion.

HORTON, Reginald Charles, b. Aldershot, e. Chatham, Kent, r. Luddesdowns, Kent, S/5436, RIFLEMAN, Died, France & Flanders, 26/12/15, Rifle Brigade (The Prince Consort's Own), 10th Battalion.

HOSKINS, George Charles, b. Aldershot, Hants, e. Guildford, Surrey, r. Tottenham Court Road, L/5367, L/CPL., Killed in action, France & Flanders, 23/10/14, Queen's (Royal West Surrey Regiment), 1st Battalion.

HOSKINS, Reginald, b. Aldershot, e. Gloucester, r. Axminster, Devon, 19924, PRIVATE, Killed in action, Gallipoli, 30/11/15, FORMERLY 58467, ROYAL FIELD ARTILLERY., Duke of Edinburgh's (Wiltshire Regiment), 5th Battalion.

HOWCUTT, William Henry, b. Aldershot, e. Devizes, Wilts, r. Pewsey, Wilts, 27766, PRIVATE, Killed in action, France & Flanders, 04/10/17, Prince Albert's (Somerset Light Infantry), 8th Battalion.

Sort Order : Surname, Christian Name(s)

SURNAME,Christian Name(s),Born,Enlisted,Residence,Number,RANK,Cause,Place,Date of Death,ADDITIONAL TEXT,Regiment,Battalion

HOWELL, William, b. Aldershot, e. Marylebone , r. Aldershot, L/16620, PRIVATE, Killed in action, France & Flanders, 24/04/17, Royal Fusiliers (City of London Regiment), 2nd Battalion.

HOYLE, Henry Lewis, b. Aldershot, Hants, e. Beverley , r. Gilberdyke, 38151, PRIVATE, Killed in action, France & Flanders, 07/09/18, East Yorkshire Regiment, 10th Battalion.

HUGGINS, Clement George, b. Aldershot, Hants, e. Norwich, Norfolk, 7026, PRIVATE, Killed in action, France & Flanders, 01/07/15, Norfolk Regiment, 1st Battalion.

HUGHES, Bertie, b. Aldershot, Hants, e. Sunderland , r. Durham, 25365, PRIVATE, Died, France & Flanders, 07/07/16, Royal Inniskilling Fusiliers, 2nd Battalion.

HUGHES, Thomas, b. Aldershot, e. Middlesbrough, 5948, PRIVATE, Killed in action, France & Flanders, 15/05/15, Alexandra, Princess of Wales's Own (Yorkshire Regiment), 2nd Battalion.

HUME, Henry, b. Aldershot, e. Newcastle , r. Gateshead, 3/10357, C/SGT., Died, Home, 03/09/16, Durham Light Infantry, Depot.

HUNT, Frederick Arthur, b. Aldershot, Hants, e. Aldershot , r. Aldershot, 1235, CPL., Killed in action, India, 15/07/15, Household Cavalry and Cavalry of the Line (incl. Yeomanry and Imperial Camel Corps), 21st Lancers (Empress of India's).

HUNT, Thomas Hankins, b. Aldershot, Hants, e. Secunderabad, India, 68462, A/BDR., Died, Home, 02/03/15, Royal Horse Artillery and Royal Field Artillery.

HUNTER, Arthur Edward, b. Aldershot, e. Sheffield, 61164, PRIVATE, Died, Home, 26/05/17, FORMERLY 25491, K.O.Y.L.I., Durham Light Infantry, 1st Battalion.

HUNWICK, Charles William, b. Aldershot, Hants, e. Colchester, Essex, 41899, GUNNER, Died, Egypt, 19/08/16, Royal Horse Artillery and Royal Field Artillery.

HUTCHINGS, William Thomas, b. Aldershot, Hants, e. Farnham, Surrey , r. Ash Vale, Surrey, G/22544, A/SGT., Died of wounds, France & Flanders, 04/04/17, Queen's (Royal West Surrey Regiment), 6th Battalion.

HYDE, Frank Etheridge, b. Aldershot, Hants, e. Brighton, Sussex , r. Burgess Hill, Sussex, 205624, PRIVATE, Killed in action, France & Flanders, 11/08/18, FORMERLY 244, ROYAL ARMY MEDICAL CORPS., Dorsetshire Regiment, 1st Battalion.

HYNDS, Frederick, b. Aldershot, e. Shaftesbury St., N. , r. Pentonville, 280161, L/CPL, Died, France & Flanders, 25/07/18, London Regiment, 4th (City of London) Battalion (Royal Fusiliers).

JACKSON, Michael John, b. Aldershot, e. Aldershot, 26814, PRIVATE, Killed in action, France & Flanders, 26/10/17, Devonshire Regiment, 9th (Service) Battalion.

JAMES, James Philip Arthur, b. Aldershot, e. Brecon, 10266, A/SGT., Killed in action, France & Flanders, 27/12/14, South Wales Borderers, 1st Battalion.

JARRETT, William Albert, b. Aldershot, e. Kingston-on-Thames , r. Aldershot, G/80171, PRIVATE, Died of wounds, France & Flanders, 12/09/18, Royal Fusiliers (City of London Regiment), 23rd Battalion.

JARVIS, Henry, b. Aldershot, e. Kasauli, India , r. Dukinfield, Cheshire, 5333, PRIVATE, Died, Mesopotamia, 16/07/16, Manchester Regiment, 1st Battalion.

JOHNSON, Arthur, b. Aldershot, e. London, 24840, SPR., Killed in action, France & Flanders, 30/06/18, (70TH FIELD COY., R.E.)., Corps of Royal Engineers.

JOHNSTON, Henry Alexander, b. Aldershot, Hants, e. Dublin, 5638, PRIVATE, Killed in action, France & Flanders, 25/04/15, King's Own (Yorkshire Light Infantry), 1st Battalion.

JOLLIFFE, Charles Henry, b. Aldershot, Hants, e. Leeds, 510683, CPL., Died, Home, 21/05/18, FORMERLY 2615, W. YORKS REGT., Labour Corps.

JONES, Arthur, b. Aldershot, Hants, e. Preston, 10954, A/CPL., Died of wounds, France & Flanders, 02/01/15, Loyal North Lancashire Regiment, 1st Battalion.

JONES, Henry, b. Aldershot, Hants, e. Belfast, 12957, RIFLEMAN, Died of wounds, France & Flanders, 23/08/16, Royal Irish Rifles, 9th Battalion.

JONES, Percy John, b. Aldershot, e. St. Paul's Churchyard, London , r. New Southgate, Middx., 14536, CPL., Killed in action, France & Flanders, 16/09/16, Duke of Cornwall's Light Infantry, 6th Battalion.

Sort Order : Surname, Christian Name(s)

SURNAME,Christian Name(s),Born,Enlisted,Residence,Number,RANK,Cause,Place,Date of Death,ADDITIONAL TEXT,Regiment,Battalion

JONES, Reginald Philip, b. Aldershot, e. London , r. Atherstone, Warwicks, 48600, C.S.M., Died, Mesopotamia, 25/06/17, FORMERLY 7829, R. SUSSEX REGT., Welsh Regiment, 8th Battalion.

JONES, William Frederick, b. Aldershot, Hants, e. Guildford, Surrey , r. Ash Vale, Surrey, L/11083, PRIVATE, Killed in action, France & Flanders, 14/07/16, Queen's (Royal West Surrey Regiment), 6th Battalion.

JOSEPHSON, Edmund George, b. Aldershot, e. Aldershot, 32154, CPL., Died of wounds, Home, 03/03/19, Devonshire Regiment, 2nd Battalion.

KEAREY, Thomas Henry, b. Aldershot, e. Hartley Wintney , r. Aldershot, 17559, PRIVATE, Killed in action, France & Flanders, 09/08/16, Hampshire Regiment, 2nd Battalion.

KEELING, George Albert, b. Aldershot, e. Winchester , r. Walham Green, Middx., 6/1223, RIFLEMAN, Killed in action, France & Flanders, 13/07/16, King's Royal Rifle Corps, 8th Battalion.

KELLY, Thomas Henry, b. Aldershot, e. Cardiff , r. Streatham, Surrey, 12270, PRIVATE, Died of wounds, France & Flanders, 27/07/16, M.M., Welsh Regiment, 2nd Battalion.

KEMP, Charles Henry, b. Aldershot, e. Hammersmith , r. West Kensington, 592419, RIFLEMAN, Killed in action, France & Flanders, 11/09/17, London Regiment, 18th (County of London) Battalion (London Irish Rifles).

KENNEALLY, Jeremiah, b. Aldershot, e. Cork , r. Cork, 4781, PRIVATE, Killed in action, Gallipoli, 02/05/15, Royal Munster Fusiliers, 1st Battalion.

KERCHEY, Albert George, b. Aldershot, Hants, e. Ebbw Vale, Mon, 21175, PRIVATE, Killed in action, France & Flanders, 16/01/16, South Wales Borderers, 10th Battalion.

KERCHV, Charles, b. Aldershot, e. Park Royal , r. Ash Vale, Surrey, T/308904, DVR., Died, France & Flanders, 11/11/18, Royal Army Service Corps.

KERSHAW, Charles Edward, b. Aldershot, e. West Kirby, Ches., 1193, PRIVATE, Died of wounds, At Sea, 24/08/15, Cheshire Regiment, 1/4th Battalion.

KIMBER, William, b. Aldershot, Hants, e. Guildford, Surrey , r. Ash Vale, Surrey, G/7928, PRIVATE, Killed in action, France & Flanders, 05/04/18, Queen's (Royal West Surrey Regiment), 6th Battalion.

KINGCOTE, Walter, b. Aldershot, Hants, e. Manchester , r. Hulme, Lancs, 1719, RIFLEMAN, Killed in action, France & Flanders, 27/10/14, King's Royal Rifle Corps, 1st Battalion.

KIRCHER, Cecil, b. Aldershot, Hants, e. Guildford, Surrey , r. Cobham, Surrey, G/4045, PRIVATE, Killed in action, France & Flanders, 25/09/15, Queen's (Royal West Surrey Regiment), 8th Battalion.

KNIGHT, Albert, b. Aldershot, Hants, e. Dover , r. Aldershot, 29574, L/CPL, Killed in action, France & Flanders, 09/04/18, Princess Victoria's (Royal Irish Fusiliers), 1st Battalion.

KNIGHT, George William, b. Aldershot, Hants, e. Warwick , r. Stockton, Warwick, 11790, RFN. (L/CORP.), Killed in action, France & Flanders, 27/07/16, King's Royal Rifle Corps, 1st Battalion.

KNOWLES, Reginald, b. Aldershot, Hants, e. Stratford, E., Essex , r. Leytonstone, N.E., Essex, 41703, CPL., Killed in action, France & Flanders, 11/04/18, FORMERLY 26940, NORTHANTS REGT., Princess Victoria's (Royal Irish Fusiliers), 1st Battalion.

LAPPIN, John George, b. Aldershot, e. Cambridge, 7587, PRIVATE, Killed in action, France & Flanders, 20/07/16, Suffolk Regiment, 2nd Battalion.

LARKIN, John, b. Aldershot, Hants, e. Guildford, Surrey , r. Aldershot, L/6727, C.S.M., Killed in action, France & Flanders, 11/01/16, Queen's (Royal West Surrey Regiment), 1st Battalion.

LAVENDER, Alfred Patrick, b. Aldershot, e. Sheffield, 13955, PRIVATE, Killed in action, France & Flanders, 25/09/16, Prince of Wales's Own (West Yorkshire Regiment), 1st Battalion.

LAW, Arthur William, b. Aldershot, e. London , r. Southall, 11731, L/CPL, Killed in action, France & Flanders, 13/01/16, Household Cavalry and Cavalry of the Line (incl. Yeomanry and Imperial Camel Corps), Corps of Hussars. 3rd (King's Own) Hussars.

LEACH, William Albert, b. Aldershot, e. Bedford , r. Dunstable, 7995, SERGT., Killed in action, France & Flanders, 22/03/18, Bedfordshire Regiment, 2nd Battalion.

LEARY, Albert, b. Aldershot, Hants, e. Bermondsey, Surrey , r. Bermondsey, S/800, PRIVATE, Died of wounds, France & Flanders, 15/10/15, Queen's (Royal West Surrey Regiment), 6th Battalion.

Sort Order : Surname, Christian Name(s)

SURNAME,Christian Name(s),Born,Enlisted,Residence,Number,RANK,Cause,Place,Date of Death,ADDITIONAL TEXT,Regiment,Battalion

LEMON, Frederick, b. Aldershot, Hants, e. Winchester , r. Aldershot, Hants, 204804, PRIVATE, Killed in action, France & Flanders, 02/10/18, Hampshire Regiment, 15th (Service) Battalion.

LEMON, Henry, b. Aldershot, Hants, e. Winchester , r. Aldershot, Hants, 26903, PRIVATE, Killed in action, France & Flanders, 20/09/17, Hampshire Regiment, 15th (Service) Battalion.

LESLIE, Archibald, b. Aldershot, e. Burslem, Staffs , r. Hanley, Staffs, 8763, PRIVATE, Killed in action, Mesopotamia, 09/04/16, Prince of Wales's (North Staffordshire Regiment), 7th Battalion.

LEVICK, George Thomas, b. Aldershot, e. Sheffield, 52507, PRIVATE, Killed in action, France & Flanders, 29/09/18, King's Own (Yorkshire Light Infantry), 2nd Battalion.

LIEBRECHT, Thomas Frederick, b. Aldershot, e. Dublin , r. Dublin, 6877, PRIVATE, Died of wounds, Home, 22/11/18, Household Cavalry and Cavalry of the Line (incl. Yeomanry and Imperial Camel Corps), 4th (Queen's Own) Hussars.

LIGHT, Richard John, b. Aldershot, e. Aldershot, 38254, L/CPL, Killed in action, France & Flanders, 25/09/15, FORMERLY SS/5, R.A.S.C., Welsh Regiment, 2nd Battalion.

LOCKE, Arthur Albert, b. Aldershot, e. Hastings, Sussex, 28827, SPR., Killed in action, France & Flanders, 15/08/18, (237TH FIELD COY., R.E.)., Corps of Royal Engineers.

LOMAS, Albert Henry, b. Aldershot, e. Woolwich, Kent , r. Charlton, Kent, 9891, PRIVATE, Died of wounds, France & Flanders, 13/03/15, Devonshire Regiment, 2nd Battalion.

LOW, Sidney James, b. Aldershot, Hants, e. New Romney, Kent , r. Littleton-on-Sea, Kent, G/9048, L/CPL, Killed in action, France & Flanders, 21/03/18, Buffs (East Kent Regiment), 1st Battalion.

LOWEN, George John, b. Aldershot, Hants, e. Dublin, L/8231, SERGT., Killed in action, France & Flanders, 19/07/15, Duke of Cambridge's Own (Middlesex Regiment), 4th Battalion.

LUSH, William Henry, b. Aldershot, Hants, e. Aldershot, Hants, 5965, PRIVATE, Killed in action, France & Flanders, 30/10/14, Household Cavalry and Cavalry of the Line (incl. Yeomanry and Imperial Camel Corps), Corps of Dragoons. 1st King's Dragoon Guards.

MACE, George, b. Aldershot, e. Addlestone , r. Addlestone, 32390, PRIVATE, Died, Home, 04/12/16, FORMERLY 20144, ROYAL WEST SURREY REGT., Royal Defence Corps.

MACSWEENEY, Davis, b. Aldershot, Hants, e. Seaforth, Lancs, 50762, BDR., Died of wounds, France & Flanders, 30/03/16, Royal Horse Artillery and Royal Field Artillery.

MAHER, George, b. Aldershot, e. Kingston-on-Thames , r. Chelsea, London, 9260, L/CPL, Died of wounds, France & Flanders, 27/09/17, Worcestershire Regiment, 2nd Battalion.

MAKIN, Edward, b. Aldershot, Hants, e. Leeds, 42787, PRIVATE, Killed in action, France & Flanders, 08/10/17, Manchester Regiment, 2/7th Battalion.

MANNS, John, b. Aldershot, Hants, e. Park Royal, 41935, PRIVATE, Killed in action, France & Flanders, 23/09/18, FORMERLY T4/236470, R.A.S.C., Suffolk Regiment, 15th Battalion.

MANSBRIDGE, Richard, b. Aldershot, e. Belfast , r. Belfast, G/55240, PRIVATE, Died, France & Flanders, 17/01/18, FORMERLY T/4/059029, R.A.S.C., Royal Fusiliers (City of London Regiment), 23rd Battalion.

MANSFIELD, Francis, b. Aldershot, e. Tipperary, 4486, SGT. DRMR., Died, Home, 11/05/16, Prince of Wales's Leinster Regiment (Royal Canadians), 4th Battalion.

MANT, W. G., b. Aldershot, e. Aldershot , r. Knaphill, Surrey, 14156, DVR., Killed in action, France & Flanders, 29/09/18, (H.Q., 2ND DIV. ENGINEERS, R.E.)., Corps of Royal Engineers.

MARKS, George William, b. Aldershot, Hants, e. Gravesend, Kent , r. Northfleet, Kent, 37246, L/SGT, Killed in action, France & Flanders, 28/08/18, Prince of Wales's Volunteers (South Lancashire Regiment), 2/4th Battalion.

MARKS, William, b. Aldershot, e. Saffron Walden , r. Saffron Walden, 3/1515, PRIVATE, Killed in action, France & Flanders, 24/09/17, Essex Regiment, 1st Battalion.

MARSHALL, Arthur, b. Aldershot, Hants, e. Winchester , r. Aldershot, Steeles, Hants, 5192, PRIVATE, Killed in action, France & Flanders, 26/08/14, Hampshire Regiment, 1st Battalion.

MARSHALL, Edward, b. Aldershot, Hants, e. Winchester , r. Aldershot, Hants, 5827, SERGT., Killed in action, France & Flanders, 12/05/17, Hampshire Regiment, 1st Battalion.

Sort Order : Surname, Christian Name(s)

SURNAME,Christian Name(s),Born,Enlisted,Residence,Number,RANK,Cause,Place,Date of Death,ADDITIONAL TEXT,Regiment,Battalion

MARSHALL, George Walter, b. Aldershot, e. Portsmouth, 38788, L/SGT, Died of wounds, France & Flanders, 13/03/18, Hampshire Regiment, 2nd Battalion.

MARSHALL, Harold Edward George, b. Aldershot, e. London , r. West Kensington, MS/2828, PRIVATE, Died, Home, 12/08/15, Royal Army Service Corps.

MARSHALL, William Henry, b. Aldershot, Hants, e. Aldershot, Hants, 8001, PRIVATE, Killed in action, Palestine, 02/11/17, Hampshire Regiment, 1/8th (T.F.) Battalion.

MARTIN, George, b. Aldershot, Hants, e. Reading, Berks, 83802, BDR., Died of wounds, France & Flanders, 10/10/15, Royal Horse Artillery and Royal Field Artillery.

MARTIN, Henry George, b. Aldershot, Hants, e. Aldershot, Hants, 25489, PRIVATE, Killed in action, France & Flanders, 28/03/18, Hampshire Regiment, 1st Battalion.

MASON, Alfred, b. Aldershot, e. Aldershot, G/6028, PRIVATE, Killed in action, British Expeditionary Force, 25/09/15, Royal Sussex Regiment, 9th Battalion.

MASON, John, b. Aldershot, e. Salford, Lancs , r. Seedley, Lancs, 2236, PRIVATE, Killed in action, Gallipoli, 06/06/15, Lancashire Fusiliers, 1/8th Battalion.

MATTHEWS, Charles Henry, b. Aldershot, e. London , r. Akershot, Hants, 47730, RIFLEMAN, Killed in action, France & Flanders, 21/09/18, FORMERLY 17124, R.F.C., Rifle Brigade (The Prince Consort's Own), 2/10th London Regiment.

MATTHEWS, Edward, b. Aldershot, e. Bordon, Hants , r. Aldershot, 9562, PRIVATE, Killed in action, France & Flanders, 21/03/18, Prince Albert's (Somerset Light Infantry), 6th Battalion.

MAYHEAD, Frederick, b. Aldershot, e. Aldershot , r. Ashvale, Surrey, 6217, CPL., Killed in action, France & Flanders, 21/05/15, Worcestershire Regiment, 3rd Battalion.

MCBRIDE, Edward George, b. Aldershot, Hants, e. Sittingbourne, Kent, T.F.2585, PRIVATE, Killed in action, France & Flanders, 14/04/15, Duke of Cambridge's Own (Middlesex Regiment), 1/8th (T.F.) Battalion.

MCCORMACK, Albert, b. Aldershot, Hants, e. Guildford, Surrey , r. Brighton, Sussex, G/1598, PRIVATE, Killed in action, France & Flanders, 01/07/16, Queen's (Royal West Surrey Regiment), 7th Battalion.

MCGRANE, Charles, b. Aldershot, e. Dublin, 8376, CPL., Killed in action, France & Flanders, 01/07/16, Royal Dublin Fusiliers, 1st Battalion.

MCGREGOR, Thomas S., b. Aldershot, e. Glasgow, 47676, PRIVATE, Killed in action, France & Flanders, 12/04/18, Royal Scots Fusiliers, 1st Battalion.

MCGUIRE, James, b. Aldershot, e. Bristol, 10137, PRIVATE, Killed in action, France & Flanders, 24/05/16, Prince Albert's (Somerset Light Infantry), 6th Battalion.

MCKENZIE, William Alfred, b. Aldershot, Hants, e. London, 28257, MUSICIAN, Died, Gibraltar, 24/10/18, Royal Garrison Artillery.

MCLEAN, Walter, b. Aldershot, Hants, e. Guildford, Surrey , r. Aldershot, G/9167, PRIVATE, Died of wounds, France & Flanders, 12/11/14, Queen's (Royal West Surrey Regiment), 2nd Battalion.

MEADE, Harry, b. Aldershot, e. Finsbury, Middx. , r. Clerkenwell, Middx., S/21022, RIFLEMAN, Killed in action, France & Flanders, 20/09/17, Rifle Brigade (The Prince Consort's Own), 11th Battalion.

MEE, George, b. Aldershot, Hants, e. Chilwell, Notts , r. Nottingham, 2550, PRIVATE, Killed in action, France & Flanders, 16/09/16, Sherwood Foresters (Nottinghamshire and Derbyshire Regiment), 2nd Battalion.

MEEHAN, Frank, b. Aldershot, e. Tralee, Co. Kerry , r. Cork, 7849, SERGT., Killed in action, France & Flanders, 09/05/15, Royal Munster Fusiliers, 2nd Battalion.

MERRITT, Percy Harold, b. Aldershot, e. Aldershot , r. Plumstead, Kent, 1952, RIFLEMAN, Killed in action, France & Flanders, 26/08/14, Rifle Brigade (The Prince Consort's Own), 1st Battalion.

METCALF, Richard, b. Aldershot, e. Ashton-Under-Lyne, Lancs , r. Salford, Lancs, 7989, PRIVATE, Killed in action, France & Flanders, 16/09/14, Manchester Regiment, 2nd Battalion.

MILES, Frederick Arthur, b. Aldershot, Hants, e. Yateley, Hants , r. Blackwater, Hants, 1875, PRIVATE, Died of wounds, Mesopotamia, 22/01/16, Hampshire Regiment, 1/4th (T.F.) Battalion.

MILES, George, b. Aldershot, e. Guildford, Surrey , r. Blackwater, Hants, 9672, A/CPL., Died of wounds, France & Flanders, 16/10/16, Hampshire Regiment, 2nd Battalion.

Sort Order : Surname, Christian Name(s)

SURNAME,Christian Name(s),Born,Enlisted,Residence,Number,RANK,Cause,Place,Date of Death,ADDITIONAL TEXT,Regiment,Battalion

MILLER, John, b. Aldershot, Hants, e. Guildford, Surrey , r. Chertsey, Surrey, L/5477, SERGT., Died, Home, 15/02/16, Queen's (Royal West Surrey Regiment), 3rd Battalion.

MILLER, William, b. Aldershot, e. Southwark, Surrey , r. Waterloo, Surrey, 128359, PIONEER, Killed in action, France & Flanders, 01/07/16, FORMERLY 22258, YORKS L.I. (5TH BATTN., SPEC. BDE., R.E.)., Corps of Royal Engineers.

MILNE, Henry, b. Aldershot, Hants, e. Deptford, S/3229, A/SGT., Killed in action, France & Flanders, 13/03/16, Gordon Highlanders, 1st Battalion.

MILTON, Charles Lewis, b. Aldershot, e. Preston, Lancs , r. Goosnargh, Preston, 50785, L/CPL, Killed in action, Russia, 09/02/19, King's (Liverpool Regiment), 17th Battalion.

MOGFORD, Alexander Charles, b. Aldershot, e. Ilford , r. East Ham, SPTS/4008, PRIVATE, Died of wounds, France & Flanders, 04/08/16, Royal Fusiliers (City of London Regiment), 23rd Battalion.

MOLLOY, Edward, b. Aldershot, Hants, e. Caversham, Berks, 8907, PRIVATE, Died, Mesopotamia, 31/08/16, Oxfordshire and Buckinghamshire Light Infantry, 1st Battalion.

MONAGHAN, Edwin James, b. Aldershot, e. Fulham, Middx., 9946, PRIVATE, Killed in action, France & Flanders, 28/09/15, Princess Charlotte of Wales's (Royal Berkshire Regiment), 1st Battalion.

MOODY, Henry Hardy, b. Aldershot, e. London, 8637, L/CPL, Died of wounds, Russia, 15/09/19, Devonshire Regiment, 2nd Battalion.

MOORE, Albert, b. Aldershot, e. Winchester , r. Winchester, 8110, RIFLEMAN, Died of wounds, France & Flanders, 12/05/15, Rifle Brigade (The Prince Consort's Own), 1st Battalion.

MOORE, Arthur William, b. Aldershot, Hants, e. Guildford, Surrey , r. Aldershot, G/5621, PRIVATE, Killed in action, France & Flanders, 14/07/16, Queen's (Royal West Surrey Regiment), 2nd Battalion.

MOORE, Frederick, b. Aldershot, e. Cairo, Egypt , r. Woolwich, Kent, 4271, L/CPL, Killed in action, France & Flanders, 25/08/16, Rifle Brigade (The Prince Consort's Own), 2nd Battalion.

MOORE, James A., b. Aldershot, Hants, e. Stirling , r. Aldershot, 10966, DRUMMER, Died, Home, 23/06/17, Royal Scots Fusiliers, Depot.

MOULDS, Charles, b. Aldershot, Hants, e. Birmingham, 241377, PRIVATE, Killed in action, France & Flanders, 03/12/17, Royal Warwickshire Regiment, 2/6th Battalion.

MUNCEY, Richard Patrick, b. Aldershot, e. Westminster, Middx. , r. Hornsery, Middx., 70661, A/SGT., Died, Malta, 13/11/15, (H.Q. SIGNAL COY., 9TH ARMY CORPS. R.E.)., Corps of Royal Engineers.

MURPHY, James, b. Aldershot, e. Dublin , r. Aldershot, 11105, PRIVATE, Killed in action, Gallipoli, 25/04/15, Royal Dublin Fusiliers, 1st Battalion.

NEEDHAM, William St. Clair, b. Aldershot, e. Aldershot, Hants, 69608, TRUMPETER, Killed in action, France & Flanders, 14/09/14, Royal Horse Artillery and Royal Field Artillery.

NEWELL, Robert James, b. Aldershot, Hants, e. Aldershot, Han Ts, 200451, PRIVATE, Killed in action, Mesopotamia, 24/02/17, Hampshire Regiment, 1/4th (T.F.) Battalion.

NEWELL, Walter Henry, b. Aldershot, Hants, e. Winchester , r. Aldershot, Hants, 9650, PRIVATE, Killed in action, France & Flanders, 13/05/15, Hampshire Regiment, 1st Battalion.

NEWMAN, Herbert Edward, b. Aldershot, e. Winchester , r. Alresford, Hants, 35755, PRIVATE, Killed in action, France & Flanders, 15/04/18, Duke of Edinburgh's (Wiltshire Regiment), 6th Battalion.

NEWNHAM, Albert Edward Victor, b. Aldershot, e. Chichester, L/10100, PRIVATE, Died of wounds, British Expeditionary Force, 16/10/14, Royal Sussex Regiment, 2nd Battalion.

NORTON, Alfred Robert Henry, b. Aldershot, e. Plymouth, 24161, PRIVATE, Killed in action, France & Flanders, 19/07/16, Gloucestershire Regiment, 14th (Service) Battalion (West of England).

OATWAY, Thomas William, b. Aldershot, Hampshire, e. Stratford , r. Battersea, Surrey, 1486, DRILL SGT., Killed in action, France & Flanders, 14/09/14, Coldstream Guards.

O'BYRNE, Edward, b. Aldershot, e. Tralee, Co Kerry , r. Listowel, Co. Kerry, 3644, L/CPL, Killed in action, France & Flanders, 09/09/16, Royal Munster Fusiliers, 8th Battalion.

O'CONNOR, Charles, b. Aldershot, e. Guildford, Surrey , r. Aldershot, 8337, L/CPL, Killed in action, Gallipoli, 26/04/15, Hampshire Regiment, 2nd Battalion.

Sort Order : Surname, Christian Name(s)

SURNAME,Christian Name(s),Born,Enlisted,Residence,Number,RANK,Cause,Place,Date of Death,ADDITIONAL TEXT,Regiment,Battalion

O'CONNOR, Erward, b. Aldershot, Hants, e. Bustard Camp, Hants , r. Aldershot, Hants, 200823, PRIVATE, Killed in action, Mesopotamia, 04/02/17, Hampshire Regiment, 1/4th (T.F.) Battalion.

OFFLEY, Alfred, b. Aldershot, e. Bury St. Edmunds, 6233, PRIVATE, Killed in action, France & Flanders, 09/04/15, Suffolk Regiment, 2nd Battalion.

O'HALLORAN, William Henry, b. Aldershot, Hants, e. Newcastle-on-Tyne, 24/236, SERGT., Died, France & Flanders, 01/07/16, Northumberland Fusiliers, 24th Battalion (Tyneside Irish).

OLIVER, Frank, b. Aldershot, e. Aldershot, 43615, PRIVATE, Killed in action, France & Flanders, 11/01/17, Royal Welsh Fusiliers, 1st Battalion.

ORANGE, Percy James, b. Aldershot, e. Aldershot, 564388, L/CPL., Died, France & Flanders, 06/11/18, FORMERLY 30637, HANTS REGT., Labour Corps.

O'SULLIVAN, Patrick, b. Aldershot, e. Cork, 10896, PRIVATE, Killed in action, Gallipoli, 29/06/15, Royal Dublin Fusiliers, 1st Battalion.

PALING, Thomas, b. Aldershot, Hants, e. London , r. Purley, Surrey, 8126, CPL., Died of wounds, Home, 14/11/16, D.C.M., Leicestershire Regiment, 1st Battalion.

PAMPLIN, Archibald Stanley, b. Aldershot, e. Canning Town, London, 10610, SERGT., Killed in action, Gallipoli, 08/08/15, Gloucestershire Regiment, 7th (Service) Battalion.

PARKER, Frank Herbert, b. Aldershot, e. Chatham, Kent , r. Wainscott, Kent, 12820, A/C.S.M., Killed in action, France & Flanders, 27/05/18, D.C.M. (7TH FIELD COY., R.E.)., Corps of Royal Engineers.

PARKER, Stanley John Ernest, b. Aldershot, e. Woolwich, Kent , r. Erith, Kent, 42179, PIONEER, Killed in action, France & Flanders, 09/10/15, (70TH FIELD COY., R.E.)., Corps of Royal Engineers.

PARSONS, Edward William, b. Aldershot, Hants, e. Guildford, Surrey , r. Seal, Nr. Farnham, Surrey, L/9194, SERGT., Killed in action, France & Flanders, 30/10/14, Queen's (Royal West Surrey Regiment), 2nd Battalion.

PATRICK, Pereival Herbert, b. Aldershot, Hants, e. Kingston, Surrey, 18833, PRIVATE, Killed in action, France & Flanders, 28/09/15, East Surrey Regiment, 2nd Battalion.

PATRICK, Richard Melton, b. Aldershot, e. Norwich , r. Brampton, Norfolk, 20886, PRIVATE, Died of wounds, Home, 23/05/17, FORMERLY 9460, NORFOLK REGT., Essex Regiment, 1st Battalion.

PAYNE, Henry, b. Aldershot, e. Dublin, 10164, PRIVATE, Died of wounds, France & Flanders, 03/05/15, Royal Dublin Fusiliers, 2nd Battalion.

PEGG, Albert, b. Aldershot, Hants, e. Bustard Camp, Hants , r. Aldershot, Hants, 200826, PRIVATE, Killed in action, Mesopotamia, 21/01/16, Hampshire Regiment, 1/4th (T.F.) Battalion.

PENTLAND, William Henry, b. Aldershot, Hants, e. Lurgan, Co. Armagh , r. Portadown, Co. Armagh, 17842, PRIVATE, Killed in action, France & Flanders, 01/07/16, Princess Victoria's (Royal Irish Fusiliers), 9th Battalion.

PEPPER, Ernest, b. Aldershot, e. Harwich, Essex , r. Colchester, 3/872, CPL., Killed in action, France & Flanders, 01/07/16, Essex Regiment, 2nd Battalion.

PETTS, Ernest Henry, b. Aldershot, Hants, e. Canterbury, Kent , r. Canterbury, Kent, L/8632, SERGT., Killed in action, France & Flanders, 03/05/15, Buffs (East Kent Regiment), 2nd Battalion.

PHILLIPS, Albert George, b. Aldershot, e. Stratford, Essex , r. Dowlais, Glam., 10870, PRIVATE, Died of wounds, France & Flanders, 27/09/15, Welsh Regiment, 2nd Battalion.

PHILLIPS, Sidney Richard, b. Aldershot, Hants, e. Swindon, Wilts, 306970, PRIVATE, Killed in action, France & Flanders, 08/08/18, FORMERLY 640, WILTSHIRE (T) ROYAL ENGINCERS., Tank Corps.

PIKE, Frederick, b. Aldershot, Hants, e. Winchester , r. Aldershot, Hants, 26977, PRIVATE, Died of wounds, France & Flanders, 09/06/17, Hampshire Regiment, 15th (Service) Battalion.

PILLEY, John Lincoln, b. Aldershot, e. York , r. Curragh, 12091, L/CPL, Killed in action, France & Flanders, 27/01/16, Household Cavalry and Cavalry of the Line (incl. Yeomanry and Imperial Camel Corps), 18th (Queen Mary's Own Royal) Hussars.

PINK, Harry, b. Aldershot, e. Winchester , r. Alton, Hants, 9044, PRIVATE, Died of wounds, Gallipoli, 20/05/15, Hampshire Regiment, 2nd Battalion.

PITCH, William, b. Aldershot, e. Warley, Essex , r. Brentwood, Essex, 6612, PRIVATE, Died of wounds, France & Flanders, 11/03/15, Essex Regiment, 2nd Battalion.

Sort Order : Surname, Christian Name(s)

SURNAME,Christian Name(s),Born,Enlisted,Residence,Number,RANK,Cause,Place,Date of Death,ADDITIONAL TEXT,Regiment,Battalion

PITTOCK, George Edward, b. Aldershot, Hants, e. Gosport, Hants, S/5723, A/S.Q.M.S., Died, East Africa, 03/12/16, Royal Army Ordnance Corps.

POPEJOY, Bert Samuel, b. Aldershot, e. Aldershot, r. Aldershot, 72, SERGT., Killed in action, France & Flanders, 21/03/18, Rifle Brigade (The Prince Consort's Own), 8th Battalion.

PORTER, Ernest James, b. Aldershot, Hants, e. Farnham, Surrey, 25924, PRIVATE, Killed in action, France & Flanders, 03/04/18, Royal Warwickshire Regiment, 2/6th Battalion.

PORTER, John Henry, b. Aldershot, Hants, e. Mill Hill, Middlesex, L/10146, CPL., Killed in action, France & Flanders, 16/02/17, Duke of Cambridge's Own (Middlesex Regiment), 1st Battalion.

PORTER, Samuel, b. Aldershot, Hants, e. Aldershot, 645, L/CPL., Died of wounds, France & Flanders, 15/04/18, Northumberland Fusiliers, 1st Battalion.

PRATT, Alfred Henry, b. Aldershot, Hants, e. Axminster, Devons, r. Sidmouth, Devons, 36178, CPL., Died of wounds, France & Flanders, 22/03/18, FORMERLY 24939, DEVONSHIRE REGT., Leicestershire Regiment, 11th Battalion.

PRETTY, Ernest George, b. Aldershot, e. Hounslow, r. Aldershot, L/11641, PRIVATE, Killed in action, France & Flanders, 15/10/14, Royal Fusiliers (City of London Regiment), 4th Battalion.

PRETTY, Frederick, b. Aldershot, Hants, e. Guildford, Surrey, r. Aldershot, L/6726, PRIVATE, Killed in action, France & Flanders, 31/10/14, Queen's (Royal West Surrey Regiment), 1st Battalion.

PRICE, Arthur Richard, b. Aldershot, e. Coventry, 24854, CPL., Died, France & Flanders, 30/03/18, Gloucestershire Regiment, 13th (Service) Battalion (Forest of Dean) (Pioneers).

PRING, Leonard Fred, b. Aldershot, e. Cork, 2631, PRIVATE, Killed in action, France & Flanders, 18/11/16, Manchester Regiment, 2nd Battalion.

PRITCHARD, George Harold, b. Aldershot, e. London, r. Battersea, 533465, PRIVATE, Died of wounds, France & Flanders, 15/09/17, London Regiment, 15th (County of London) Battalion (P.W.O. Civil Service Rifles).

PRITCHARD, James Henry, b. Aldershot, e. Hull, 20906, PRIVATE, Killed in action, France & Flanders, 22/03/18, East Yorkshire Regiment, 1st Battalion.

PRIVETT, Arthur Edward, b. Aldershot, e. London, r. Petersfield, 391952, RIFLEMAN, Killed in action, France & Flanders, 23/09/18, London Regiment, 9th (County of London) Battalion (Queen Victoria's Rifles).

PRYANT, Richard, b. Aldershot, e. Hackney, r. Clapton, 2899, PRIVATE, Died, Home, 19/05/17, FORMERLY 20058, 10TH LONDON REGT., Royal Defence Corps.

PULLEN, Thomas, b. Aldershot, e. Guildford, r. Farncombe, P/17, SERGT., Died, Salonika, 29/08/16, Corps of Military Police, Mounted Branch.

RAISON, George Hurst, b. Aldershot, Hants, e. Aldershot, 162, SERGT., Killed in action, France & Flanders, 13/10/14, Northumberland Fusiliers, 1st Battalion.

RANDALL, John, b. Aldershot, Hants, e. Guildford, Surrey, r. Frimley, Surrey, G/43051, PRIVATE, Died of wounds, France & Flanders, 12/04/17, FORMERLY G/6972, ROYAL WEST SURREY REGT., Duke of Cambridge's Own (Middlesex Regiment), 4th Battalion.

RAWLINGS, James, b. Aldershot, e. London, r. Southwark, London, 8684, PRIVATE, Died of wounds, France & Flanders, 25/10/15, Prince of Wales's (North Staffordshire Regiment), 1st Battalion.

RAYNES, John William, b. Aldershot, Hants, e. Pontefract, Yorks, 36039, TPR., Killed in action, France & Flanders, 14/03/15, Royal Horse Artillery and Royal Field Artillery.

READ, Edwin Arthur, b. Aldershot, e. St. Pancras, Middx., r. Hampstead, Middx., A/203163, RIFLEMAN, Killed in action, France & Flanders, 06/11/16, FORMERLY S/16686, RIFLE BRIG., King's Royal Rifle Corps, 16th Battalion.

READ, Henry Arthur, b. Aldershot, e. Bristol, 31582, PRIVATE, Died of wounds, France & Flanders, 06/11/18, Devonshire Regiment, 8th (Service) Battalion.

READER, Stanley William, b. Aldershot, Hants, e. London, 34059, B.Q.M.S., Died, Home, 15/01/18, Royal Horse Artillery and Royal Field Artillery.

REID, George Frederick, b. Aldershot, e. Chatham, Kent, r. Canterbury, Kent, 25249, SPR., Died, Home, 04/04/15, (30TH FORT. COY., R.E.), Corps of Royal Engineers.

REID, Samuel, b. Aldershot, Hampshire, e. Glasgow, Lanarks, r. Stirling, 510, CPL., Died of wounds, France & Flanders, 12/07/17, Princess Louise's (Argyll & Sutherland Highlanders), 11th Battalion.

Sort Order : Surname, Christian Name(s)

SURNAME,Christian Name(s),Born,Enlisted,Residence,Number,RANK,Cause,Place,Date of Death,ADDITIONAL TEXT,Regiment,Battalion

REYNOLDS, Robert Stanley, b. Aldershot, Hants, e. Norwich , r. Aldershot, Hants, 3/4530, PRIVATE, Killed in action, Gallipoli, 21/08/15, Hampshire Regiment, 10th Battalion.

RICHARDSON, Hector, b. Aldershot, e. London , r. York, 6683, CPL., Killed in action, France & Flanders, 24/08/14, Household Cavalry and Cavalry of the Line (incl. Yeomanry and Imperial Camel Corps), 18th (Queen Mary's Own Royal) Hussars.

RICHARDSON, W. H. E., b. Aldershot, Hants, e. Edinburgh , r. Whittington, Salop, 8332, PRIVATE, Died of wounds, France & Flanders, 19/05/16, Sherwood Foresters (Nottinghamshire and Derbyshire Regiment), 10th Battalion.

RILEY, William George, b. Aldershot, e. Leeds, 305713, PRIVATE, Killed in action, France & Flanders, 19/09/17, Prince of Wales's Own (West Yorkshire Regiment), 11th Battalion.

ROBERTSON, George, b. Aldershot, Hants, e. Perth , r. Edinburgh, 19276, PRIVATE, Killed in action, France & Flanders, 25/09/15, FORMERLY 11965, SCOTS GREYS., Leicestershire Regiment, 2nd Battalion.

ROBINSON, James Henry, b. Aldershot, e. Shorncliffe, 9131, L/CPL, Killed in action, Gallipoli, 02/05/15, South Wales Borderers, 2nd Battalion.

ROBINSON, William Charles James Edwin, b. Aldershot, Hants, e. Aldershot, Hants, 8018, CPL., Killed in action, France & Flanders, 09/08/16, Hampshire Regiment, 2nd Battalion.

ROSE, William Henry, b. Aldershot, e. Poole, Dorset , r. Aldershot, 205033, PRIVATE, Killed in action, France & Flanders, 24/04/18, Devonshire Regiment, 2nd Battalion.

ROUTLEY, Francis Robert, b. Aldershot, Hants, e. Sandwich, Kent , r. Sandwich, Kent, L/9513, L/CPL, Killed in action, France & Flanders, 03/05/17, Queen's (Royal West Surrey Regiment), 6th Battalion.

ROWLANDS, John Henry, b. Aldershot, Hants, e. Winchester, 47962, A/CPL., Died, E.E.F., 25/06/18, Devonshire Regiment, 5th (P.O.W.) Battalion (Territorials).

RYAN, Thomas Martin, b. Aldershot, Hants, e. London , r. Gosport, Hants, 604, B.S.M., Killed in action, France & Flanders, 04/04/18, Royal Garrison Artillery.

SALES, Charles Walter, b. Aldershot, Hants, e. Chatham, Kent , r. Aldershot, Hants, 8496, SERGT., Killed in action, France & Flanders, 25/09/15, Oxfordshire and Buckinghamshire Light Infantry, 5th Battalion.

SAVAGE, Stuart George Victor, b. Aldershot, e. Bristol , r. Bristol, S/26770, A/S/SGT., Died of wounds, France & Flanders, 03/07/17, Royal Army Service Corps.

SCOTT, Reynold, b. Aldershot, Hants, e. Aldershot, Hants, 203410, PRIVATE, Killed in action, France & Flanders, 16/10/18, Hampshire Regiment, 15th (Service) Battalion.

SEABY, John Edward, b. Aldershot, Hants, e. Northampton, 43901, PRIVATE, Died of wounds, France & Flanders, 12/09/18, Lincolnshire Regiment, 8th Battalion.

SEAL, William Ernest, b. Aldershot, e. Bury St. Edmunds, 6829, SERGT., Killed in action, France & Flanders, 30/09/15, Suffolk Regiment, 2nd Battalion.

SHEA, John, b. Aldershot, Hants, e. Guildford, Surrey , r. Fareham, Hants, S/54, L/CPL, Killed in action, France & Flanders, 13/04/18, Queen's (Royal West Surrey Regiment), 1st Battalion.

SHEIL, James Wilfred, b. Aldershot, Hants, e. London , r. South Ealing, Middlesex, 1837, PRIVATE, Died of wounds, France & Flanders, 13/03/15, Manchester Regiment, 1st Battalion.

SHRUBB, Herbert Charles, b. Aldershot, Hants, e. Guildford, Surrey , r. Chilworth, Surrey, G/30192, PRIVATE, Killed in action, France & Flanders, 19/09/18, Queen's (Royal West Surrey Regiment), 7th Battalion.

SIMPSON, Charles, b. Aldershot, Hants, e. Wallsend-on-Tyne, 27/1350, C.S.M., Killed in action, France & Flanders, 01/07/16, Northumberland Fusiliers, 27th Battalion (Tyneside Irish).

SIMPSON, Charles John, b. Aldershot, e. Walker-on-Tyne, 1927, L/CPL, Died, France & Flanders, 24/05/15, Northumberland Fusiliers, 1/5th Battalion (Territorial).

SINGLETON, George Tilbury, b. Aldershot, Hants, e. Meerut, India, 13831, GUNNER, Died of wounds, France & Flanders, 05/04/18, M.M., Royal Horse Artillery and Royal Field Artillery.

SMITH, Frank Edward, b. Aldershot, Hants, e. Aldershot, Hants, 1885, PRIVATE, Died, Home, 01/11/16, Hampshire Regiment, 1/4th (T.F.) Battalion.

SMITH, Frederick George, b. Aldershot, Hants, e. Guildford, Surrey , r. Aldershot, L/8144, SERGT., Killed in action, France & Flanders, 23/04/17, Queen's (Royal West Surrey Regiment), 1st Battalion.

Sort Order : Surname, Christian Name(s)

SURNAME,Christian Name(s),Born,Enlisted,Residence,Number,RANK,Cause,Place,Date of Death,ADDITIONAL TEXT,Regiment,Battalion

SMITH, George Goldsworth, b. Aldershot, e. York, 49934, GUNNER, Died of wounds, France & Flanders, 20/07/16, Royal Horse Artillery and Royal Field Artillery.

SMITH, John, b. Aldershot, Hants, e. Hounslow, Middx. , r. Isleworth, Middx., G/4005, PRIVATE, Died of wounds, France & Flanders, 09/03/16, Queen's (Royal West Surrey Regiment), 1st Battalion.

SMITH, John, b. Aldershot, Hants, e. Belfast, 711894, DVR., Killed in action, France & Flanders, 27/12/17, Royal Horse Artillery and Royal Field Artillery, Territorial Force.

SMITH, Joseph Robert Coade, b. Aldershot, e. Colchester , r. Mullingar, Ireland, T/31221, CPL., Killed in action, France & Flanders, 11/08/18, Royal Army Service Corps.

SMITH, Leslie John, b. Aldershot, e. Buxton, 23596, GDSN., Killed in action, France & Flanders, 14-17/09/16, Grenadier Guards, 3rd Battalion.

SMITH, Percival George, b. Aldershot, Hants, e. Bury-St.-Edmunds, Suffolk, 320907, PRIVATE, Killed in action, France & Flanders, 19/08/18, Norfolk Regiment, 12th Battalion.

SMITH, Richard Charles, b. Aldershot, e. York Town, 11650, GDSN., Killed in action, France & Flanders, 27/06/17, FORMERLY 1ST BATTN., ROYAL BERKS., Grenadier Guards, 3rd Battalion.

SMITH, Samuel, b. Aldershot, Hants, e. Hamilton, Lanarks , r. Preston, Lancs, 5490, SERGT., Killed in action, France & Flanders, 22/02/15, Princess Louise's (Argyll & Sutherland Highlanders), 2nd Battalion.

SMITH, William, b. Aldershot, e. Aldershot , r. Aldershot, 25407, PRIVATE, Died, Mesopotamia, 15/07/16, FORMERLY 22292, HAMPSHIRE REGIMENT., Duke of Edinburgh's (Wiltshire Regiment), 5th Battalion.

SMYTHE, Christopher, b. Aldershot, Hants, e. Bromley, Kent , r. Swanley Junction, Kent, G/816, CPL., Killed in action, France & Flanders, 07/08/17, M.M., Queen's Own (Royal West Kent Regiment), 7th Battalion.

SNELLING, Jack, b. Aldershot, Hants, e. Guildford, Surrey , r. Aldershot, G/409, PRIVATE, Died of wounds, France & Flanders, 08/10/15, Queen's (Royal West Surrey Regiment), 6th Battalion.

SOFFE, Harry, b. Aldershot, Hants, e. Aldershot, Hants, 9537, PRIVATE, Killed in action, France & Flanders, 26/04/15, Hampshire Regiment, 1st Battalion.

SPEAKMAN, Edward Joseph Edmund, b. Aldershot, Hants, e. Aldershot, Hants, 381154, PRIVATE, Killed in action, France & Flanders, 20/07/18, Hampshire Regiment, 2/4th (T.F.) Battalion.

SPENDER, Walter, b. Aldershot, Hants, e. Derby , r. Sevenoaks, Kent, 6601, SERGT., Killed in action, France & Flanders, 14/02/16, Sherwood Foresters (Nottinghamshire and Derbyshire Regiment), 10th Battalion.

SPICER, Albert Ley, b. Aldershot, Hants, e. Lydd, Kent, 21738, PRIVATE, Died of wounds, France & Flanders, 19/08/17, East Surrey Regiment, 12th Battalion.

SPIERS, Frederick Charles, b. Aldershot, e. London, Middlesex , r. Hounslow, Middlesex, 7972, SERGT., Killed in action, France & Flanders, 14/12/14, Prince Albert's (Somerset Light Infantry), 1st Battalion.

SPILLER, Charles, b. Aldershot, e. Folkestone, 62632, GUNNER, Died, India, 20/08/15, Royal Horse Artillery and Royal Field Artillery.

SPILLER, John, b. Aldershot, Hants, e. Guildford, Surrey , r. Aldershot, 9011, PRIVATE, Killed in action, France & Flanders, 11/02/15, Bedfordshire Regiment, 2nd Battalion.

SPRINGHAM, Alexander, b. Aldershot, e. Aldershot, Hants, 64421, BDR., Killed in action, France & Flanders, 17/07/16, Royal Horse Artillery and Royal Field Artillery.

STAGG, Albert Edward, b. Aldershot, e. Taunton, 240052, SERGT., Killed in action, Egypt, 23/11/17, Prince Albert's (Somerset Light Infantry), 1/5th Battalion.

STAMP, Percy, b. Aldershot, e. London, 71218, CPL., Died of wounds, France & Flanders, 12/10/17, Royal Horse Artillery and Royal Field Artillery.

STANLEY, Robert James, b. Aldershot, Hants, e. Dublin , r. Tipton, Staffs, 5523, C/SGT., Killed in action, France & Flanders, 21/12/14, Manchester Regiment, 1st Battalion.

STANWAY, Thomas Henry, b. Aldershot, Hants, e. Conway, Carnarvon , r. Frodingham, Lincs, 699, C.Q.M.S., Died of wounds, France & Flanders, 03/09/18, M.S.M., Loyal North Lancashire Regiment, 1st Battalion.

STEPHENS, Frederick Henry, b. Aldershot, e. Aldershot, 21459, CPL., Killed in action, France & Flanders, 04/07/16, FORMERLY 8739, HANTS REGT., Machine Gun Corps, (Infantry).

Sort Order : Surname, Christian Name(s)

SURNAME,Christian Name(s),Born,Enlisted,Residence,Number,RANK,Cause,Place,Date of Death,ADDITIONAL TEXT,Regiment,Battalion

STEWART, George, b. Aldershot, Hants, e. Norwich, Norfolk, 1675, PRIVATE, Died of wounds, Gallipoli, 25/08/15, Royal Army Medical Corps, (Territorial Force.)

STOKES, Folliott Arthur, b. Aldershot, Hants, e. Kingston, Surrey , r. Dublin, Ireland, 6355, PRIVATE, Killed in action, France & Flanders, 08/05/15, East Surrey Regiment, 2nd Battalion.

STONE, William, b. Aldershot, Hants, e. Highgate, Middlesex, T.F.243001, PRIVATE, Killed in action, France & Flanders, 18/11/17, Duke of Cambridge's Own (Middlesex Regiment), 1st Battalion.

STOVOLD, Frederick, b. Aldershot, Hants, e. Guildford, Surrey , r. Bramley, Surrey, L/10862, PRIVATE, Died of wounds, Home, 10/02/15, Queen's (Royal West Surrey Regiment), 2nd Battalion.

STRANGE, Andrew, b. Aldershot, e. Woolwich , r. Woolwich, T4/238671, DVR., Died, Home, 23/10/18, Royal Army Service Corps.

STRANGWARD, Herbert, b. Aldershot, e. Norwich , r. Norwich, 20981, PRIVATE, Killed in action, France & Flanders, 28/04/16, FORMERLY 17849, NORFOLK REGT., Essex Regiment, 1st Battalion.

STYLES, Albert Henry, b. Aldershot, Hants, e. Aldershot, 41265, PRIVATE, Killed in action, France & Flanders, 22/04/18, FORMERLY 8/7380, T. RES. BN., Duke of Cornwall's Light Infantry, 1st Battalion.

STYLES, Henry Ernest, b. Aldershot, e. Aldershot, 26533, PIONEER, Died, France & Flanders, 12/07/18, FORMERLY 9022, SOM. L.I. (4TH SIGNAL COY., R.E.)., Corps of Royal Engineers.

SUMNER, Edward, b. Aldershot, Hants, e. Aldershot, 69271, PRIVATE, Killed in action, France & Flanders, 19/08/17, Royal Army Medical Corps.

SUMPSTER, Alfred Charles, b. Aldershot, e. Aldershot, 5528, C.S.M., Died, Mesopotamia, 05/07/16, (3RD SAPPERS & MINERS, R.E.)., Corps of Royal Engineers.

SUTTON, Henry, b. Aldershot, e. Finsbury, Middx. , r. East Finchley, Middx., A/1053, RIFLEMAN, Died of wounds, France & Flanders, 19/08/16, King's Royal Rifle Corps, 7th Battalion.

SWEETMAN, Arthur, b. Aldershot, Hants, e. Woolwich, Kent , r. Plumstead, Kent, S/10829, PRIVATE, Killed in action, France & Flanders, 25/05/15, Buffs (East Kent Regiment), 1st Battalion.

SYCAMORE, Ernest, b. Aldershot, Hants, e. Gillingham, Kent , r. Knowle, Warwick, 12525, CPL., Died of wounds, France & Flanders, 18/05/18, FORMERLY 3089, HOUSEHOLD BATTN., Irish Guards, 1st Battalion.

TALO, William James, b. Aldershot, Hants, e. London , r. Aberdeen, 8193, DRUMMER, Died, Mesopotamia, 29/10/16, Leicestershire Regiment, 2nd Battalion.

TANNER, Frank, b. Aldershot, Hants, e. Guildford, Surrey , r. Aldershot, S/5833, PRIVATE, Killed in action, France & Flanders, 16/05/15, Queen's (Royal West Surrey Regiment), 2nd Battalion.

TAYLOR, Charles Albert, b. Aldershot, Hants, e. Guildford, Surrey , r. Aldershot, G/6825, L/CPL, Killed in action, France & Flanders, 31/07/17, Queen's (Royal West Surrey Regiment), 2nd Battalion.

TAYLOR, John, b. Aldershot, Hants, e. Grantham, 1671, PRIVATE, Killed in action, France & Flanders, 13/10/15, Lincolnshire Regiment, 4th Battalion.

TEBBUTT, Henry Edward, b. Aldershot, e. Aldershot, 38662, PRIVATE, Killed in action, France & Flanders, 27/04/18, FORMERLY 381262, HANTS REGT., Princess Charlotte of Wales's (Royal Berkshire Regiment), 2nd Battalion.

TEW, William Charles, b. Aldershot, Hants, e. Mill Hill, Middlesex, L/13821, PRIVATE, Killed in action, France & Flanders, 07/08/15, Duke of Cambridge's Own (Middlesex Regiment), 3rd Battalion.

THIRKETTLE, J. W. H., b. Aldershot, Hants, e. Westminster, Middx. , r. South Norwood, Surrey, 568072, SERGT., Died, Home, 10/11/18, (S.S.T.C., BEDFORD, R.E.)., Corps of Royal Engineers.

THOMAS, Harry, b. Aldershot, Hants, e. Woolwich , r. Plumstead, 98291, L/CPL, Killed in action, France & Flanders, 30/11/17, FORMERLY 36267, K.R.R.C., Machine Gun Corps, (Infantry).

THOMPSON, Edward William, b. Aldershot, e. Kensington , r. Wandsworth, 3018, PRIVATE, Killed in action, France & Flanders, 02/07/16, London Regiment, 13th (County of London) Battalion (Princess Louise's Kensington Battalion).

THOMPSON, John Robert William, b. Aldershot, Hampshire, e. London , r. Hampstead, 9517, L/CPL, Killed in action, France & Flanders, 10/03/15, Cameronians (Scottish Rifles), 2nd Battalion.

THORNTON, Richard, b. Aldershot, e. Aldershot, Hants, 614, CPL., Died of wounds, France & Flanders, 06/11/14, Northumberland Fusiliers, 1st Battalion.

Sort Order : Surname, Christian Name(s)

SURNAME,Christian Name(s),Born,Enlisted,Residence,Number,RANK,Cause,Place,Date of Death,ADDITIONAL TEXT,Regiment,Battalion

TILTMAN, Charles, b. Aldershot, Hants, e. Aldershot, Hants , r. Swindon, Wilts, 24901, PRIVATE, Killed in action, France & Flanders, 01/11/16, Hampshire Regiment, 14th (Service) Battalion.

TIMMS, William Henry, b. Aldershot, Hants, e. Hartley Wintney, Hants , r. Aldershot, Hants, 17455, PRIVATE, Killed in action, Gallipoli, 06/08/15, Hampshire Regiment, 2nd Battalion.

TOMKINS, Arthur Victor, b. Aldershot, Hants, e. Guildford, Surrey , r. Ash Vale, Surrey, 8621, PRIVATE, Killed in action, France & Flanders, 21/03/18, Duke of Edinburgh's (Wiltshire Regiment), 2nd Battalion.

TOMKINS, Charles Edward, b. Aldershot, e. Aldershot , r. Aldershot, 23174, PRIVATE, Killed in action, France & Flanders, 21/03/18, Duke of Edinburgh's (Wiltshire Regiment), 2nd Battalion.

TROWBRIDGE, Charles Edward, b. Aldershot, e. Andover , r. Andover, Hants, 5643, RIFLEMAN, Died of wounds, France & Flanders, 10/05/15, Rifle Brigade (The Prince Consort's Own), 2nd Battalion.

TRUSSLER, Henry George, b. Aldershot, Hants, e. Reading, 8340, A/SGT., Killed in action, France & Flanders, 16/04/17, Cameronians (Scottish Rifles), 1st Battalion.

TUPPEN, Alexander David, b. Aldershot, e. York, 1284, CPL., Killed in action, France & Flanders, 01/08/15, Prince of Wales's Own (West Yorkshire Regiment), 1/5th Battalion.

TURNER, Charles, b. Aldershot, e. Leeds , r. Leeds, 171197, A/CPL., Killed in action, France & Flanders, 21/03/18, Prince of Wales's Own (West Yorkshire Regiment), 1st Battalion.

TURNER, Edward, b. Aldershot, Hants, e. Queenborough, Kent, 45960, L/CPL, Killed in action, France & Flanders, 25/04/18, FORMERLY 232086, R.E., Lancashire Fusiliers, 19th Battalion.

TURNER, Henry Dennis, b. Aldershot, e. Kingston-on-Thames, 9137, CPL., Killed in action, France & Flanders, 07/07/17, Royal Horse Artillery and Royal Field Artillery.

TURNER, Thomas Sidney, b. Aldershot, e. Aldershot , r. Farnham, T/34215, DVR., Died, France & Flanders, 07/12/16, Royal Army Service Corps.

TURNER, William James, b. Aldershot, Hants, e. London , r. Clapham Junction, 5378, PRIVATE, Died of wounds, France & Flanders, 01/09/14, Household Cavalry and Cavalry of the Line (incl. Yeomanry and Imperial Camel Corps), 2nd Dragoon Guards (Queen's Bays).

VAUGHAN, Frank Bertram, b. Aldershot, Hants, e. Kingston, Surrey, 10888, PRIVATE, Killed in action, France & Flanders, 20/04/15, East Surrey Regiment, 1st Battalion.

VENESS, George Frederick, b. Aldershot, Hants, e. Manchester , r. Moston, Lancs, 41642, PRIVATE, Killed in action, France & Flanders, 12/04/18, South Wales Borderers, 5th Battalion.

VILLIERS, Arthur Edward, b. Aldershot, e. Aldershot, Hants, 67371, GUNNER, Killed in action, France & Flanders, 12/10/17, Royal Horse Artillery and Royal Field Artillery.

VIRGO, James, b. Aldershot, Hants, e. Woolwich, Kent , r. Plumstead, Kent, S/6541, PRIVATE, Killed in action, France & Flanders, 09/01/15, Queen's (Royal West Surrey Regiment), 2nd Battalion.

WAITE, Stanley, b. Aldershot, Hants, e. Erith, Kent , r. Northumberland Heath, Kent, 534126, PRIVATE, Died, Home, 28/10/18, Royal Army Medical Corps, (Territorial Force.)

WAKE, Henry, b. Aldershot, Hants, e. Fermoy, Ireland, 52373, SERGT., Killed in action, France & Flanders, 05/02/18, D.C.M., Royal Horse Artillery and Royal Field Artillery.

WALKER, James Henry, b. Aldershot, e. Abingdon, Berks , r. Chilton, Berks, 41275, PRIVATE, Killed in action, France & Flanders, 30/11/17, Princess Charlotte of Wales's (Royal Berkshire Regiment), 5th Battalion.

WALKER, John, b. Aldershot, e. Rotherham , r. Rotherham, 10107, CPL., Killed in action, France & Flanders, 21/02/15, Household Cavalry and Cavalry of the Line (incl. Yeomanry and Imperial Camel Corps), 20th Hussars.

WALLWORK, Thomas, b. Aldershot, e. Rochdale, Lancs , r. Pendleton, Lancs, 3386, PRIVATE, Killed in action, France & Flanders, 08/05/15, FORMERLY 4511, LANCS FUS., Prince of Wales's Volunteers (South Lancashire Regiment), 2nd Battalion.

WALSH, John Charles, b. Aldershot, e. Woolwich, Kent , r. Deal, Kent, 4864, RIFLEMAN, Killed in action, France & Flanders, 19/11/17, Rifle Brigade (The Prince Consort's Own), 2nd Battalion.

WALSH, Thomas, b. Aldershot, Hants, e. Galway , r. Ballyglunin, 9239, PRIVATE, Killed in action, France & Flanders, 05/11/14, Connaught Rangers, 1st Battalion.

Sort Order : Surname, Christian Name(s)

SURNAME,Christian Name(s),Born,Enlisted,Residence,Number,RANK,Cause,Place,Date of Death,ADDITIONAL TEXT,Regiment,Battalion

WARNES, William, b. Aldershot, Hants, e. Cresswell, Staffs, 96681, GUNNER, Died of wounds, France & Flanders, 19/03/16, Royal Horse Artillery and Royal Field Artillery.

WATERS, George William, b. Aldershot, e. Winchester , r. Aldershot, 6/569, L/CPL, Killed in action, France & Flanders, 03/10/17, Rifle Brigade (The Prince Consort's Own), 1st Battalion.

WATTS, Edgar Frederick, b. Aldershot, Hants, e. Woking, 9412, SERGT., Died, France & Flanders, 03/03/19, South Wales Borderers, 1st Battalion.

WATTS, Edmund, b. Aldershot, Hants, e. Guildford, Surrey , r. Aldershot, Hants, 8319, PRIVATE, Killed in action, Gallipoli, 14/07/15, Hampshire Regiment, 2nd Battalion.

WEBB, Frederick, b. Aldershot, Hants, e. Newcastle-on-Tyne, 3141, PRIVATE, Died of wounds, France & Flanders, 22/02/15, Northumberland Fusiliers, 2nd Battalion.

WELLS, Walter, b. Aldershot, Hants, e. Woolwich, Kent , r. Arundel, Sussex, 93253, L/SGT, Killed in action, France & Flanders, 05/10/18, FORMERLY 03425, A.O.C., Sherwood Foresters (Nottinghamshire and Derbyshire Regiment), 11th Battalion.

WELSH, Arthur Charles, b. Aldershot, Hants, e. Canterbury, Kent , r. Woolwich, Kent, L/6992, SERGT., Killed in action, France & Flanders, 06/03/16, Buffs (East Kent Regiment), 6th Battalion.

WEST, Albert, b. Aldershot, Hants, e. Mountain Ash, Glam , r. Wells, Somerset, 4/4063, A/SGT., Died, Home, 09/07/18, FORMERLY 24683, WELCH REGT., South Wales Borderers, 51st (Grad) Battalion.

WEST, William James, b. Aldershot, Hants, e. Gt. Missenden , r. Stoney Stratford, Bucks, 51275, PRIVATE, Died of wounds, France & Flanders, 05/09/18, FORMERLY 2061, R.A.M.C., Cheshire Regiment, 1st Battalion.

WESTLAKE, William John A., b. Aldershot, Hants, e. Woolwich, Kent, A/1222, ARMR/S/SGT., Died, At Sea, 28/03/15, Royal Army Ordnance Corps.

WHITE, Henry Victor Ralph, b. Aldershot, Hants, e. Allahabad, India , r. Hanley, Staffs, 7588, DRUMMER, Killed in action, France & Flanders, 25/09/15, South Staffordshire Regiment, 2nd Battalion.

WHITE, William Frank, b. Aldershot, e. Guildford, Surrey, 2065, SERGT., Died, France & Flanders, 26/09/16, FORMERLY 8139, ROYAL WEST SURREYS., Northumberland Fusiliers, 2nd Battalion.

WICKES, Ernest Alfred, b. Aldershot, Hants, e. Lambeth, Surrey , r. South Lambeth, Surrey, G/4154, PRIVATE, Killed in action, France & Flanders, 15/07/16, Queen's (Royal West Surrey Regiment), 1st Battalion.

WILD, George Henry, b. Aldershot, e. Bury, St. Edmunds , r. Ilford, Essex, 2848, PRIVATE, Died, India, 24/09/16, Lancashire Fusiliers, 1st Battalion

WILDGOOSE, Herbert Eustace, b. Aldershot, Hampshire, e. Hull, Yorkshire, 262, A/L/CPL., Killed in action, France & Flanders, 09/05/15, Black Watch (Royal Highlanders), 2nd Battalion.

WILKINSON, Arthur, b. Aldershot, e. Aldershot , r. Aldershot, 25198, PRIVATE, Died of wounds, Mesopotamia, 15/12/17, FORMERLY 22250, HAMPSHIRE REGIMENT., Duke of Edinburgh's (Wiltshire Regiment), 5th Battalion.

WILLANS, Albert, b. Aldershot, e. Uxbridge , r. Uxbridge, L/16718, PRIVATE, Killed in action, France & Flanders, 06/08/16, Royal Fusiliers (City of London Regiment), 9th Battalion.

WILLIAMS, Harry Allnut, b. Aldershot, e. Hounslow , r. Hillingdon Heath Middx., 16031, L/CPL, Killed in action, France & Flanders, 24/05/15, Royal Fusiliers (City of London Regiment), 3rd Battalion.

WILLIAMSON, Bert, b. Aldershot, Hants, e. Hartley Wintney, Hants , r. Aldershot, Hants, 34206, PRIVATE, Died of wounds, France & Flanders, 31/08/18, Hampshire Regiment, 1st Battalion.

WILLIS, William David Turvy, b. Aldershot, Hants, e. Hampton Court, Middlesex , r. Hounslow, Middlesex, T.F.3749, CPL., Died of wounds, France & Flanders, 19/10/16, Duke of Cambridge's Own (Middlesex Regiment), 1/8th (T.F.) Battalion.

WILLMENT, Charles Frank, b. Aldershot, e. Guildford, Surrey , r. Mottisfont, Hants, 38908, DVR., Died, France & Flanders, 29/10/18, (K.K. CABLE SECTION, R.E.)., Corps of Royal Engineers.

WILLMOTT, Albert John, b. Aldershot, e. Bristol, 201678, CPL., Died, France & Flanders, 18/06/17, Gloucestershire Regiment, 2/4th (City of Bristol) Battalion, Territorial.

WILSON, Richard, b. Aldershot, Hants, e. London, Middx., S/8758, PRIVATE, Died of wounds, France & Flanders, 12/10/15, Seaforth Highlanders (Ross-shire Buffs, the Duke of Albany's), 7th Battalion.

Sort Order : Surname, Christian Name(s)

SURNAME,Christian Name(s),Born,Enlisted,Residence,Number,RANK,Cause,Place,Date of Death,ADDITIONAL TEXT,Regiment,Battalion

WYATT, Ernest, b. Aldershot, e. Winchester , r. Winchester, 3197, RIFLEMAN, Died of wounds, France & Flanders, 11/09/15, Rifle Brigade (The Prince Consort's Own), 3rd Battalion.

YEOMAN, Roland Sounes, b. Aldershot, Hants, e. Woolwich, Kent , r. Croydon, Surrey, 18118, L/CPL, Killed in action, France & Flanders, 16/08/16, East Surrey Regiment, 9th Battalion.

YOUNG, Albert, b. Aldershot, Hants, e. Camberley, Surrey , r. Camberley, T/205827, SERGT., Killed in action, France & Flanders, 29/07/18, Queen's (Royal West Surrey Regiment), 2/4th Battalion.

YOUNG, John Fred, b. Aldershot, Hants, e. Woolwich, Kent, 82826, GUNNER, Killed in action, Mesopotamia, 12/03/16, Royal Horse Artillery and Royal Field Artillery.

Sort Order : Surname, Christian Name(s)

SURNAME,Christian Name(s),Born,Enlisted,Residence,Number,RANK,Cause,Place,Date of Death,ADDITIONAL TEXT,Regiment,Battalion

ADAMS, James, b. Aldershot, e. Aldershot, 307679, PRIVATE, Killed in action, France & Flanders, 08/08/18, FORMERLY 59693, ROYAL FLYING CORPS., Tank Corps.

ALDEN, Frederick William, b. Aldershot, e. Aldershot, r. Gosport, 9862, C.S.M., Died, France & Flanders, 09/08/16, King's (Liverpool Regiment), 1st Battalion.

ASPINALL, Reginald Clarence, b. Aldershot, e. Aldershot, r. Portsmouth, Hants, 8052, L/CPL, Killed in action, France & Flanders, 07/11/14, Hampshire Regiment, 1st Battalion.

BARNETT, Percy, b. Aldershot, e. Aldershot, 9018, L/CPL, Died, France & Flanders, 25/02/15, Royal Welsh Fusiliers, 1st Battalion.

BARNETT, Walter Edward, b. Aldershot, Hants, e. Aldershot, 13584, PRIVATE, Killed in action, France & Flanders, 07/07/16, FORMERLY 20777, HUSSARS., Dorsetshire Regiment, 6th Battalion.

BENNETT, Thomas, b. Aldershot, Hants, e. Aldershot, Hants, 9994, PRIVATE, Killed in action, France & Flanders, 25/02/15, Prince of Wales's Leinster Regiment (Royal Canadians), 1st Battalion.

BERRY, Harold, b. Aldershot, Hants, e. Aldershot, 10926, PRIVATE, Died of wounds, France & Flanders, 19/09/14, Highland Light Infantry, 2nd Battalion.

BONE, Frank James, b. Aldershot, Hants, e. Aldershot, 25145, PRIVATE, Killed in action, France & Flanders, 10/08/17, FORMERLY 24951, Y. HASSARS OF THE LINE., Princess Victoria's (Royal Irish Fusiliers), 8th Battalion.

BOYER, Ernest Earl, b. Aldershot, Hants, e. Aldershot, 33284, GUNNER, Died, Turkey, 31/10/16, Royal Horse Artillery and Royal Field Artillery.

BRANT, William, b. Aldershot, e. Aldershot, r. Cove, 995, A/CPL., Died, Home, 09/06/16, Corps of Military Police, Foot Branch.

BROWN, Francis Anthony, b. Aldershot, Hants, e. Aldershot, r. King's Lynn, Norfolk, 92322, PRIVATE, Killed in action, France & Flanders, 20/09/17, FORMERLY T/90322, R.A.S.C., Sherwood Foresters (Nottinghamshire and Derbyshire Regiment), 16th Battalion.

CAMPBELL, Alan George, b. Aldershot, Hants, e. Aldershot, 3/7124, R.S.M., Killed in action, France & Flanders, 25/09/15, Gordon Highlanders, 8th Battalion.

CARVER, Frederick John, b. Aldershot, Hants, e. Aldershot, Hants, 200422, PRIVATE, Died, Egypt, 03/08/17, Hampshire Regiment, 2/5th (T.F.) Battalion.

COMFORT, George Henry Harding, b. Aldershot, e. Aldershot, 33296, PRIVATE, Died of wounds, France & Flanders, 08/12/17, Princess Charlotte of Wales's (Royal Berkshire Regiment), 1st Battalion.

COPPLESTONE, Frank, b. Aldershot, e. Aldershot, r. Barnstaple, Devon, 5844, L/CPL, Killed in action, France & Flanders, 30/08/15, Worcestershire Regiment, 3rd Battalion.

COX, Harry, b. Aldershot, Hants, e. Aldershot, 20286, PRIVATE, Killed in action, France & Flanders, 15/11/16, Gloucestershire Regiment, 1/5th Battalion (Territorial).

COX, Harry, b. Aldershot, Hants, e. Aldershot, 200214, PRIVATE, Killed in action, Mesopotamia, 23/02/17, Hampshire Regiment, 1/4th (T.F.) Battalion.

COX, Joseph, b. Aldershot, Hants, e. Aldershot, r. Frimley, Hants, 9240, PRIVATE, Killed in action, Mesopotamia, 31/12/16, Dorsetshire Regiment, 2nd Battalion.

DALLAS, Stanley, b. Aldershot, e. Aldershot, r. Aldershot, P/1975, A/SGT., Killed in action, France & Flanders, 23/03/18, Corps of Military Police, Foot Branch.

DELANEY, Charles, b. Aldershot, Hants, e. Aldershot, 10312, PRIVATE, Killed in action, France & Flanders, 26/08/14, Royal Inniskilling Fusiliers, 2nd Battalion.

DODD, Archie, b. Aldershot, e. Aldershot, 10087, PRIVATE, Died, France & Flanders, 05/09/18, Worcestershire Regiment, 2nd Battalion.

DUNN, Edward, b. Aldershot, Hants, e. Aldershot, Hants, 25038, L/CPL, Killed in action, France & Flanders, 11/04/17, Hampshire Regiment, 1st Battalion.

EDWARDS, Frederick James, b. Aldershot, Hants, e. Aldershot, Hants, r. Alresford, Hants, 10031, PRIVATE, Killed in action, France & Flanders, 20/10/16, Hampshire Regiment, 2nd Battalion.

ELFLETT, Andrews, b. Aldershot, Hants, e. Aldershot, Hants, 8877, L/CPL, Killed in action, France & Flanders, 02/10/18, Hampshire Regiment, 15th (Service) Battalion.

Sort Order : Surname, Christian Name(s)

SURNAME,Christian Name(s),Born,Enlisted,Residence,Number,RANK,Cause,Place,Date of Death,ADDITIONAL TEXT,Regiment,Battalion

FAITHFUL, Percy Reginald, b. Aldershot, e. Aldershot , r. Alton, 267050, CPL., Killed in action, France & Flanders, 28/08/17, Gloucestershire Regiment, 2/6th Battalion (Territorials).

FINCH, Arthur, b. Aldershot, e. Aldershot, 31478, PRIVATE, Killed in action, France & Flanders, 26/09/17, Hampshire Regiment, 14th (Service) Battalion.

FISHER, George, b. Aldershot, e. Aldershot, 267049, L/CPL, Killed in action, France & Flanders, 19/08/17, Gloucestershire Regiment, 2/6th Battalion (Territorials).

FRANKLIN, Albert, b. Aldershot, e. Aldershot , r. Aldershot, 1919, RIFLEMAN, Died, France & Flanders, 03/04/15, Rifle Brigade (The Prince Consort's Own), 1st Battalion.

GARDNER, William George Sylvester, b. Aldershot, e. Aldershot , r. Liphook, Hants, 9194, PRIVATE, Died of wounds, France & Flanders, 26/11/14, Devonshire Regiment, 1st Battalion.

GARNETT, John Edward, b. Aldershot, e. Aldershot, 12646, L/SGT, Killed in action, France & Flanders, 26/09/16, Grenadier Guards, 2nd Battalion

GILDING, Edward Guelph, b. Aldershot, Hants, e. Aldershot, 8456, SERGT., Killed in action, France & Flanders, 31/07/17, Northamptonshire Regiment, 2nd Battalion.

GILL, Alfred Charles, b. Aldershot, e. Aldershot , r. Eastleigh, Hants, M/27685, A/CPL., Died, France & Flanders, 20/02/16, Royal Army Service Corps.

GODDARD, Harry, b. Aldershot, Hants, e. Aldershot, Hants, 8671, CPL., Killed in action, France & Flanders, 26/08/14, Hampshire Regiment, 1st Battalion.

GORMAN, Thomas, b. Aldershot, e. Aldershot , r. Alton, 8835, SERGT., Killed in action, France & Flanders, 02/04/17, Alexandra, Princess of Wales's Own (Yorkshire Regiment), 2nd Battalion.

GRAHAM, Ronald Leonard, b. Aldershot, e. Aldershot , r. Potterslane, Surrey, 10698, PRIVATE, Killed in action, Gallipoli, 30/04/15, Royal Dublin Fusiliers, 1st Battalion.

GREEN, John, b. Aldershot, Hants, e. Aldershot, 19844, A/Q.M.S., Died, France & Flanders, 10/05/17, Royal Army Medical Corps.

GREGORY, William Alexander, b. Aldershot, Hants, e. Aldershot, Hants, 7535, SPR., Died, France & Flanders, 15/10/18, (350TH E. & M. COY., R.E.)., Corps of Royal Engineers.

HALL, Alfred William, b. Aldershot, Hants, e. Aldershot, Han Ts, 331266, RIFLEMAN, Killed in action, Palestine, 19/04/17, Hampshire Regiment, 1/8th (T.F.) Battalion.

HART, Albert, b. Aldershot, e. Aldershot , r. Ash Vale, Surrey, 19834, CPL., Killed in action, Mesopotamia, 09/03/17, FORMERLY 10971, WORCS REGT. (72ND FIELD COY., R.E.), Corps of Royal Engineers.

HEATH, William James Henry, b. Aldershot, Hants, e. Aldershot, Hants, 14681, SPR., Killed in action, France & Flanders, 05/03/17, (15TH FIELD COY., R.E.), Corps of Royal Engineers.

HOPPITT, Charles, b. Aldershot, Hants, e. Aldershot, 23106, PRIVATE, Killed in action, France & Flanders, 23/10/16, Hampshire Regiment, 1st Battalion.

HUNT, Frederick Arthur, b. Aldershot, Hants, e. Aldershot , r. Aldershot, 1235, CPL., Killed in action, India, 15/07/15, Household Cavalry and Cavalry of the Line (incl. Yeomanry and Imperial Camel Corps), 21st Lancers (Empress of India's).

JACKSON, Michael John, b. Aldershot, e. Aldershot, 26814, PRIVATE, Killed in action, France & Flanders, 26/10/17, Devonshire Regiment, 9th (Service) Battalion.

JOSEPHSON, Edmund George, b. Aldershot, e. Aldershot, 32154, CPL., Died of wounds, Home, 03/03/19, Devonshire Regiment, 2nd Battalion.

LIGHT, Richard John, b. Aldershot, e. Aldershot, 38254, L/CPL, Killed in action, France & Flanders, 25/09/15, FORMERLY SS/5, R.A.S.C., Welsh Regiment, 2nd Battalion.

LUSH, William Henry, b. Aldershot, Hants, e. Aldershot, Hants, 5965, PRIVATE, Killed in action, France & Flanders, 30/10/14, Household Cavalry and Cavalry of the Line (incl. Yeomanry and Imperial Camel Corps), Corps of Dragoons. 1st King's Dragoon Guards.

MANT, W. G., b. Aldershot, e. Aldershot , r. Knaphill, Surrey, 14156, DVR., Killed in action, France & Flanders, 29/09/18, (H.Q., 2ND DIV. ENGINEERS, R.E.), Corps of Royal Engineers.

Sort Order : Surname, Christian Name(s)

SURNAME,Christian Name(s),Born,Enlisted,Residence,Number,RANK,Cause,Place,Date of Death,ADDITIONAL TEXT,Regiment,Battalion

MARSHALL, William Henry, b. Aldershot, Hants, e. Aldershot, Hants, 8001, PRIVATE, Killed in action, Palestine, 02/11/17, Hampshire Regiment, 1/8th (T.F.) Battalion.

MARTIN, Henry George, b. Aldershot, Hants, e. Aldershot, Hants, 25489, PRIVATE, Killed in action, France & Flanders, 28/03/18, Hampshire Regiment, 1st Battalion.

MASON, Alfred, b. Aldershot, e. Aldershot, G/6028, PRIVATE, Killed in action, British Expeditionary Force, 25/09/15, Royal Sussex Regiment, 9th Battalion.

MAYHEAD, Frederick, b. Aldershot, e. Aldershot , r. Ashvale, Surrey, 6217, CPL., Killed in action, France & Flanders, 21/05/15, Worcestershire Regiment, 3rd Battalion.

MERRITT, Percy Harold, b. Aldershot, e. Aldershot , r. Plumstead, Kent, 1952, RIFLEMAN, Killed in action, France & Flanders, 26/08/14, Rifle Brigade (The Prince Consort's Own), 1st Battalion.

NEEDHAM, William St. Clair, b. Aldershot, e. Aldershot, Hants, 69608, TRUMPETER, Killed in action, France & Flanders, 14/09/14, Royal Horse Artillery and Royal Field Artillery.

NEWELL, Robert James, b. Aldershot, Hants, e. Aldershot, Han Ts, 200451, PRIVATE, Killed in action, Mesopotamia, 24/02/17, Hampshire Regiment, 1/4th (T.F.) Battalion.

OLIVER, Frank, b. Aldershot, e. Aldershot, 43615, PRIVATE, Killed in action, France & Flanders, 11/01/17, Royal Welsh Fusiliers, 1st Battalion.

ORANGE, Percy James, b. Aldershot, e. Aldershot, 564388, L/CPL, Died, France & Flanders, 06/11/18, FORMERLY 30637, HANTS REGT., Labour Corps.

POPEJOY, Bert Samuel, b. Aldershot, e. Aldershot , r. Aldershot, 72, SERGT., Killed in action, France & Flanders, 21/03/18, Rifle Brigade (The Prince Consort's Own), 8th Battalion.

PORTER, Samuel, b. Aldershot, Hants, e. Aldershot, 645, L/CPL, Died of wounds, France & Flanders, 15/04/18, Northumberland Fusiliers, 1st Battalion.

RAISON, George Hurst, b. Aldershot, Hants, e. Aldershot, 162, SERGT., Killed in action, France & Flanders, 13/10/14, Northumberland Fusiliers, 1st Battalion.

ROBINSON, William Charles James Edwin, b. Aldershot, Hants, e. Aldershot, Hants, 8018, CPL., Killed in action, France & Flanders, 09/08/16, Hampshire Regiment, 2nd Battalion.

SCOTT, Reynold, b. Aldershot, Hants, e. Aldershot, Hants, 203410, PRIVATE, Killed in action, France & Flanders, 16/10/18, Hampshire Regiment, 15th (Service) Battalion.

SMITH, Frank Edward, b. Aldershot, Hants, e. Aldershot, Hants, 1885, PRIVATE, Died, Home, 01/11/16, Hampshire Regiment, 1/4th (T.F.) Battalion.

SMITH, William, b. Aldershot, e. Aldershot , r. Aldershot, 25407, PRIVATE, Died, Mesopotamia, 15/07/16, FORMERLY 22292, HAMPSHIRE REGIMENT., Duke of Edinburgh's (Wiltshire Regiment), 5th Battalion.

SOFFE, Harry, b. Aldershot, Hants, e. Aldershot, Hants, 9537, PRIVATE, Killed in action, France & Flanders, 26/04/15, Hampshire Regiment, 1st Battalion.

SPEAKMAN, Edward Joseph Edmund, b. Aldershot, Hants, e. Aldershot, Hants, 381154, PRIVATE, Killed in action, France & Flanders, 20/07/18, Hampshire Regiment, 2/4th (T.F.) Battalion.

SPRINGHAM, Alexander, b. Aldershot, e. Aldershot, Hants, 64421, BDR., Killed in action, France & Flanders, 17/07/16, Royal Horse Artillery and Royal Field Artillery.

STEPHENS, Frederick Henry, b. Aldershot, e. Aldershot, 21459, CPL., Killed in action, France & Flanders, 04/07/16, FORMERLY 8739, HANTS REGT., Machine Gun Corps, (Infantry).

STYLES, Albert Henry, b. Aldershot, Hants, e. Aldershot, 41265, PRIVATE, Killed in action, France & Flanders, 22/04/18, FORMERLY 8/7380, T. RES. BN., Duke of Cornwall's Light Infantry, 1st Battalion.

STYLES, Henry Ernest, b. Aldershot, e. Aldershot, 26533, PIONEER, Died, France & Flanders, 12/07/18, FORMERLY 9022, SOM. L.I. (4TH SIGNAL COY., R.E.), Corps of Royal Engineers.

SUMNER, Edward, b. Aldershot, Hants, e. Aldershot, 69271, PRIVATE, Killed in action, France & Flanders, 19/08/17, Royal Army Medical Corps.

SUMPSTER, Alfred Charles, b. Aldershot, e. Aldershot, 5528, C.S.M., Died, Mesopotamia, 05/07/16, (3RD SAPPERS & MINERS, R.E.), Corps of Royal Engineers.

Bibliography

The Story of the Royal Garrison Church W.M., May and Co 1924
Bygone Aldershot T. Childerhouse, Phillimore and Co Ltd 1984
Aldershot Through Time Paul Vickers, Amberley 2012.
Camberley at War Ken Clarke 1984
Images of Aldershot Stephen Phillips and Vivien Owen, Breedon Books 1998
Aldershot Past Stephen Phillips and Dicken, Phillimore 2000
Aldershot Review John Walters, Jarolds 1970
Aldershot Buses Peter Holmes, Waterfront Publishers 1992
The Book of Aldershot Tim Childerhouse, Baron
Pubs of Aldershot Peter Palmer, Aldershot Historical and Archaeology Society
Prim. Aldershot Margaret Collier and Rosalind Sherwood, Tentmakers 2010
Images of England – Aldershot Ian Maine and Jim White, Tempus Publishing
    Ltd
The Story of Aldershot Lieutenant-Colonel Cole, Southern Books (Aldershot)
    Ltd
The Aldershot Review John Walters, Jarrolds
The Aldershot Aeronauts Tim Childerhouse 1994.
Behind the Lines Nicholas Boyack, Allen and Unwin Port Nicholas Press
Liphook Bramshott and the Canadians Bramshott and Liphook Preservation
    Society
The Chief: Douglas Haig and the British Army Aurum Press 2011
Horace Smith-Dorrien – Memories of Forty Eight Year's Service Pickle
    Publishing 1925
Journal of The Royal Electrical/Mechanical Engineers April 1986
Kitchener's Lost Boys John Oakes, The History Press
The Little General Richard Holmes, Jonathan Cape 1981
Command and Morale Gary Sheffield, Pen and Sword 2014
Aldershot News
Sheldrake Military Gazette

Index